Criminal Psychology Step by Step

Understanding the Minds Behind the Crimes: Decoding the
Layers of Criminal Motivation

Brian Blanda

Preface

Crime has fascinated and terrified humanity for centuries. From ancient civilizations grappling with theft and violence to modern societies tackling cybercrime and white-collar fraud, the study of criminal behavior has always been essential. But what truly drives a person to commit a crime? Is it nature or nurture? Are criminals born or made? These are the questions at the heart of this book.

This book is designed to take you on a structured, logical look through the fascinating realities of criminal psychology. Whether you're a student, a professional, or simply someone interested in the complexities of human behavior, this book provides a step-by-step breakdown of the psychological principles behind crime. We'll explore theories, case studies, and real-world applications that reveal the motivations, thought processes, and behaviors of criminals.

Why This Book?

The field of criminal psychology is broad, touching on everything from biological predispositions to social influences, personality disorders, and even the impact of economic pressures. Rather than offering scattered insights, this book presents a structured, easy-to-follow guide that builds upon itself. Each chapter is designed to cover a unique aspect of criminal psychology.

One of the biggest misconceptions about crime is that it is purely an act of will—something that people consciously choose without external or internal influences. However, research in psychology and neuroscience has shown that criminal behavior is often a product of a complex mix of genetics, environment, personality, and opportunity. By breaking down these layers step by step, we can begin to understand why certain individuals engage in criminal acts while others, despite facing similar circumstances, do not.

What You'll Learn

In **Chapter 1**, we lay the groundwork by defining criminal psychology and exploring how it differs from related fields like criminology and forensic psychology. We also look at the methodologies used to study criminal minds and discuss ethical concerns in this field.

Chapter 2 goes into the theoretical foundations of criminal behavior, exploring major psychological perspectives such as psychodynamic theory, behavioral and cognitive models, social learning theories, and even evolutionary explanations.

Moving into **Chapter 3**, we explore the biological roots of criminal behavior—how genetics, brain structures, hormones, and neurotransmitters influence aggression, impulsivity, and criminal tendencies. Understanding these factors helps us see crime not just as a moral failing but as a phenomenon with deep biological underpinnings.

From biology, we shift to personality and mental health in **Chapter 4**. Here, we examine how personality disorders like antisocial personality disorder and psychopathy shape criminal behavior. We also look at the intersection of trauma, mental illness, and criminal acts.

No discussion of crime is complete without looking at the **social and environmental factors** that shape criminality, which we explore in **Chapter 5**. We analyze how family upbringing, peer influences, socioeconomic conditions, and cultural norms contribute to criminal behavior.

Chapter 6 then categorizes crimes based on their psychological underpinnings, helping us understand how violent crimes differ from financial and white-collar crimes or victimless crimes. Each category is explored through the lens of psychology, revealing the different motivations and triggers for each type.

Once we understand the foundations of criminal behavior, we move into profiling and analysis in **Chapter 7**. This chapter covers crime scene analysis, behavioral profiling, victimology, geographic profiling, and even the growing field of cybercrime profiling.

Understanding why criminals commit crimes is only half the picture—we also need to understand the **triggers and motivations** behind specific offenses. **Chapter 8** goes into intrinsic and extrinsic motivators, the impact of emotions, economic pressures, substance abuse, and ideological motivations.

The book then turns toward real-world applications in **Chapter 9**, which explores investigative psychology and interrogation techniques. Here, we discuss interviewing methods, deception detection, and advanced tools like polygraphs and brain imaging technologies.

Of course, no discussion of criminal psychology is complete without addressing what happens after a crime is committed. **Chapter 10** looks at rehabilitation, recidivism, and crime prevention strategies. We explore therapeutic approaches, community reintegration programs, and policies designed to reduce repeat offenses.

Finally, we examine the **future of criminal psychology** in **Chapter 11**, looking at the impact of AI, cyberpsychology, globalization, and forensic research innovations. The book concludes with a historical timeline of major developments in criminal psychology and a glossary of essential terms.

Who Should Read This Book?

This book is for anyone curious about the science behind crime. Whether you're a psychology student, a law enforcement professional, a legal expert, or just someone fascinated by true crime, this book provides insights that are both educational and engaging.

If you're a **student**, this book gives you a structured way to learn about criminal psychology without feeling overwhelmed. It introduces you to key theories, research findings, and real-world applications.

If you're a **law enforcement or legal professional**, understanding criminal psychology can help you analyze offender behavior, improve investigative techniques, and make informed decisions about rehabilitation and punishment.

If you're an **educator or researcher**, this book provides a well-rounded introduction to the field, covering both classic and contemporary theories.

And if you're simply **a true crime enthusiast**, this book will deepen your understanding of the psychological elements behind the cases you follow, moving beyond sensationalized media portrayals to a more scientific perspective.

Final Thoughts

Crime is a complex and evolving phenomenon. While it's easy to label criminals as simply "bad people," the reality is far more nuanced. This book doesn't justify or excuse criminal behavior, but it does seek to explain it. From understanding the psychological roots of crime, we can better prevent it, rehabilitate offenders, and support victims.

Criminal psychology is a field where science meets real-world impact, and by studying it, we gain insight into both human nature and the structures that shape our society. I hope this book challenges you, informs you, and above all, deepens your understanding of the criminal mind.

Topical Outline

Chapter 1: Foundations of Criminal Psychology
- Defining Criminal Psychology and Its Scope
- Distinguishing Criminal Psychology from Criminology
- Interdisciplinary Approaches: Merging Psychology, Sociology, and Law
- Research Methodologies Specific to Criminal Behavior
- Ethical Considerations in Studying Criminal Minds
- The Role and Responsibilities of the Criminal Psychologist
- Contemporary Challenges in Field Applications

Chapter 2: Theoretical Perspectives in Criminal Behavior
- Psychodynamic Theories and the Unconscious Drivers of Crime
- Behavioral and Cognitive Models: Learning and Decision-Making
- Social Learning and Environmental Influences on Offending
- Evolutionary and Biological Frameworks for Understanding Crime

Chapter 3: Biological Underpinnings of Criminality
- Genetic Influences and Heritability Factors
- Neurobiological Contributions to Aggression and Impulsivity
- Brain Structure Variations and Their Link to Criminal Behavior
- Neurotransmitter Imbalances and Behavioral Dysregulation
- Hormonal Effects on Aggression and Decision-Making

Chapter 4: Personality, Psychopathology, and Crime
- Personality Traits Predisposing Individuals to Criminality
- Antisocial Personality Disorder: Diagnostic Criteria and Manifestations
- Psychopathy: Emotional Deficits and Behavioral Patterns
- The Influence of Narcissistic and Borderline Traits
- Mental Illness: Intersection of Psychopathology and Criminal Behavior
- Impact of Trauma and Adverse Childhood Experiences

Chapter 5: Environmental and Social Influences
- Family Dynamics and Early Socialization in Offending
- Socioeconomic Disparities and Crime Correlation
- Peer Group Influence and the Formation of Gang Culture
- Cultural Norms and Deviance in Varying Societal Contexts

Chapter 6: The Psychology of Crime in Various Categories
- Crimes Against Persons (Violent Crimes)
- Crimes Against Property
- Inchoate Crimes
- Statutory Crimes
- Financial Crimes (White-Collar Crimes)
- Crimes Against Morality (Victimless Crimes)

Chapter 7: Criminal Behavior Analysis and Profiling

Table of Contents

Chapter 1: Foundations of Criminal Psychology

Defining Criminal Psychology and Its Scope

Criminal psychology is the study of the thoughts, emotions, and behaviors of individuals who commit crimes. It examines why people break the law, how their minds work before, during, and after an offense, and whether their behavior can be predicted, altered, or prevented. The field combines **psychology, law, forensic science, and criminology** to create a structured understanding of the criminal mind. Unlike general psychology, which focuses on mental health and behavior in a broad sense, criminal psychology is concerned with the specific motivations, cognitive distortions, and emotional responses of offenders.

The **primary goal** of criminal psychology is to analyze and explain criminal behavior. Psychologists in this field assess the **risk factors** that make someone more likely to commit a crime. These factors include **biological predispositions, personality traits, childhood trauma, social influences, and mental health conditions**. Some offenders have antisocial tendencies from a young age, while others are shaped by their environment or specific life experiences. Criminal psychologists study these variables to determine what pushes an individual toward criminal activity.

Another key focus is understanding the **mental state of offenders**. In criminal trials, a defendant's psychological condition is often questioned. Criminal psychologists assess whether a person was mentally competent at the time of a crime or whether mental illness had a role in their actions. The legal system depends on this analysis to determine responsibility, intent, and appropriate sentencing. In some cases, these evaluations decide whether an individual is fit to stand trial or if they require psychiatric treatment instead of incarceration.

Criminal psychology is also used in **offender profiling**. By analyzing past crimes, psychologists help law enforcement predict future offenses, identify patterns, and develop profiles of unknown criminals. These profiles include **behavioral patterns, likely personality traits, decision-making processes, and emotional responses**. Profiling helps investigators understand how a criminal thinks, which can narrow down suspects and lead to faster arrests.

The **scope of criminal psychology** extends beyond profiling and investigations. Psychologists in this field also work in **correctional facilities, rehabilitation centers, mental health institutions, and academic research**. They develop treatment programs for offenders, study the effectiveness of rehabilitation efforts, and provide therapy for individuals who have committed crimes. Understanding the psychology of offenders helps create strategies for reducing recidivism, which refers to the likelihood of a person reoffending after being released from prison.

One of the most critical aspects of criminal psychology is studying the **different types of offenders**. Not all criminals think or behave the same way. Some commit crimes due to impulsivity, while others plan their actions carefully. Some are driven by financial desperation, while others act out of anger, revenge, or psychological disorders. Serial offenders, for example, have **different cognitive and emotional patterns** compared to someone who commits a crime in the heat of the moment. Understanding these differences helps in both prevention and treatment.

Criminal psychology is also concerned with **victimology**, the study of victims and their relationships with offenders. Some criminals choose their victims based on specific characteristics, while others act randomly. Analyzing victim-offender interactions helps psychologists determine how criminals justify their actions and whether their behavior follows a pattern. Understanding victim selection is especially useful in cases of serial offenses, violent crimes, and domestic abuse.

Beyond individual offenders, criminal psychology also examines **societal factors** that contribute to crime. Poverty, lack of education, childhood neglect, and exposure to violence all increase the likelihood of criminal behavior. Psychologists in this field work alongside criminologists to explore **how different environments shape behavior**. While some individuals are born with psychological traits that make them more prone to crime, external influences often determine whether those traits lead to actual offenses.

Another area where criminal psychology is applied is **jury selection and courtroom behavior**. The way a defendant behaves in court can influence a jury's perception of guilt or innocence. Criminal psychologists sometimes work as consultants, advising legal teams on how a defendant should present themselves, how witnesses might react under pressure, and how different jury members are likely to interpret evidence. Their expertise ensures that psychological biases are accounted for in legal proceedings.

The **application of criminal psychology in law enforcement** has expanded in recent years, particularly with advances in technology. Police now use **behavioral analysis, artificial intelligence, and psychological assessments** to predict criminal activity and improve interrogation techniques. Criminal psychologists contribute to these efforts by refining techniques for **detecting deception, assessing credibility, and understanding a suspect's mental state**.

The **future of criminal psychology** includes deeper integration with neuroscience and artificial intelligence. Brain imaging technology is being used to study **how the brains of offenders function differently from non-offenders**. Advances in machine learning are allowing researchers to analyze massive amounts of behavioral data to detect early warning signs of criminal tendencies. The more science advances, the more precise criminal psychology becomes in explaining and predicting criminal actions.

Criminal psychology is not just about catching criminals. It is about **understanding why crime happens**, preventing future offenses, and improving the justice system's approach to dealing with offenders. Whether used in police work, courtrooms, correctional facilities, or research, this field **combines psychological science with real-world application** to address crime at its root causes.

Distinguishing Criminal Psychology from Criminology

Criminal psychology and criminology both examine crime, but they focus on different aspects of it. Criminal psychology studies the thoughts, emotions, and behaviors of individuals who commit crimes, while criminology looks at crime as a broader social phenomenon. The two fields often overlap, but they differ in methodology, focus, and application.

Criminal psychology is rooted in **individual analysis**. It seeks to understand the motivations behind a person's criminal behavior. Psychologists in this field assess personality traits, mental disorders, cognitive processes, and emotional triggers that contribute to criminal acts. They analyze **why** a person commits a crime, how they justify their actions, and how their psychological state influences their behavior. Criminal psychologists often work in clinical settings, law enforcement, corrections, and academia, conducting assessments and offering treatment to offenders.

Criminology, in contrast, **examines crime at the societal level**. It looks at crime patterns, social causes, and the effectiveness of laws and criminal justice policies. Criminologists study statistics, economic conditions, education levels, family structures, and cultural influences to understand what leads to higher crime rates. Rather than focusing on individual offenders, criminology explores how crime develops within communities and what can be done to reduce it.

The **methods** used in these fields also differ. Criminal psychologists rely on clinical assessments, forensic interviews, case studies, and psychological testing.

They use tools like the Hare Psychopathy Checklist (PCL-R) to assess traits associated with psychopathy, or the MMPI-2 to evaluate personality disorders. They apply psychological theories such as cognitive distortions, behavioral conditioning, and attachment theory to explain criminal behavior.

Criminologists, on the other hand, focus on **data analysis and large-scale studies**. They use crime statistics, demographic surveys, and sociological theories to identify crime trends. Criminologists might analyze data from the Uniform Crime Reports (UCR) or the National Crime Victimization Survey (NCVS) to determine how factors like unemployment or urbanization affect crime rates. They rely on theories like strain theory, which suggests that crime results from social pressure to achieve success, or routine activity theory, which explains crime based on opportunities and lack of deterrents.

Criminal psychology is more **practical and application-based**, while criminology is **theoretical and research-driven**. A criminal psychologist might work with law enforcement to create an offender profile, assess a suspect's mental state, or determine if a defendant is fit to stand trial. They help police and legal professionals understand the psychological aspects of crime. Criminologists, by contrast, analyze policies and recommend legal reforms. They might study whether harsher sentencing reduces crime or how economic downturns impact crime rates.

One of the key distinctions is **how they view crime prevention**. Criminal psychologists focus on rehabilitation and treatment. They assess offenders, recommend therapy or counseling, and develop intervention programs to reduce

3

recidivism. Their goal is to understand **how an individual criminal thinks and acts**, and whether that behavior can be modified.

Criminologists take a **broader approach**. They study how different **laws, policing strategies, and social programs** affect crime rates. Instead of working with individual offenders, they evaluate entire communities, prisons, and legal systems to determine what policies work best. A criminologist might examine how changes in gun laws impact violent crime or whether community policing reduces gang violence.

Despite these differences, criminal psychology and criminology often **intersect**. Both fields contribute to criminal investigations, policymaking, and corrections. A criminal psychologist might work with a criminologist to analyze patterns in serial offenses. A criminologist might use psychological theories to explain crime trends.

Both fields also work toward the **same goal**: understanding and reducing crime. While criminal psychology does this by analyzing the **individual**, criminology does it by analyzing **society**. Their combined knowledge helps shape everything from investigative techniques to rehabilitation programs to crime prevention policies.

Interdisciplinary Approaches: Merging Psychology, Sociology, and Law

Criminal psychology is not a self-contained discipline. It relies on insights from psychology, sociology, and law to fully understand criminal behavior, justice systems, and rehabilitation efforts. Each of these fields contributes a distinct perspective. Psychology focuses on individual cognition, emotions, personality traits, and mental health. Sociology looks at the broader social structures, cultural dynamics, and group behaviors that contribute to crime. Law provides the framework for defining criminal acts, determining guilt, and administering justice. These disciplines do not operate separately; they work together to create a full picture of crime and criminal behavior. Without this interdisciplinary approach, criminal psychology would lack the depth needed to analyze, predict, and manage criminal activity effectively.

Psychology: The Mind of the Criminal

Criminal psychology originates in traditional psychological studies of behavior and cognition. It examines **why criminals think the way they do**, how emotions and personality traits influence their actions, and whether these behaviors can be modified or prevented. It also assesses **how mental illness, childhood trauma, substance abuse, and personality disorders** contribute to criminal activity.

One of the most studied aspects of criminal psychology is **cognitive distortions**, which are biased ways of thinking that allow criminals to justify their actions. Offenders frequently use cognitive distortions to shift blame, minimize the consequences of their actions, or dehumanize their victims. For example, a fraudster may believe that "everyone cheats" or that "big companies deserve to be scammed." A violent offender may convince themselves that their victim provoked them. Identifying and addressing these thought patterns is critical in rehabilitation.

Another key psychological component is **impulse control and emotional regulation**. Some criminals, particularly violent offenders, struggle with controlling their emotions and making rational decisions in high-stress situations. Neuroscientific research suggests that individuals with **underdeveloped prefrontal cortices**, the area of the brain responsible for decision-making, are more prone to impulsive behavior. Many violent crimes are committed in moments of extreme emotional arousal—anger, jealousy, or fear—rather than through premeditated planning.

Psychologists also study **antisocial personality disorder and psychopathy**, two conditions commonly associated with criminal behavior. Individuals with **antisocial personality disorder (ASPD)** often disregard societal norms, have little empathy for others, and engage in manipulative or aggressive behavior. **Psychopathy**, a more severe condition, is characterized by **a lack of remorse, shallow emotional responses, and an inability to form deep personal relationships**. Many serial offenders and career criminals exhibit traits of psychopathy, though not all psychopaths engage in criminal activity.

Another major psychological factor influencing crime is **early childhood experiences**. Studies show that **abuse, neglect, unstable family environments, and exposure to violence at a young age** increase the likelihood of engaging in criminal behavior later in life. The cycle of violence hypothesis suggests that children who experience or witness violence are more likely to become violent themselves. Early interventions, such as therapy and behavioral programs, can help mitigate these risks.

Sociology: The Social Causes of Crime

While psychology focuses on the individual, sociology examines crime as a social phenomenon. It investigates how environmental, economic, and cultural factors influence criminal behavior. Sociologists do not see crime as simply the result of individual psychology; they view it as a **product of social structures, inequalities, and cultural expectations**.

One of the foundational sociological theories in criminal psychology is social learning theory, which suggests that people learn criminal behavior by observing and imitating others. This is particularly evident in gang culture, organized crime, and domestic violence cycles. If a person grows up in an environment where criminal activity is normalized, they are more likely to adopt similar behaviors. This is why high-crime neighborhoods often produce higher rates of offenders.

Strain theory provides another sociological explanation for crime. This theory states that people commit crimes when they experience a gap between their goals and their ability to achieve them through legitimate means. For example, someone living in poverty may resort to theft or fraud when they see no other way to obtain financial stability. The greater the **economic disparity**, the higher the crime rate tends to be. Societies with extreme wealth inequality often experience higher rates of theft, fraud, and violent crime.

Labeling theory explores how being identified as a criminal affects an individual's future behavior. When someone is convicted of a crime and labeled a criminal, society often treats them differently, limiting their job opportunities and social standing. This can lead to **a self-fulfilling prophecy**, where the individual continues committing crimes because they feel they have no other path in life.

Sociology also examines **how laws are enforced differently across different social groups**. Studies show that **racial, economic, and gender biases** influence how individuals are prosecuted and sentenced. A wealthier individual may receive a lighter sentence for the same crime compared to someone from a lower-income background. Understanding these disparities is crucial for making the justice system fairer.

Law: The Structure That Defines Crime

Psychology and sociology help us understand **why people commit crimes**, but law provides the **boundaries that classify, prosecute, and punish crime**. Without legal structures, crime would be an abstract concept with no practical application.

The legal system defines what constitutes a crime and establishes different levels of culpability. For instance, not all homicides are treated the same—murder, manslaughter, and self-defense each carry different legal consequences based on intent and circumstances. Criminal psychology assists in determining these distinctions, particularly in evaluating an offender's **mental state, level of intent, and ability to understand right from wrong**.

One of the most significant contributions of criminal psychology to law is **the evaluation of criminal responsibility**. The legal concept of **mens rea (criminal intent)** determines whether a person had the mental capacity to commit a crime. Forensic psychologists assess whether an offender was aware of their actions or if **mental illness, intoxication, or cognitive impairment** affected their intent. Courts rely on these evaluations in cases where defendants claim insanity or diminished capacity.

Psychology also helps shape **sentencing and rehabilitation efforts**. Some offenders are deemed too dangerous to be rehabilitated and are given life sentences. Others may receive **treatment-based alternatives**, such as therapy, probation, or restorative justice programs. Courts must decide whether punishment or rehabilitation is the more appropriate response based on an individual's psychological profile.

Another area where psychology and law merge is in **jury selection and courtroom behavior**. The way evidence is presented, the emotional appeal of a case, and even the body language of a defendant can influence jury decisions. Legal teams use psychological research to **understand juror biases, prepare witnesses for testimony, and present arguments in a way that resonates with the jury**.

Law enforcement also benefits from this interdisciplinary approach. **Behavioral profiling, interrogation techniques, and deception detection** rely on psychological insights. The legal system establishes guidelines on how psychological evidence can be used in court and ensures that investigative methods remain ethical and legally sound.

A Unified Approach to Crime

Criminal psychology cannot function without **the combined knowledge of psychology, sociology, and law**. These disciplines do not compete with one another—they enhance each other. Psychology explains **individual motives and mental processes**, sociology provides **a broad understanding of crime as a social issue**, and law gives **the structure for defining and addressing criminal acts**.

Without sociology, criminal psychology would lack context. Without psychology, law enforcement would struggle to understand criminal behavior on an individual level. Without legal structures, psychology and sociology would not have practical applications in crime prevention, investigation, and justice.

The most effective approaches to **crime prevention, investigation, and rehabilitation** come from integrating these disciplines. Whether analyzing serial offenders, improving prison systems, or developing legal policies, the combination of these fields **creates a more complete and effective approach to understanding and addressing crime**.

Research Methodologies Specific to Criminal Behavior

Understanding criminal behavior requires systematic research. Criminal psychology relies on a combination of **quantitative and qualitative methods** to analyze offenders, crime patterns, and the effectiveness of various interventions. Unlike traditional psychological studies, which often take place in controlled laboratory environments, research in criminal psychology frequently involves real-world data collected from offenders, law enforcement agencies, court records, and correctional facilities. These methodologies help psychologists answer key questions: What motivates criminal acts? How do psychological disorders influence criminal behavior? Can future crimes be predicted based on behavioral patterns?

Experimental and Observational Research in Criminal Psychology

One of the most controlled research methods in criminal psychology is the **experimental method**. This approach allows researchers to isolate specific variables and test their influence on behavior. However, ethical concerns make it nearly impossible to conduct experiments that directly involve criminal activity. Instead, researchers use controlled settings to simulate criminal decision-making processes. For example, studies on **aggression and violence** often involve exposing participants to violent media or controlled conflict situations to measure their responses. While these studies cannot perfectly replicate real-life criminal behavior, they help psychologists understand **risk factors** such as **impulsivity, desensitization to violence, and moral disengagement**.

Another commonly used approach is observational research, where researchers study offenders in natural settings such as prisons, juvenile detention centers, and rehabilitation facilities. Unlike experimental methods, observational research does not manipulate variables; it records behavior as it naturally occurs. Researchers examine how **inmates interact, how aggression manifests, or how psychological conditions develop in long-term incarceration**. This method provides important insights into **recidivism rates, the effectiveness of rehabilitation programs, and the long-term psychological impact of criminal behavior**.

Case Studies: In-Depth Analysis of Offenders

Case studies involve detailed, **in-depth analysis of individual offenders**, often focusing on serial criminals, violent offenders, or individuals with rare psychological conditions. Researchers gather data from interviews, court documents, forensic evidence, and psychological assessments to reconstruct an offender's background, thought process, and motivations. This method has been instrumental in profiling criminals such as serial killers, sex offenders, and fraudsters.

One of the most well-known case study methodologies is **criminal profiling**, in which psychologists analyze past crimes to determine behavioral patterns. Profilers use detailed case studies to construct psychological models that help law enforcement **anticipate the actions of unknown offenders**. However, case studies have limitations—they provide deep insight into **one individual or a small group** but cannot always be generalized to the broader criminal population.

Surveys and Self-Report Studies

Criminal psychology often relies on self-reports from offenders, victims, and witnesses to gather data on criminal behavior. Surveys, questionnaires, and structured interviews allow researchers to assess the thoughts, experiences, and motivations of individuals involved in criminal activity. Self-report studies have been useful in examining juvenile delinquency, substance abuse, and white-collar crime, where official crime data may be incomplete.

However, self-report studies come with **significant challenges**. Offenders may **lie, exaggerate, or withhold information** to manipulate the results. Many criminals do not accurately recall or acknowledge their own behaviors, especially in cases involving psychopathy or antisocial personality disorder. To mitigate these risks, researchers use **anonymous surveys, cross-check responses with official crime records, and employ psychological deception detection techniques**.

Victim surveys provide a different perspective by gathering data on **unreported crimes, trauma responses, and the effectiveness of law enforcement interventions**. Many crimes, particularly sexual offenses and domestic abuse, are **underreported** due to fear, shame, or distrust in the justice system. Victimization surveys help fill in the gaps left by official crime statistics.

Longitudinal Studies: Tracking Criminal Behavior Over Time

Longitudinal research is one of the most comprehensive methods for studying criminal behavior. It involves **tracking individuals over extended periods**, sometimes from childhood to adulthood, to examine how **risk factors, life experiences, and psychological traits influence criminal tendencies**. These studies help researchers identify patterns and **predict which individuals are most at risk of engaging in criminal behavior**.

One famous longitudinal study is the **Cambridge Study in Delinquent Development**, which followed **411 boys from childhood into adulthood** to determine which factors contributed to persistent criminal activity. Findings from such studies have shown that **early exposure to violence, lack of parental supervision, and poor school performance** significantly increase the likelihood of future criminal behavior.

The advantage of longitudinal studies is their ability to demonstrate **cause-and-effect relationships** over time. Unlike one-time surveys or case studies, they provide a **clear picture of how criminal behavior develops**. However, these studies are expensive, time-consuming, and difficult to maintain, as participants may drop out or become untraceable over the years.

Meta-Analysis: Combining Data from Multiple Studies

Criminal psychologists often conduct meta-analyses, which involve reviewing and combining findings from multiple studies to identify consistent patterns across research. This method is particularly useful for evaluating the effectiveness of rehabilitation programs, law enforcement strategies, and crime prevention efforts.

For example, a meta-analysis on **the effectiveness of anger management programs in reducing violent crime** might examine dozens of studies to determine whether these interventions actually reduce aggression. By pooling data from multiple sources, researchers can reach **stronger conclusions** than any single study could provide.

The Use of Neuroscience and Psychophysiology in Criminal Psychology

Modern research has incorporated **brain imaging and physiological testing** to explore the neurological aspects of criminal behavior. Techniques such as **functional MRI (fMRI), electroencephalography (EEG), and cortisol level testing** allow researchers to analyze brain activity and stress responses in offenders.

fMRI studies have shown that **violent offenders often exhibit reduced activity in the prefrontal cortex**, which is responsible for impulse control, decision-making, and ethical reasoning. Similarly, studies on **psychopaths** indicate abnormalities in the **amygdala**, the brain region linked to fear and emotional processing. These findings suggest that some individuals may be **neurologically predisposed to aggression or lack of empathy**.

Psychophysiological research also examines **heart rate variability, skin conductance, and hormonal responses** to stress and aggression. Offenders with **low resting heart rates and reduced physiological responses to stress** are more likely to engage in violent crime. These findings contribute to **biopsychosocial models of criminal behavior**, which integrate biological, psychological, and social factors to explain why some individuals are more prone to criminal activity than others.

Ethical and Legal Considerations in Criminal Psychology Research

Research in criminal psychology faces significant ethical challenges. Studying criminal behavior requires access to sensitive data, including criminal records, psychological evaluations, and confidential interviews with offenders and victims. Researchers must ensure that their studies do not violate privacy rights, exploit vulnerable individuals, or expose participants to psychological harm.

Another challenge is the **informed consent process**. Many studies involve **prison populations, juvenile offenders, or individuals with mental illness**, raising concerns about whether participants fully understand the risks of participation. Researchers must follow strict guidelines to ensure ethical integrity, such as obtaining approval from Institutional Review Boards (IRBs) and using anonymous or de-identified data whenever possible.

Finally, researchers must be aware of the **legal implications** of their findings. If a psychologist uncovers information about a planned crime or a previously undisclosed offense, they may be legally obligated to report it to authorities. Balancing **confidentiality, public safety, and ethical research practices** remains a challenge in the field.

Advancing the Study of Criminal Behavior

Criminal psychology continues to evolve with advancements in **technology, data analysis, and neuroscience**. The integration of **machine learning algorithms, AI crime prediction models, and biometric analysis** is changing the way researchers study criminal behavior. However, no single method can fully explain why crime occurs. The most effective research relies on **multiple methodologies**, combining **psychological theories, sociological insights, and legal frameworks** to create a deeper, more accurate understanding of criminal behavior.

Ethical Considerations in Studying Criminal Minds

Studying criminal behavior presents unique ethical challenges. Unlike other areas of psychology, criminal psychology deals with individuals who have committed acts of violence, fraud, abuse, and other serious offenses. Researchers must balance **the need for scientific knowledge with the rights, safety, and dignity of offenders, victims, and society**. The ethical concerns in this field are complex, involving issues of confidentiality, informed consent, potential harm, and the legal responsibilities of researchers. Without strict ethical standards, research in criminal psychology could easily cross the line into **exploitation, bias, or violation of human rights**.

Confidentiality and Privacy in Criminal Psychology Research

Confidentiality is one of the **biggest ethical challenges** in criminal psychology. Researchers often have access to **criminal records, psychological assessments,**

court documents, and personal histories of offenders. This information is highly sensitive, and improper handling can lead to serious legal and social consequences.

Offenders may reveal details about previously undisclosed crimes, ongoing criminal activity, or plans to harm others during research studies. Psychologists must decide whether to maintain confidentiality or report the information to authorities. In most jurisdictions, researchers and clinicians are legally obligated to break confidentiality if they believe a person poses an immediate threat to themselves or others. However, drawing the line between hypothetical risk and genuine danger is difficult.

Victim confidentiality is also a major concern. Many victims, particularly those of **sexual violence, domestic abuse, and human trafficking**, do not want their experiences made public. Researchers must ensure that **victim identities remain anonymous**, even when publishing case studies or statistical analyses. Some victims may consent to interviews for research purposes, but their participation should be handled with extreme care to **avoid retraumatization**.

To protect privacy, criminal psychologists often use **de-identified data**, where personal details are removed, or aggregate data, which presents trends rather than individual case studies. Researchers must also secure their data against breaches, ensuring that sensitive information is **encrypted, stored securely, and only accessible to authorized individuals**.

Informed Consent and Vulnerable Populations

Obtaining informed consent is a fundamental ethical requirement in psychology. However, criminal psychology involves **prisoners, juveniles, individuals with mental illnesses, and those in coercive environments**, raising concerns about **whether their consent is truly voluntary**.

Prisoners may feel pressured to participate in research, either to gain **favorable treatment, reduced sentences, or privileges** within the correctional system. Some may not fully understand their rights, particularly if they have **low literacy levels or cognitive impairments**. Researchers must ensure that participants understand the nature of the study, their right to withdraw, and that refusal will not result in punishment or loss of benefits.

Juvenile offenders pose additional challenges. Many young offenders come from **unstable backgrounds, abusive households, or have limited education**, making it difficult for them to understand the implications of participating in research. In most cases, parental or legal guardian consent is required. However, **in cases of parental neglect or abuse, obtaining parental consent may not be ethical or feasible**.

When dealing with **offenders with severe mental illnesses**, researchers must evaluate **whether the participant is mentally competent** to give informed consent. Individuals with **schizophrenia, severe intellectual disabilities, or dissociative disorders** may not fully comprehend the risks of participating in a study. In such cases, additional ethical oversight is required.

Deception and Psychological Harm in Criminal Research

Some psychological studies involve **deception**, where participants are not fully informed of the study's true purpose to prevent biased responses. In criminal psychology, deception is **rarely justified** due to the potential **psychological distress, distrust, or legal complications** it may cause. Offenders may feel manipulated if they later discover they were misled, and victims may feel exploited if they believe their trauma was used for academic purposes.

Psychologists must also consider the potential **harm their research may cause to participants**. Certain studies, particularly those involving violent offenders, **may trigger past trauma, aggression, or distress**. Asking offenders to recall details of their crimes in detail can reinforce **antisocial thought patterns, increase aggression, or desensitize them to violence**.

Similarly, victim interviews can be **emotionally distressing**. Even if a victim consents to participating in a study, discussing their experience may cause flashbacks, anxiety, depression, or suicidal thoughts. Researchers must have protocols in place to provide psychological support, referrals to therapy, and the option to withdraw from the study at any time.

Bias in Criminal Psychology Research

Bias can easily distort research in criminal psychology. If studies **focus disproportionately on certain demographic groups**, they can reinforce **racial, socioeconomic, and gender-based stereotypes** about crime. For example, early psychological studies on crime often **overrepresented lower-income, minority offenders**, leading to biased assumptions about the causes of criminal behavior.

Selection bias is another issue. Many studies in criminal psychology rely on **convicted offenders**, meaning they exclude criminals who were never caught. This can create a misleading picture of criminal behavior. White-collar criminals, cybercriminals, and high-status offenders are often underrepresented in research because they are less likely to be prosecuted compared to violent street offenders.

To counteract bias, researchers must ensure their **samples are representative of the entire criminal population**, including both violent and non-violent offenders, first-time and repeat offenders, and individuals from diverse racial and economic backgrounds. Studies should also be peer-reviewed and replicated to ensure their findings are not based on flawed assumptions.

Ethical Dilemmas in Criminal Profiling and Law Enforcement Research

Criminal psychology is widely used in **law enforcement investigations, criminal profiling, and interrogation techniques**. However, applying psychological research to police work comes with ethical risks.

One of the **most controversial issues** is the use of **psychological coercion in interrogations**. Some law enforcement agencies use tactics based on psychological principles, such as maximization (exaggerating evidence to pressure a confession) and minimization (downplaying the severity of the crime to encourage admission).

While these techniques can produce confessions, they also increase the risk of false confessions, particularly among juveniles and individuals with intellectual disabilities.

Criminal profiling raises additional ethical concerns. While profiling can help law enforcement **narrow down suspects**, it can also lead to **racial or gender-based discrimination**. For example, early FBI profiling techniques focused heavily on white male serial offenders, making it less effective at identifying female, minority, or international offenders. Law enforcement agencies must ensure that profiling methods are based on empirical research rather than outdated stereotypes.

The use of **predictive policing algorithms** based on psychological and sociological research is another area of ethical debate. Some jurisdictions use AI-driven crime prediction models that analyze **past criminal behavior, demographic data, and social conditions** to predict where crime is most likely to occur. However, these systems can reinforce systemic biases if the data they are trained on is already skewed. If crime reports disproportionately come from low-income neighborhoods, predictive policing may wrongly target these areas, increasing racial profiling and over-policing.

Balancing Ethics with the Need for Research

Criminal psychology research is essential for understanding **offender behavior, preventing crime, and improving rehabilitation efforts**. However, the **potential risks to participants, the justice system, and society** must always be considered. Ethical research in this field requires **protecting privacy, ensuring informed consent, preventing psychological harm, and avoiding bias**.

Researchers must also recognize the **real-world consequences** of their findings. If psychological research is misused, it can lead to false confessions, discriminatory policies, or unethical interrogation practices. Criminal psychology has the potential to improve law enforcement, rehabilitation, and legal decision-making, but only if it is conducted with strict ethical oversight.

The Role and Responsibilities of the Criminal Psychologist

Criminal psychologists analyze the thoughts, emotions, and behaviors of individuals involved in crime. Their work extends far beyond profiling criminals for law enforcement. They assess offenders, provide expert testimony in court, develop rehabilitation programs, and study the psychological factors that contribute to criminal behavior. Their expertise is applied in investigations, legal proceedings, corrections, and research, making them an essential part of the justice system.

Conducting Psychological Assessments of Offenders

One of the primary responsibilities of a criminal psychologist is evaluating offenders. Courts, law enforcement, and correctional institutions rely on these assessments to determine **mental competency, risk levels, and rehabilitation potential**. These evaluations help decide whether an individual is fit to stand trial, if they meet the legal criteria for insanity, or if they pose an ongoing threat to society.

Psychologists use structured interviews, psychological testing, and historical analysis to assess an offender's mental state. Standard tools include the **Minnesota Multiphasic Personality Inventory (MMPI-2)** for personality disorders, the **Hare Psychopathy Checklist-Revised (PCL-R)** for evaluating psychopathy, and risk assessment tools like the **HCR-20** to predict violent recidivism. These evaluations help courts make informed sentencing decisions, particularly in cases where mental illness is a factor.

Criminal psychologists also assess juveniles involved in the justice system. Young offenders present unique challenges because their **cognitive development, impulse control, and emotional regulation are not yet fully matured**. Evaluating whether a juvenile offender can be rehabilitated or whether they should be tried as an adult requires careful psychological examination.

Expert Testimony in Criminal Trials

Criminal psychologists frequently provide **expert testimony** in court. Their role is to help judges and juries understand **the psychological aspects of a case**, such as whether a defendant was mentally competent at the time of the crime or if a witness's memory is reliable.

A significant portion of expert testimony revolves around **insanity defenses**. In some cases, defendants claim they were legally insane at the time of the crime, meaning they were unable to distinguish right from wrong. Psychologists evaluate whether the defendant meets the criteria for insanity under legal standards such as the **M'Naghten Rule** or the **Durham Rule**, which vary by jurisdiction. These assessments can determine whether the individual should be sent to a psychiatric facility instead of prison.

Psychologists also testify about **false confessions**, which occur when suspects admit to crimes they did not commit due to **coercion, intimidation, or mental impairment**. Research has shown that certain interrogation techniques increase the likelihood of false confessions, particularly among individuals with **low IQ, mental illness, or extreme stress responses**. Expert testimony in these cases helps courts understand how confessions can sometimes be unreliable.

Criminal Profiling and Investigative Psychology

Although criminal profiling is often portrayed in movies and television, it represents only a small fraction of a criminal psychologist's work. When profiling is used, it involves analyzing past offenses to identify patterns, behavioral traits, and potential risk factors in an unknown suspect.

Behavioral profiling is based on **crime scene analysis, victimology, and statistical comparisons to previous offenders**. It helps law enforcement predict a suspect's potential background, age range, personality traits, and likelihood of reoffending. However, profiling is not an exact science—it is a tool that can narrow down investigative leads but cannot replace direct evidence.

Psychologists also work on **geographic profiling**, which analyzes the locations of crimes to identify where an offender is most likely to live or operate. Serial offenders often display patterns in where they commit their crimes, and understanding these patterns can assist law enforcement in predicting their movements.

Rehabilitation and Treatment of Offenders

Criminal psychologists contribute to the **treatment and rehabilitation of offenders** in prisons, psychiatric hospitals, and parole programs. Many offenders, particularly those with **antisocial personality disorder, substance abuse problems, or impulse control disorders**, require psychological intervention to reduce the risk of reoffending.

Therapeutic programs include **anger management, cognitive-behavioral therapy (CBT), and relapse prevention training**. CBT is widely used to help offenders recognize **distorted thinking patterns**, such as minimizing the impact of their crimes or blaming others for their actions. By challenging these thought patterns, therapy aims to reduce future criminal behavior.

Sex offenders often undergo **specialized rehabilitation programs** that focus on impulse control, empathy training, and relapse prevention. However, research has shown that treatment effectiveness varies widely depending on the offender's psychological makeup, level of remorse, and willingness to change.

In correctional facilities, psychologists help develop **risk assessment and intervention strategies**. They determine which inmates are likely to reoffend, who might benefit from therapy, and who poses a danger to themselves or others. These evaluations impact parole decisions, sentence reductions, and security classifications within prisons.

Research and Academic Contributions

Criminal psychologists also conduct research to improve **law enforcement strategies, legal policies, and rehabilitation efforts**. They study topics such as **criminal decision-making, the impact of childhood trauma on future offending, and the effectiveness of different sentencing policies**.

Longitudinal studies track offenders over years or even decades to identify patterns in **recidivism, behavioral changes, and rehabilitation outcomes**. These studies provide data that influence how criminal justice systems handle different types of offenders.

Some psychologists specialize in witness memory research, examining how stress, time delays, and interrogation techniques affect the accuracy of eyewitness testimony. Studies have shown that memory is highly malleable, and even confident witnesses can recall events inaccurately. These findings have led to changes in **how police lineups are conducted, how witnesses are questioned, and how much weight courts give to eyewitness testimony**.

Working with Law Enforcement and Crisis Negotiation

Some criminal psychologists work directly with law enforcement agencies as **consultants, hostage negotiators, or crisis intervention specialists**. In hostage situations, for example, psychologists analyze the behavior of **the hostage-taker**, determine their likely motivations, and help law enforcement develop negotiation strategies.

In crisis intervention, psychologists assist police in dealing with **mentally unstable individuals who may pose a danger to themselves or others**. Law enforcement officers often lack the training to handle psychiatric crises, and psychologists help de-escalate situations to avoid unnecessary violence or incarceration.

Psychologists also help law enforcement develop training programs on recognizing mental illness, de-escalation tactics, and communication strategies for dealing with offenders. Given that a significant percentage of individuals in the criminal justice system have **mental health conditions**, this training is essential for both public safety and ethical policing.

Ethical and Legal Responsibilities

Because their work directly affects legal decisions, psychologists in the criminal justice system **must adhere to strict ethical guidelines**. They must ensure their evaluations are **objective, scientifically valid, and not influenced by personal biases or external pressures**.

One of the most difficult ethical dilemmas involves **dual loyalty**—balancing the needs of the legal system with the well-being of the individual being assessed. For example, a prison psychologist might be asked to determine whether an inmate is fit for release, but if the inmate is also their patient, they must ensure their recommendations are **based on clinical judgment rather than institutional pressure**.

Psychologists must also avoid **overstepping their expertise**. They can provide insights into an offender's mental state, but they cannot determine **legal guilt or innocence**—that remains the responsibility of the courts. They must also ensure their findings are communicated clearly, avoiding psychological jargon that could be misinterpreted by judges, juries, or attorneys.

A Multi-Faceted Role in the Justice System

The work of a criminal psychologist **spans multiple areas**, from offender assessment and rehabilitation to legal consultation and crisis intervention. They analyze **why crimes occur, how offenders think, and how the justice system can respond more effectively**. Their research helps shape sentencing policies, prison reforms, and investigative techniques, while their clinical work provides treatment and risk management strategies for offenders.

Understanding crime requires more than legal knowledge—it requires insight into human behavior, motivation, and mental health. Criminal psychologists bring that expertise, ensuring that the justice system not only punishes crime but also works toward prevention, rehabilitation, and ethical decision-making.

Contemporary Challenges in Field Applications

Criminal psychology continues to evolve, but professionals in the field face growing challenges in applying psychological principles to law enforcement, the legal system, and offender rehabilitation. New types of crime, changing societal attitudes, and limitations in research and technology create obstacles that impact the effectiveness of criminal psychologists. From ethical concerns to emerging crime trends, these challenges force psychologists to adapt and refine their methods.

The Complexity of Predicting Criminal Behavior

One of the most difficult aspects of criminal psychology is predicting **who will commit a crime and when**. Risk assessments help determine whether an offender is likely to reoffend, but no method can guarantee accurate predictions. Factors influencing criminal behavior—mental illness, substance abuse, trauma, and social environment—are complex and interact in unpredictable ways.

Psychological tools like the **HCR-20 (Historical, Clinical, Risk Management)** are widely used to assess the risk of violence, but even the best tools are not foolproof. Some offenders show **no warning signs before committing violent acts**, while others with high-risk profiles never act on criminal impulses. Misjudging a person's risk level can have serious consequences. Overestimating risk leads to unnecessary imprisonment or overly restrictive parole conditions, while underestimating risk can put the public in danger.

Another issue is the **false positive problem**—labeling someone as dangerous when they are not. Many individuals with **antisocial personality traits or aggressive tendencies never commit crimes**, and excessive reliance on risk assessments can lead to **stigmatization and legal overreach**. Psychologists must constantly refine their methods while acknowledging the **inherent uncertainty in predicting human behavior**.

The Rise of Cybercrime and Digital Offenses

Traditional psychological models were developed based on **physical crimes**, but the rise of cybercrime has introduced new challenges. Many cybercriminals do not fit the **typical psychological profiles** of violent offenders. Unlike street criminals, hackers and online fraudsters often operate in isolation, lack direct contact with victims, and may not experience the same **moral and emotional responses** as those who commit face-to-face crimes.

Cybercriminals range from **teenagers engaging in online vandalism to sophisticated financial fraudsters**. Some are motivated by financial gain, others by ideology, and some by curiosity or boredom. The **absence of physical confrontation** makes it harder to study their behavior using traditional forensic psychology methods. Law enforcement agencies are still developing **psychological models that accurately explain cybercriminal motivations** and identify risk factors for digital offenses.

Additionally, online environments allow criminals to operate **anonymously** or under false identities, making psychological assessments difficult. Unlike traditional offenders, cybercriminals often **do not have criminal records, violent tendencies, or histories of delinquency**. They might be highly intelligent individuals who rationalize their actions as victimless crimes. Criminal psychologists must develop new frameworks that account for **the unique cognitive and social aspects of cybercrime**.

The Effectiveness of Rehabilitation Programs

Rehabilitation is a key goal of the criminal justice system, but determining what **works and what doesn't** remains a challenge. Some offenders respond well to therapy and education programs, while others **show no improvement or even become more dangerous after release**. Understanding which offenders can be rehabilitated and how to structure effective treatment programs is a major issue in the field.

One complication is that many rehabilitation programs were developed based on **research with non-criminal populations**. Traditional therapy models, such as **cognitive-behavioral therapy, dialectical behavior therapy (DBT), and psychodynamic therapy**, are effective for general mental health treatment but may not work the same way for offenders, especially those with **antisocial or psychopathic traits**.

For individuals with **psychopathy**, rehabilitation is particularly difficult. Many standard therapies focus on **developing empathy, impulse control, and emotional regulation**, but research suggests that psychopaths do not respond to treatment in the same way as other offenders. In some cases, therapy even makes them more manipulative by improving their ability to fake remorse and deceive authorities. Criminal psychologists must continuously adjust rehabilitation programs to fit different offender profiles.

The lack of **long-term follow-up studies** is another issue. Many rehabilitation programs measure success based on **whether an offender completes a program or shows improvement in the short term**, but recidivism rates often tell a different story. An offender who appears reformed in a controlled setting may return to crime once reintegrated into society. Developing effective methods for measuring long-term rehabilitation success remains one of the biggest challenges in the field.

The Ethical Dilemmas of Criminal Psychology

Criminal psychologists often work in situations where **ethics and legal obligations conflict**. They must balance the rights of offenders with the need to protect society, and their work can sometimes lead to **unintended harm**.

One major ethical concern is **bias in psychological evaluations**. Even though forensic assessments are designed to be objective, **unconscious biases** can still affect evaluations. Studies show that factors such as **race, gender, and socioeconomic status** can influence risk assessments, sentencing recommendations, and parole decisions. If psychological tools are not carefully calibrated, they may reinforce systemic biases in the justice system.

Another ethical issue involves **dual relationships**. A psychologist who evaluates an offender for a court case may later be asked to provide treatment in a prison setting. This creates a **conflict of interest**, as the psychologist must remain neutral in their assessments while also trying to help the offender rehabilitate. Courts and correctional institutions must establish **clear guidelines to prevent ethical conflicts in forensic psychology**.

Criminal psychologists also face **legal and moral dilemmas when dealing with dangerous offenders**. If an offender **confesses to planning a future crime**, psychologists must decide whether to break confidentiality and report it. In cases where there is no clear evidence of immediate danger, this decision becomes legally and ethically complex. Reporting **false or vague threats** can **unfairly harm** an offender's legal standing, but failing to act on a credible threat can lead to **preventable violence**.

The Challenge of Mental Illness in the Criminal Justice System

A **significant percentage of incarcerated individuals have mental health conditions**, yet prisons are **not equipped to handle psychiatric disorders effectively**. Many offenders who need psychiatric care end up in the prison system instead of mental health facilities due to gaps in legal and healthcare systems. Criminal psychologists must navigate the blurred line between criminal behavior and mental illness, determining when an individual should be treated rather than punished.

Certain mental illnesses, such as **schizophrenia, bipolar disorder, and PTSD**, can impair judgment and contribute to criminal actions. However, not all individuals with these conditions commit crimes, and **not all criminals with mental illness are incapable of understanding their actions**. Criminal psychologists must carefully distinguish **between criminal intent and impaired mental functioning**, ensuring that justice is served fairly.

Additionally, many mentally ill offenders do not receive proper treatment while incarcerated. Prisons are often **overcrowded, understaffed, and focused on punishment rather than rehabilitation**. Psychologists working in these environments must advocate for **mental health interventions, medication access, and specialized treatment programs** to reduce the likelihood of **repeat offenses among mentally ill inmates**.

Adapting to New Challenges in Criminal Psychology

As crime evolves, so must the field of criminal psychology. New forms of crime, ethical concerns, and **limitations in forensic research** all present obstacles that psychologists must address. The challenges are significant, but they also push the field to develop better assessment tools, improve rehabilitation methods, and refine ethical guidelines. Criminal psychology is constantly adapting, ensuring that law enforcement, the courts, and correctional systems are informed by psychological research that is as accurate, fair, and effective as possible.

Chapter 2: Theoretical Perspectives in Criminal Behavior

Psychodynamic Theories and the Unconscious Drivers of Crime

Psychodynamic theories suggest that criminal behavior stems from unconscious conflicts, early childhood experiences, and unresolved psychological tensions. These theories originate from Sigmund Freud's work in psychoanalysis, which argues that human behavior is shaped by deep, hidden forces within the mind. Criminal psychologists who take a psychodynamic approach believe that **crime is not a rational choice but an expression of unconscious desires, fears, or unresolved childhood trauma**.

Freud divided the human psyche into three components: the **id, ego, and superego**. The id represents primal desires and impulses, the ego mediates between desires and reality, and the superego enforces moral standards. When these forces are out of balance, behavior can become dysfunctional. Some criminals act out because their **id dominates**—seeking instant gratification without concern for consequences. Others commit crimes because their **superego is too weak**, failing to regulate impulses effectively. In contrast, an overly rigid superego can lead to repression and aggression, which may surface in violent or anti-social behavior.

Early childhood experiences also shape later behavior. Freud believed that psychological development occurs in stages, and disruptions in these stages can lead to **fixations and maladaptive behaviors**. For example, a child who experiences neglect, abuse, or inconsistent discipline may struggle to develop proper emotional regulation. They may seek out crime as a way to assert control, express repressed anger, or gain attention.

Attachment theory, an extension of psychodynamic ideas, suggests that early relationships with caregivers shape a person's emotional stability. Children who grow up in **unstable, neglectful, or abusive environments** may develop **insecure attachment styles**, which are linked to aggression, manipulation, and criminal behavior. Research shows that many offenders, particularly violent criminals, **experienced severe childhood trauma, abandonment, or inconsistent caregiving**. These early disruptions interfere with the development of empathy, trust, and self-control, increasing the likelihood of criminal behavior in adulthood.

Unresolved trauma can lead to **repetition compulsion**, a concept in psychodynamic theory that explains why some individuals **reenact past conflicts through crime**. For example, a person who was physically abused as a child may later commit violent crimes, unconsciously reliving their own victimization. Others may turn to **theft, fraud, or manipulation as a means of gaining control**, compensating for feelings of powerlessness experienced in childhood.

Freud's defense mechanisms also provide insight into criminal behavior. When people experience deep psychological distress, they use defense mechanisms to cope. **Denial, rationalization, projection, and displacement** are common among offenders. A person who commits domestic violence may **rationalize** their actions by blaming their partner's behavior. A fraudster may **deny** any wrongdoing, insisting that everyone else is just as dishonest. An aggressive offender may **project** their own insecurities onto others, justifying violent acts as self-defense.

Psychoanalytic explanations of crime also emphasize the concept of **guilt and unconscious punishment-seeking**. Some offenders, particularly those with deeply internalized guilt, may **unconsciously commit crimes as a way of punishing themselves**. This is seen in repeat offenders who sabotage their own chances at rehabilitation or commit crimes that ensure their own capture. Their behavior reflects **an unconscious desire for punishment**, stemming from unresolved guilt, self-hatred, or early childhood conditioning.

Another area where psychodynamic theory is applied in criminal psychology is **serial offending and violent crimes with ritualistic elements**. Some serial killers and violent offenders exhibit patterns that suggest **deep-rooted psychological fixations**. They may engage in repetitive behaviors, symbolic acts, or ritualistic violence that reflects internal conflicts. Some experts argue that **these crimes serve as a way for offenders to process, relive, or symbolically resolve childhood traumas**.

Critics of psychodynamic theories argue that these explanations **are difficult to test scientifically**. The unconscious mind cannot be measured directly, making it challenging to prove or disprove many of Freud's ideas. However, modern research supports **some key psychodynamic principles**, particularly the impact of early childhood trauma, attachment issues, and defense mechanisms in criminal behavior.

Contemporary forensic psychology integrates psychodynamic concepts with other approaches. While early Freudian ideas about sexuality and psychosexual stages have been largely abandoned, **the role of unconscious motivations, childhood experiences, and psychological conflict remains relevant** in criminal profiling, offender therapy, and forensic assessments.

In therapy, psychodynamic approaches help offenders explore **the roots of their behavior**, identify unresolved emotions, and develop healthier coping mechanisms. Techniques such as free association, dream analysis, and guided self-reflection are used in forensic settings to uncover unconscious motivations. However, traditional psychoanalysis is **rarely used in criminal psychology due to its long duration and lack of immediate behavioral interventions**. Instead, **short-term psychodynamic therapy** is sometimes integrated into rehabilitation programs, particularly for offenders with histories of trauma, deep-seated anger, or self-destructive tendencies.

One of the most influential extensions of psychodynamic theory in criminal psychology is the work of John Bowlby on **attachment and delinquency**. Bowlby's studies on juvenile offenders found that those with histories of early separation, neglect, or lack of maternal attachment were more likely to engage in **theft, aggression, and antisocial behavior**. This research reinforced the idea that early relational experiences shape moral development and impulse control.

Psychodynamic theories remain an important framework for understanding the deeper psychological forces behind crime. While they do not provide **a complete explanation for criminal behavior**, they offer insights into **how early** experiences, unconscious conflicts, and emotional disturbances shape an individual's path toward offending.

Behavioral and Cognitive Models: Learning and Decision-Making

Behavioral and cognitive theories explain criminal behavior by examining **how people learn to commit crimes and how they make decisions**. Unlike psychodynamic theories, which focus on unconscious motivations, these models emphasize **observable behaviors, thought patterns, and environmental influences**. Criminal behavior is not seen as the result of hidden psychological conflicts but rather as **a learned response to rewards, punishments, and cognitive distortions**.

Behaviorism and the Learning of Criminal Behavior

Behaviorists argue that all human actions, including crime, are shaped by **reinforcement and punishment**. Behavior is learned through interactions with the environment rather than being driven by unconscious forces or innate predispositions.

One of the most influential behavioral models is **operant conditioning**, developed by B.F. Skinner. This theory suggests that behaviors are strengthened when they are **rewarded** and weakened when they are **punished**. If a person steals and successfully avoids detection, they experience **reinforcement**, making them more likely to repeat the behavior. If they are caught and face severe consequences, they may be less likely to steal again.

Criminal behavior often persists because it is **reinforced in various ways**. A drug dealer may continue selling because of the financial rewards, while a gang member may feel a sense of **power, belonging, or status** from committing violent acts. Even when criminals face legal consequences, **if the rewards outweigh the punishments in their minds**, they are likely to reoffend.

Punishment is not always effective in changing behavior. Studies show that **inconsistent punishment**—where some crimes go unpunished while others result in severe consequences—makes it harder for people to learn from their actions. If an offender **gets away with multiple crimes before facing consequences**, they may see punishment as unpredictable rather than a deterrent. This explains why some habitual offenders continue committing crimes despite multiple arrests.

Classical conditioning, another behavioral concept, explains how **emotional responses become associated with crime**. A person who commits **violent acts in a stressful situation** may later experience an automatic surge of aggression when faced with similar stressors. If someone **associates stealing with excitement**, they may develop an emotional attachment to the thrill of the crime itself, independent of material gain.

Social Learning Theory and Crime as a Modeled Behavior

Albert Bandura expanded behaviorism by introducing **social learning theory**, which argues that people learn by **observing and imitating others**. Crime is not just reinforced by direct rewards but also **modeled by peers, media, and societal influences**.

Criminal behavior is often **learned from family members, friends, or role models**. If a child grows up in a household where theft, violence, or deception are normal, they are more likely to **adopt these behaviors as acceptable ways to solve problems**. Studies show that children of incarcerated parents have **a higher likelihood of becoming offenders themselves**, not necessarily because of genetics but because they learn criminal behavior as **a survival strategy**.

Gang culture provides an example of **criminal behavior being socially reinforced**. Young recruits observe older gang members engaging in violent acts and earning respect, money, or power. They learn that **violence is rewarded within their peer group**. Even if they fear law enforcement, **the immediate social benefits of gang membership outweigh the long-term risks**.

The media also has a role in social learning. Glorification of crime in movies, music, and social media can normalize criminal behavior, especially when it is portrayed as exciting or profitable. While most people can distinguish fiction from reality, individuals who lack strong moral reasoning or impulse control may be more susceptible to imitating criminal acts.

Differential association theory, developed by Edwin Sutherland, further expands on social learning by arguing that **criminal behavior is learned through communication and association with deviant individuals**. The more time a person spends with offenders, the more likely they are to adopt **criminal values, techniques, and justifications**.

Cognitive Theories: How Criminals Think

Cognitive models shift the focus from **behavior to thought processes**. They examine how criminals **interpret situations, justify their actions, and make decisions**. Many offenders engage in **cognitive distortions**, which are faulty or biased ways of thinking that allow them to commit crimes without guilt.

One common distortion is **minimization**, where offenders **downplay the severity of their crimes**. A fraudster may convince themselves that stealing from a large corporation is not truly harmful. A violent offender may claim that their victim "deserved it."

Another distortion is **blaming external factors**. Criminals may justify their actions by **blaming society, their upbringing, or their victims**. A burglar may rationalize stealing by believing that the rich do not deserve their wealth. A domestic abuser may insist that their partner provoked them.

Cognitive psychology also explains **how criminals assess risk and reward**. Research shows that **many offenders do not engage in logical cost-benefit** analysis. Instead of carefully weighing the **risks of getting caught against the potential rewards**, they often act impulsively, focusing on immediate gratification. This is particularly true for **violent crimes, drug-related offenses, and impulsive thefts**.

The **rational choice theory**, however, suggests that some criminals **do make calculated decisions** based on risk assessment. White-collar criminals, for example, often engage in detailed planning, ensuring that their fraudulent activities remain undetected. Organized crime members may carefully **strategize their actions, weigh risks, and eliminate threats to their operations**.

Research also shows that individuals with low self-control are more prone to crime. The General Theory of Crime, developed by Gottfredson and Hirschi, argues that most crimes are committed by individuals **who seek immediate gratification, lack patience, and have difficulty delaying rewards**. These traits are often formed in childhood, influenced by parenting style, discipline, and environmental stability.

Cognitive-Behavioral Approaches in Rehabilitation

Cognitive and behavioral theories have shaped modern offender rehabilitation programs. Cognitive-behavioral therapy (CBT) is widely used in correctional settings to help offenders **identify and change distorted thinking patterns**.

CBT programs focus on **impulse control, moral reasoning, and empathy training**. Offenders learn to recognize their **automatic thoughts and beliefs that contribute to criminal behavior**. For example, a violent offender may be taught to **pause and assess their emotions before reacting aggressively**. A repeat thief may be encouraged to **reframe their thinking about entitlement and consequences**.

Behavioral interventions, such as **token economies in prisons**, reinforce positive behavior by **rewarding compliance and discouraging rule-breaking**. Programs that use **structured rewards and consequences** have been shown to reduce recidivism in certain offender populations.

Why Some Criminals Do Not Learn from Punishment

If crime is learned behavior, why do some offenders **not change despite repeated arrests**? Research shows that **chronic offenders often experience "criminal hardening"**, where they become **desensitized to punishment and view incarceration as an expected part of life**.

For some, punishment **loses its deterrent effect** when they develop **cognitive defenses** against it. They may see prison as a place to strengthen criminal connections or use their experiences to **become better at avoiding detection in the future**.

Others continue offending because **their environment reinforces crime**. If an individual is released from prison but **returns to a high-crime neighborhood** with **no job prospects**, they may see no alternative but to re-engage in criminal activity.

Criminal psychology must account for these **complex learning patterns**, which involve **a mix of reinforcement, cognitive distortions, and environmental influences**. While some offenders can be reformed through **cognitive-behavioral interventions**, others require **major shifts in their social environment and opportunities** to break the cycle of crime.

Understanding how criminals learn and think helps criminal psychologists develop better interventions, improve risk assessments, and refine rehabilitation efforts. Crime is rarely a spontaneous act with no psychological basis—it is shaped by a lifetime of learned behaviors and cognitive patterns, which can sometimes be unlearned with the right interventions.

Social Learning and Environmental Influences on Offending

Criminal behavior does not develop in isolation. People learn crime from their surroundings—family, peers, culture, and media all shape how individuals perceive criminal actions. Social learning theory explains how people adopt criminal behavior through **observation, imitation, reinforcement, and normalization**. Unlike theories that focus on unconscious drives or biological factors, this perspective sees crime as a learned behavior influenced by social environments.

How Criminal Behavior is Learned

Albert Bandura's **social learning theory** argues that people do not need to experience direct rewards or punishments to learn behavior. Instead, they can **observe others and internalize their actions**. This is especially relevant in criminal behavior, where individuals see crime being **committed, rewarded, or ignored**, leading them to adopt similar behaviors.

People learn through direct observation of role models—parents, friends, gang leaders, or even fictional characters. If a child repeatedly witnesses a parent resolving conflicts through violence, they may come to see aggression as an acceptable response to frustration. If a teenager watches peers shoplift without consequence, they may believe theft is easy and low-risk.

Reinforcement also is important. If a person commits a crime and is rewarded socially or financially, they are more likely to repeat the behavior. Gang members often receive respect, protection, or material benefits for committing crimes, reinforcing their belief that crime is an effective means of achieving success. Even if someone does not initially seek out crime, being surrounded by it normalizes criminal behavior.

The media also serves as an indirect teacher. Movies, TV shows, and online platforms glorify crime, exaggerate the rewards, and downplay the consequences. While most people can distinguish fiction from reality, repeated exposure to crime as a source of power, revenge, or financial gain can influence how some individuals justify their actions.

Family Influence and Early Socialization

A person's **upbringing and family environment** shape their likelihood of engaging in crime. Families are the first and most powerful influence on a child's behavior. If criminal activity is present, accepted, or encouraged within the household, children are more likely to adopt those behaviors.

Parental neglect, inconsistent discipline, or a lack of supervision contribute to delinquency. Children raised in unstable households, where rules are unclear or constantly shifting, struggle to develop self-control and accountability. If parents fail to enforce consequences for misbehavior, children do not learn to associate actions with punishment.

On the other hand, some parents actively encourage criminal behavior. Children of organized criminals or repeat offenders may be trained in deception, theft, or violence from an early age. Some are pressured to commit crimes as a rite of passage or a way to prove loyalty to their family or community.

Sibling influence also matters. If an older sibling is involved in crime, younger siblings may follow their example, seeing crime as a family tradition or an expected lifestyle. Studies show that delinquency often runs in families, not due to genetics but because criminal behaviors are learned and reinforced over generations.

Peer Influence and Crime as a Social Activity

During adolescence, peers become **a dominant force in shaping behavior**. Teenagers and young adults are especially susceptible to peer pressure, as belonging to a group and gaining social approval are strong motivators.

Criminal behavior is often a group activity. Many first-time offenders commit crimes with friends, gangs, or social groups rather than acting alone. The presence of others reduces personal responsibility, emboldens risky behavior, and reinforces the idea that crime is acceptable.

Gangs provide an extreme example of social learning in criminal behavior. Young members observe older members engaging in violence, drug trafficking, or theft. They learn the techniques, develop a criminal identity, and gain status by mimicking experienced criminals. Many gangs use initiation rituals that require members to commit a crime, forcing them into illegal activity as a condition of acceptance.

Social groups also create pressure to conform. If a teenager's friends engage in minor criminal activity—vandalism, shoplifting, or drug use—they may feel compelled to participate, even if they would not commit these acts alone. They fear being labeled weak, disloyal, or excluded from the group.

Neighborhood and Community Influence

Where a person grows up influences their exposure to crime. High-crime neighborhoods **normalize criminal activity, reduce trust in law enforcement, and provide fewer legitimate opportunities for success**.

People who live in **poverty-stricken areas with high unemployment** may see crime as **a necessary means of survival**. If legal jobs are scarce and residents struggle financially, illegal activities like drug dealing, theft, or fraud become **alternative economic opportunities**. When crime is the **easiest way to make money**, people rationalize their actions as a survival strategy rather than a moral failure.

The **broken windows theory** suggests that visible signs of disorder—graffiti, vandalism, abandoned buildings, and public intoxication—encourage further criminal behavior. When people see that minor crimes go unpunished, they assume larger crimes will also be ignored. Over time, neighborhoods with high levels of disorder and little enforcement experience increased crime rates.

A lack of community trust in law enforcement also fuels crime. If residents **do not believe the police will protect them or treat them fairly**, they take justice into their own hands. This contributes to gang violence, vigilante actions, and revenge-based crimes. In communities where calling the police is viewed as betraying the neighborhood, crime goes unreported, allowing offenders to continue without consequences.

Cultural Norms and Crime Acceptance

Culture determines **which behaviors are acceptable, questionable, or criminal**. In some cultures, certain acts that are illegal in one society are widely accepted in another. Understanding cultural attitudes toward crime helps explain **why some offenses are more common in certain regions or communities**.

For example, **honor-based violence** exists in societies where **family reputation and social status** take precedence over individual rights. In some cultures, acts such as revenge killings, forced marriages, or violent retaliation for perceived disrespect are justified based on tradition.

Subcultures within larger societies also influence crime rates. Some groups glorify violence, dominance, or criminal enterprise as measures of success. For instance, organized crime families, extremist groups, and some gang cultures actively promote illegal activity as part of their identity.

In contrast, cultures that emphasize **collective responsibility, strong moral education, and community involvement** tend to have lower crime rates. Societies that promote social accountability, where individuals feel connected to their community, are less likely to produce high numbers of offenders.

The Role of Socialization in Crime Prevention

Since crime is often learned behavior, **it can also be unlearned**. Criminal psychology uses social learning theory to **develop intervention strategies** that focus on **early prevention, positive reinforcement, and alternative role models**.

Programs aimed at at-risk youth emphasize mentorship, structured activities, and social support to reduce criminal influences. Early intervention programs in schools help children from unstable environments develop impulse control, moral reasoning, and conflict resolution skills.

Community policing strategies **build relationships between law enforcement and residents, increasing trust and encouraging cooperation**. When people feel that law enforcement is fair and responsive, they are more likely to report crimes and reject criminal behavior.

Rehabilitation programs for offenders use social learning principles to replace criminal reinforcement with positive reinforcement. Inmates who are surrounded by pro-social influences, trained in legitimate work skills, and connected with supportive mentors upon release are less likely to return to crime.

Crime as a Socially Learned Phenomenon

Social learning theory helps explain **why crime spreads within families, peer groups, and communities**. People commit crimes not because they are inherently bad or biologically predisposed, but because they learn that crime is acceptable, rewarding, or necessary.

By understanding how criminal behavior is acquired through observation, reinforcement, and cultural norms, criminal psychologists and policymakers can develop better crime prevention strategies, stronger rehabilitation efforts, and more effective community interventions. The challenge is breaking cycles of crime by introducing new role models, alternative opportunities, and positive social reinforcements that replace the rewards of illegal behavior.

Evolutionary and Biological Frameworks for Understanding Crime

Criminal behavior is often analyzed through psychological and sociological perspectives, but evolutionary and biological theories provide a different lens. These frameworks examine how genetics, brain structure, hormones, and survival instincts influence criminal tendencies. While crime is shaped by environment and learning, biology and evolution may create predispositions that make some individuals more likely to offend.

The Role of Genetics in Criminal Behavior

Genetic research suggests that criminal tendencies can run in families. Studies on twins, particularly those raised apart, show that identical twins have higher rates of criminal similarity than fraternal twins. If one identical twin commits a crime, the other is more likely to have similar behavior, even when raised in different environments. This suggests that genetics influence criminal behavior, though they do not determine it entirely.

Research on adopted children also supports a genetic connection. Children of biological parents with criminal histories have higher chances of offending, even when raised in non-criminal adoptive families. However, genetics alone cannot explain why some individuals with these predispositions never commit crimes. Environmental factors still are important.

Scientists have identified genes associated with aggression and impulse control. One of the most studied is the MAOA gene, sometimes called the "warrior gene." Some variations of this gene are linked to higher aggression levels, particularly when combined with childhood abuse. Individuals with low-functioning MAOA who experience early trauma are at greater risk for violent behavior. However, not everyone with this gene variation becomes a criminal, showing that biological risks need environmental triggers to activate them.

Brain Structure and Criminal Behavior

Advancements in neuroscience reveal that differences in brain structure and function may contribute to criminal tendencies. Brain scans of violent offenders show abnormalities in the prefrontal cortex, amygdala, and limbic system—areas responsible for decision-making, impulse control, and emotional regulation.

The prefrontal cortex helps regulate emotions and control impulsive actions. Studies show that individuals with damage or underdevelopment in this area struggle with self-control, risk assessment, and ethical decision-making. Many violent offenders have reduced activity in the prefrontal cortex, which may explain their lack of inhibition.

The amygdala processes emotions, particularly fear and aggression. **In some criminals, particularly those with psychopathic traits, the amygdala is smaller or less active. This can lead to reduced empathy, poor fear recognition, and an inability to emotionally connect with victims**. People with psychopathy often commit crimes without guilt or remorse, which may be linked to differences in how their brains process emotions.

The limbic system, which controls emotions and survival instincts, can also contribute to criminal behavior. Overactive limbic systems can lead to heightened aggression and emotional instability. Some offenders display excessive emotional reactivity, making them more likely to act on violent impulses.

Brain injuries can also lead to criminal behavior. Damage to the frontal lobe, particularly from head trauma, has been linked to increased aggression, poor impulse control, and antisocial behavior. Some historical cases of violent criminals have been connected to traumatic brain injuries, leading researchers to explore how physical brain damage alters personality and behavior.

Hormonal and Neurochemical Influences on Crime

Hormones and neurotransmitters regulate mood, aggression, and impulse control. Abnormal levels of certain chemicals in the brain can contribute to criminal tendencies.

Testosterone is often linked to aggression. Higher levels of testosterone are associated with increased dominance-seeking behavior, impulsivity, and risk-taking. While not all individuals with high testosterone levels become violent, studies show that many violent offenders have above-average levels. This connection is particularly strong in male offenders, who commit most violent crimes.

Cortisol, a stress hormone, also influences behavior. Low cortisol levels are linked to reduced fear responses, meaning individuals with low cortisol may not experience anxiety about punishment or social consequences. This can make them more likely to engage in reckless or antisocial behavior.

Dopamine and serotonin are influential in impulse control and pleasure-seeking behavior. Dopamine is linked to reward-seeking and risk-taking, while serotonin helps regulate mood and aggression. Low serotonin levels are found in many violent offenders, suggesting that poor emotional regulation contributes to impulsive crimes.

Neurochemical imbalances alone do not create criminals, but they can make individuals more prone to aggression, impulsivity, or risk-taking. When combined with environmental stressors, these biological factors increase the likelihood of offending.

Evolutionary Perspectives on Crime

Evolutionary psychology explains crime as an adaptation to survival pressures. Human behavior evolved in response to threats, competition, and the need to pass on genes. Some criminal behaviors can be seen as extreme versions of survival strategies that benefited early humans.

One evolutionary explanation for crime is resource competition. In prehistoric societies, individuals had to fight for food, territory, and status. Aggressive, risk-taking individuals had a survival advantage in certain situations. While modern societies have legal structures, some individuals still engage in resource-driven crimes, such as theft and fraud, as a way to secure material advantages.

Sexual competition is another factor. Evolutionary theories suggest that men commit more violent crimes than women because of biological differences in mating strategies. In ancestral environments, men who displayed dominance and aggression were more likely to secure mates and pass on their genes. This may explain why most violent crimes, including homicide and sexual assault, are committed by men. While society discourages violence, the biological drive for status and competition remains.

Cheating behaviors, such as fraud and deception, also have evolutionary roots. In early human societies, individuals who could manipulate others for personal gain had an advantage. While social structures punish deception today, the tendency to seek shortcuts to success remains. White-collar criminals, con artists, and scammers use deception in ways that mirror ancestral survival tactics.

Risk-taking behavior, often seen in criminals, also has evolutionary advantages. Taking risks can lead to high rewards, whether in hunting, warfare, or social dominance. In modern society, some individuals channel risk-taking into crime rather than socially acceptable challenges. This may explain why many criminals engage in reckless, high-stakes behavior despite the risks of punishment.

Nature vs. Nurture: The Interaction of Biology and Environment

Biological and evolutionary factors do not determine criminal behavior on their own. Genetics and brain function may create predispositions, but environment shapes whether those tendencies turn into actual crimes. A person with a genetic risk for aggression may never act violently if raised in a supportive, structured environment. Conversely, someone with no biological predisposition may become a criminal due to severe childhood trauma, social pressure, or economic hardship.

Twin studies reveal that genetic influence on crime varies depending on upbringing. Identical twins raised in different environments show different crime patterns, proving that biology is not destiny. Instead, biological risks interact with environmental triggers, such as poverty, abuse, or peer influence.

Early intervention programs recognize this interaction. Programs aimed at improving childhood development, emotional regulation, and impulse control can help counteract biological risk factors. Cognitive-behavioral therapy, social skills training, and structured environments help individuals with biological predispositions learn alternative behaviors.

The Future of Biological Research in Criminal Psychology

Advancements in neuroscience and genetics continue to shape how criminal behavior is understood. Brain imaging technology allows researchers to study how offenders' brains function differently, leading to potential early detection of risk factors. Genetic research is identifying new markers linked to aggression and impulse control.

However, ethical concerns remain. If criminal tendencies can be predicted biologically, should individuals with certain genetic markers or brain structures be treated differently? Could biological explanations for crime be used to justify harsher punishments or, conversely, to argue that offenders have less responsibility for their actions? These debates will shape the future of criminal psychology and how society balances justice with scientific understanding.

Criminal behavior is influenced by many factors, and biological perspectives offer insights into why some individuals are more prone to offending. While biology is not the sole cause of crime, it interacts with environment, upbringing, and personal choices in ways that help explain the complexity of human behavior. Understanding these biological and evolutionary factors allows criminal psychologists to develop better prevention strategies, treatment approaches, and interventions for those at risk of offending.

Chapter 3: Biological Underpinnings of Criminality

Genetic Influences and Heritability Factors

Criminal behavior is shaped by both genetics and environment. While crime is not directly inherited, research shows that genetic factors contribute to aggression, impulsivity, and antisocial behavior. The question is not whether crime is genetic but **how genetic predispositions interact with life experiences to influence criminal behavior**.

Twin and Adoption Studies: Measuring Genetic Influence

Studies on twins provide strong evidence that genetics influence criminal behavior. Identical twins share 100% of their genes, while fraternal twins share about 50%. If crime were purely environmental, identical and fraternal twins would have **similar crime rates**. But research consistently shows that **identical twins are more likely to both engage in criminal activity compared to fraternal twins**. This suggests a genetic influence.

Adoption studies further separate genetic and environmental factors. When children are adopted into non-criminal families, **their biological parents' criminal history still predicts their likelihood of offending**. If crime were purely learned, adopted children would resemble their adoptive parents. Instead, studies show that children of criminal biological parents **have a higher chance of offending, even when raised in non-criminal homes**.

One of the most famous adoption studies, conducted in Denmark, found that **boys whose biological fathers had criminal records were more likely to engage in criminal behavior than those whose biological fathers did not, even when raised in non-criminal families**. This suggests that certain genetic traits make people more vulnerable to criminal behavior, though environment still influences whether those traits lead to crime.

Genes Linked to Aggression and Criminal Behavior

Genetic research has identified specific genes associated with aggression, impulsivity, and antisocial tendencies. One of the most studied is the **MAOA gene**, sometimes called the "warrior gene." This gene regulates the breakdown of neurotransmitters like dopamine and serotonin, which influence mood and impulse control. Some people have **low-functioning MAOA**, which has been linked to increased aggression, particularly in individuals exposed to childhood abuse.

Studies show that men with **low-functioning MAOA who were abused as children are significantly more likely to engage in violent crime than those with normal MAOA function**. However, men with this gene variation who were not abused show **no significant increase in violent behavior**. This suggests that genetics create **a vulnerability rather than a direct cause of crime—** environmental triggers still matter.

Other genes linked to criminal behavior include those involved in **dopamine regulation**. Dopamine is linked to **reward-seeking and impulsivity**, and variations in dopamine-related genes are associated with **risk-taking and reduced sensitivity to punishment**. Individuals with **certain dopamine receptor gene variations** may be more likely to engage in **thrill-seeking behavior**, including criminal activity.

Heritability of Crime: How Much is Genetic?

Heritability estimates tell us how much of a trait can be attributed to genetics compared to environment. Studies on criminal behavior suggest that **genetics account for about 40-50% of the variation in antisocial behavior**, meaning that environment also has a major role.

Heritability is higher for violent crimes than for non-violent crimes. Research suggests that aggression and impulsivity are more strongly linked to genetics, while crimes like theft or fraud are influenced more by opportunity and social environment.

Psychopathy and Genetic Influence

Psychopathy is one of the strongest genetically influenced traits associated with criminal behavior. People with psychopathic traits show **low empathy, high impulsivity, and a lack of fear or guilt**. Studies show that **psychopathic tendencies are highly heritable, with estimates around 50-60%**.

Brain scans of individuals with psychopathy reveal structural differences in the amygdala (which processes emotions) and the prefrontal cortex (which regulates decision-making and impulse control). These differences suggest that some individuals are biologically predisposed to reduced emotional responses and poor impulse control, making them more likely to engage in criminal activity.

However, not all people with psychopathic traits become criminals. Some channel their traits into socially acceptable careers, such as business or politics. The difference often lies in **early social experiences, education, and environmental conditioning**.

The Interaction of Genes and Environment

Genetics create **a foundation, but environment determines how those genetic traits are expressed**. The same genetic predisposition for aggression can lead to **criminal behavior in a violent, unstable home or success in competitive sports or business in a structured, supportive environment**.

A key concept in this interaction is **gene-environment correlation**. People with genetic tendencies toward aggression may be more likely to **end up in high-risk environments**. A naturally impulsive child may seek out **thrill-seeking peers**, increasing their likelihood of engaging in crime. A person with high aggression levels may provoke hostile reactions from others, reinforcing violent behavior.

Epigenetics also shows how environment affects gene expression. Stress, trauma, and abuse can switch certain genes on or off, altering brain chemistry. Childhood neglect can increase aggression-related gene expression, making crime more likely. This means that genetics do not work alone—life experiences shape whether genetic risks turn into criminal behavior.

Genetics and Sentencing: Ethical Concerns

If genetic traits influence crime, should they be considered in sentencing and rehabilitation? Some argue that **genetic predisposition should be a mitigating factor**, meaning those with high genetic risks should receive more rehabilitation instead of just punishment. Others worry that genetic explanations could lead to **harsher sentences for people deemed biologically dangerous**, even if they have not committed a crime.

Research in this area is ongoing, but most experts agree that **genetics should never be used as the sole factor in legal decisions**. Crime is complex, and while biology contributes, social factors, personal choices, and rehabilitation potential all matter.

Future Directions in Genetic Research on Crime

Advances in genetic research may help identify **early warning signs of behavioral disorders** linked to crime. If psychologists can detect risk factors in childhood, **early intervention programs** could help reduce criminal behavior.

However, the ethical concerns surrounding genetic profiling remain significant. If people are labeled **high-risk based on genetics**, they could face **unfair treatment, discrimination, or loss of personal freedom**. Future research must balance **scientific discovery with ethical responsibility**.

Genetics provide a foundation for understanding crime, but they do not determine destiny. **A person may inherit traits that increase their likelihood of offending, but environment, upbringing, and personal choices still shape their path.** Recognizing this balance helps criminal psychologists develop better prevention, treatment, and legal strategies while avoiding oversimplified or harmful genetic explanations for crime.

Neurobiological Contributions to Aggression and Impulsivity

Criminal behavior often involves aggression and poor impulse control. Neuroscientists study how brain structures, neurotransmitters, and neural pathways influence violent and impulsive actions. While aggression can be learned through environment and socialization, neurobiological factors create predispositions that make some individuals more prone to violent behavior.

Brain Structures Involved in Aggression

The **prefrontal cortex**, **amygdala**, and **limbic system** are influential in regulating aggression and impulse control. Brain scans of violent offenders show structural and functional differences in these regions compared to non-offenders.

The **prefrontal cortex**, located in the front of the brain, helps regulate decision-making, emotional control, and long-term planning. When this area is underactive or damaged, individuals struggle to control impulses and consider consequences before acting. Studies on individuals with prefrontal cortex damage show **increased aggression, poor judgment, and higher rates of criminal behavior**.

The **amygdala**, a small structure deep in the brain, processes emotions such as fear and anger. Overactive amygdalas are linked to heightened aggression, while underactive amygdalas are associated with reduced empathy and a lack of emotional response to violence. Some violent criminals exhibit **hyperactivity in the amygdala**, leading to **exaggerated emotional reactions and impulsive violence**. Others, particularly psychopathic offenders, show **reduced amygdala activity**, contributing to emotional detachment and lack of remorse.

The **limbic system**, which includes the amygdala and other structures, controls emotional regulation and survival instincts. An overactive limbic system can make individuals **more emotionally reactive, increasing the likelihood of impulsive aggression**. People with limbic system abnormalities often have difficulty managing stress and frustration, which can lead to violent outbursts.

Neurotransmitters and Criminal Behavior

Neurotransmitters are chemicals that help transmit signals in the brain. Certain neurotransmitters regulate aggression, mood stability, and impulse control. Imbalances in these chemicals are linked to violent and criminal behavior.

Serotonin has a major role in regulating mood and aggression. Low serotonin levels are associated with **increased impulsivity, aggression, and difficulty managing emotions**. Studies show that violent criminals, particularly those with histories of impulsive aggression, often have lower serotonin levels than non-violent individuals. People with serotonin deficiencies may struggle to **control their temper, overreact to minor provocations, or act without thinking**.

Dopamine is involved in the brain's reward system and influences risk-taking behavior. High dopamine levels can increase **sensation-seeking tendencies**, making individuals more likely to engage in criminal activity for excitement or pleasure. Some offenders engage in **violent or criminal acts not just for material gain but for the thrill itself**.

Cortisol, the body's primary stress hormone, regulates responses to fear and punishment. Low cortisol levels are linked to **fearlessness and a reduced sensitivity to consequences**. Individuals with chronically low cortisol may not feel anxious about getting caught or punished, making them more likely to take risks.

Testosterone is associated with aggression and dominance-seeking behavior. High levels of testosterone are correlated with increased **aggression, impulsivity, and competitiveness**. While not all individuals with high testosterone engage in violence, research suggests that elevated testosterone **can amplify aggressive tendencies, particularly in response to provocation**.

Brain Injury and Criminal Behavior

Head injuries can dramatically alter personality, impulse control, and aggression levels. Studies on traumatic brain injuries (TBI) reveal a strong link between **frontal lobe damage and increased criminal behavior**. The frontal lobe, particularly the prefrontal cortex, is responsible for rational decision-making and emotional regulation. When damaged, individuals struggle with impulse control, display reckless behavior, and show increased aggression.

Research on violent offenders finds **higher rates of childhood head injuries compared to the general population**. Some famous criminal cases, including serial killers and violent criminals, involve histories of **brain trauma that may have contributed to their behavior**.

Neurodevelopmental Factors and Early Life Influences

Brain development in childhood and adolescence affects aggression and impulse control. Adverse childhood experiences, such as neglect, abuse, and prenatal exposure to drugs or alcohol, **can interfere with normal brain development**. Children exposed to extreme stress at a young age may develop **overactive limbic systems and underactive prefrontal cortices**, increasing their likelihood of aggressive behavior.

Neurodevelopmental disorders, including **attention-deficit/hyperactivity disorder (ADHD) and conduct disorder**, are associated with **higher rates of impulsive crime**. Individuals with ADHD often struggle with **impulse control, delayed gratification, and risk assessment**, making them more likely to engage in reckless or criminal behavior, especially if they grow up in unstable environments.

Implications for Criminal Justice and Rehabilitation

Understanding the neurobiological basis of aggression helps develop better rehabilitation and intervention strategies. Programs that focus on **impulse control, emotional regulation, and stress management** can help individuals with neurobiological vulnerabilities.

Medication and therapy targeting neurotransmitter imbalances can help manage aggression in individuals with **low serotonin or high dopamine levels**. Behavioral therapies that strengthen prefrontal cortex functioning, such as **cognitive-behavioral therapy**, help offenders learn **self-control techniques and better decision-making skills**.

Brain research is shaping the future of criminal psychology. By identifying biological risk factors early, psychologists and law enforcement professionals can develop **preventive strategies to reduce violent crime and improve rehabilitation outcomes**.

Brain Structure Variations and Their Link to Criminal Behavior

Criminal behavior has long been associated with differences in brain structure. Neuroscientists use brain imaging technology to study how structural abnormalities in the brain contribute to aggression, impulsivity, and antisocial behavior. While no single brain structure causes crime, research shows that certain areas are consistently different in offenders compared to non-offenders.

The Prefrontal Cortex: Decision-Making and Self-Control

The **prefrontal cortex**, located at the front of the brain, is responsible for **rational decision-making, impulse control, and moral reasoning**. It regulates emotions, weighs consequences, and helps people resist urges that could lead to harmful actions.

Brain scans of violent offenders show **reduced activity in the prefrontal cortex** compared to non-violent individuals. When this area is underactive, people struggle with **self-control, risk assessment, and ethical judgment**. Studies on individuals with prefrontal cortex damage reveal **higher levels of aggression, poor decision-making, and reduced ability to regulate emotions**.

One study on murderers found that their **prefrontal cortex activity was significantly lower than that of non-murderers**. This suggests that impairments in this region may increase the likelihood of impulsive violence. However, not everyone with low prefrontal cortex activity becomes a criminal. Environment, upbringing, and personal choices also influence behavior.

The Amygdala: Emotional Regulation and Aggression

The amygdala, a small almond-shaped structure deep in the brain, processes emotions such as fear, anger, and pleasure. It's important in threat detection and aggression regulation. Research shows that **abnormalities in the amygdala are linked to both impulsive and premeditated violent behavior**.

Some offenders, particularly those with **psychopathic traits**, have **smaller or underactive amygdalas**. This may explain their **lack of empathy, reduced fear response, and emotional detachment**. People with psychopathy often commit crimes **without remorse or guilt**, which could be due to their brains not processing emotional stimuli the same way as non-offenders.

Other violent criminals show hyperactivity in the amygdala, leading to overreactive emotional responses and heightened aggression. These individuals may become **easily provoked, struggle with emotional regulation, and lash out violently when under stress**.

The Limbic System and Emotional Control

The **limbic system**, which includes the amygdala and other structures, controls emotions, memory, and motivation. An overactive limbic system can make individuals **more emotionally reactive and aggressive**. Those with high limbic system activity often struggle with **anger management and impulse control**.

The hippocampus, another limbic system structure, is responsible for learning and memory. Some studies suggest that **individuals with smaller hippocampi have difficulty learning from past experiences**, meaning they may **repeat criminal behaviors despite previous punishments**.

The Corpus Callosum and Communication Between Brain Hemispheres

The corpus callosum connects the left and right hemispheres of the brain, allowing for communication between rational thought (left hemisphere) and emotional processing (right hemisphere). Studies show that **criminals, particularly those with psychopathic traits, often have thinner or less active corpus callosums**. This may contribute to **poor emotional regulation, impulsivity, and a reduced ability to feel empathy**.

Research on serial killers and violent offenders suggests that poor connectivity between the two hemispheres may prevent emotions from influencing rational thought, leading to cold, calculated violence with no emotional restraint.

Brain Differences in Psychopaths vs. Impulsive Offenders

Not all criminals have the same brain structure variations. Research distinguishes between **impulsive offenders, who act out of emotion, and psychopathic offenders, who plan crimes without emotional involvement**.

Impulsive offenders often have **reduced prefrontal cortex activity and overactive amygdalas**, making them react aggressively without thinking. These individuals commit crimes **in the heat of the moment, often due to stress, anger, or fear**.

Psychopathic offenders, on the other hand, tend to have **underactive amygdalas, reduced prefrontal connectivity, and abnormalities in the corpus callosum**. They **do not react emotionally, plan crimes carefully, and lack empathy for their victims**. Their crimes are often **strategic rather than impulsive**.

Brain Abnormalities from Injury and Trauma

Traumatic brain injuries (TBI) are linked to increased aggression and violent behavior. Damage to the **frontal lobe**—which includes the prefrontal cortex—has been found in a disproportionate number of violent offenders.

Some historical criminal cases involve individuals who **developed violent tendencies after suffering brain trauma**. One of the most famous examples is **Phineas Gage**, a railroad worker who survived an accident where an iron rod pierced his skull. After the injury, his personality changed dramatically—he became aggressive, impulsive, and socially inappropriate. This case provided early evidence that the **prefrontal cortex is crucial for self-control and decision-making**.

Studies of prison populations show that a significant number of inmates have **histories of head injuries, particularly those affecting the frontal lobe**. Brain trauma can disrupt **emotional regulation, impulse control, and moral reasoning**, making affected individuals more prone to aggression.

Neuroplasticity: Can the Brain Change?

One of the most important findings in neuroscience is that the brain can **adapt and change over time**, a concept known as **neuroplasticity**. This means that even if an individual has structural differences that predispose them to criminal behavior, therapy, training, and rehabilitation can help improve self-control and decision-making.

Cognitive-behavioral therapy (CBT) and impulse control training have been shown to increase prefrontal cortex activity and improve emotional regulation. Meditation and stress management techniques can help reduce amygdala hyperactivity, making individuals less reactive to stress and provocation.

While brain structure influences behavior, **it doesn't dictate fate**. Understanding these biological differences allows psychologists and criminal justice professionals to develop **more effective intervention strategies** that focus on **rehabilitation rather than just punishment**. By targeting brain functions that regulate impulse control, aggression, and emotional processing, many offenders can learn to manage their behavior and reduce their risk of reoffending.

Neurotransmitter Imbalances and Behavioral Dysregulation

Criminal behavior is influenced by a complex interaction of brain chemistry and external environment. Neurotransmitters—chemical messengers in the brain—are influential in regulating mood, impulse control, aggression, and decision-making. When these chemical balances are disrupted, individuals may exhibit behaviors that increase their risk of engaging in crime. While neurotransmitter imbalances alone do not cause criminal behavior, they contribute to personality traits and emotional responses that make offending more likely under certain conditions.

Serotonin is one of the most widely studied neurotransmitters in relation to aggression and impulse control. **Low levels of serotonin are consistently linked to increased aggression, irritability, and difficulty in regulating emotions**. Studies on violent offenders show that many have lower serotonin activity compared to non-violent individuals. The reason for this link is that serotonin helps regulate impulsivity and mood stability. When serotonin levels are low, individuals may struggle to control anger and frustration, making them more likely to react violently to stressors or perceived threats.

In some cases, serotonin deficiency has been associated with an inability to anticipate negative consequences, leading to reckless and antisocial behavior. This explains why some individuals continue engaging in crime despite repeated arrests or punishments. They are neurologically less sensitive to the long-term risks of their actions.

Dopamine, another important neurotransmitter, is associated with reward-seeking behavior and pleasure. **High dopamine levels are linked to sensation-seeking and risk-taking, two traits that are commonly found in offenders**.

Individuals with an overactive dopamine system may engage in crime not out of necessity but for the thrill or excitement it brings. This is particularly common in impulsive crimes such as theft, vandalism, and violent assaults. The brain's reward system reinforces behaviors that produce pleasure, and for some offenders, crime itself can become a source of stimulation. In cases of repeat offenders, particularly those involved in high-risk criminal activities like armed robbery or drug trafficking, there is evidence that the dopamine system may reinforce criminal behavior in the same way it reinforces addiction. They may feel compelled to keep committing crimes because their brain has linked crime with a sense of excitement or personal gratification.

Norepinephrine, often referred to as the stress hormone, is another neurotransmitter involved in criminal behavior. It regulates the body's response to stress and danger, affecting alertness, arousal, and emotional reactivity. Individuals with an overactive norepinephrine system are more likely to exhibit aggression and hypervigilance.

Many violent offenders show excessive norepinephrine activity, which makes them more prone to overreacting to perceived threats. This is particularly relevant in reactive aggression, where individuals lash out violently in response to anger or fear. Over time, an exaggerated stress response can lead to an individual becoming highly aggressive even in non-threatening situations, increasing the likelihood of violent crime.

Cortisol, the body's primary stress-regulating hormone, interacts with neurotransmitters to modulate emotional responses. **Research shows that individuals with chronically low cortisol levels tend to have reduced fear responses. This means they do not experience the same level of anxiety about punishment or social rejection as others. In criminal psychology, this is significant because fear of consequences is a major deterrent for crime**. If an individual has a blunted stress response, they may not feel the same level of caution or remorse when committing a crime. Low cortisol has been observed in violent offenders, particularly those who show no signs of emotional distress after committing an act of violence. Their bodies do not produce the same level of stress hormones that would typically trigger fear or guilt, making them more likely to engage in criminal behavior without hesitation.

The interaction between neurotransmitters and early life experiences is crucial in determining how these imbalances manifest in behavior. Many individuals with neurotransmitter abnormalities do not become criminals because their environment provides stability, discipline, and positive reinforcement for prosocial behavior.

However, when combined with childhood trauma, neglect, or exposure to violence, these neurochemical imbalances can **increase the risk of antisocial and aggressive tendencies**. Children who experience severe neglect or abuse often develop dysregulated neurotransmitter systems, leading to problems with emotional control and decision-making later in life. Early exposure to violence can also sensitize the brain's reward system to aggression, making violent acts feel more rewarding over time.

Substance abuse is another factor that alters neurotransmitter function and contributes to criminal behavior. Many offenders have histories of drug or alcohol abuse, which can further disrupt brain chemistry. Stimulants like cocaine and methamphetamine artificially increase dopamine levels, leading to increased risk-taking and impulsivity.

Chronic use of these substances can cause long-term changes in the brain's reward system, making individuals more prone to addiction-driven crimes such as theft, assault, and drug trafficking. Alcohol, on the other hand, reduces serotonin levels, impairing impulse control and increasing aggression. Many violent crimes, including domestic violence and homicide, are committed under the influence of alcohol because it lowers inhibitions and impairs judgment.

Psychopathy, **a condition often associated with criminal behavior, has been linked to abnormal neurotransmitter activity**. Individuals with psychopathy show reduced serotonin function, leading to emotional detachment and a lack of empathy. They also have higher dopamine activity, which contributes to their sensation-seeking and manipulative tendencies.

This combination of low serotonin and high dopamine creates individuals who are both impulsive and reward-driven, making them more likely to engage in crime for personal gain or enjoyment. Unlike impulsive offenders who act out of emotional dysregulation, psychopaths commit crimes with calculated intent. Their brains don't register distress or guilt in the same way as non-psychopathic individuals, which explains their lack of remorse even after committing serious offenses.

Brain imaging studies provide further evidence of how neurotransmitter imbalances affect behavior. Functional MRI scans of violent criminals show abnormalities in brain regions that regulate neurotransmitter activity, particularly the prefrontal cortex and amygdala. In many cases, these individuals show hyperactivity in the brain's reward system and reduced connectivity in areas responsible for impulse control. This imbalance creates a neurological environment where aggression and risk-taking are more easily triggered while emotional regulation is impaired.

While neurotransmitter imbalances do not excuse criminal behavior, they provide insight into why some individuals are more prone to impulsive, aggressive, or antisocial tendencies. Understanding these biological influences allows for better rehabilitation strategies that target brain chemistry. Medications that regulate serotonin and dopamine levels, for example, have been used in some correctional programs to help offenders manage aggression and impulsivity. Behavioral therapies that focus on impulse control and emotional regulation can also help individuals with neurotransmitter dysregulation develop alternative coping mechanisms.

Neuroscience continues to shape the field of criminal psychology, offering new ways to understand and address the biological underpinnings of crime. While social and environmental factors remain significant in shaping behavior, the role of neurotransmitters in aggression, impulse control, and decision-making cannot be ignored. Future research in this area may lead to more effective interventions that reduce recidivism by addressing the root biological causes of criminal behavior.

Hormonal Effects on Aggression and Decision-Making

Hormones regulate many aspects of human behavior, including aggression, impulse control, and risk-taking. The endocrine system, which controls hormone production, interacts with the brain to influence emotional responses and decision-making. While no hormone directly causes criminal behavior, **imbalances in certain hormones can increase aggression, impair judgment, and lower sensitivity to punishment**. Understanding how hormones influence behavior helps explain why some individuals are more prone to violent or reckless actions, especially in high-stress environments.

Testosterone is one of the most widely studied hormones in relation to aggression and criminal behavior. It is primarily associated with dominance-seeking, competition, and risk-taking. Research consistently shows that individuals with higher testosterone levels tend to exhibit increased aggression and impulsivity, especially when provoked. Studies on violent offenders and prison populations indicate that those convicted of **violent crimes, such as assault and homicide, often have elevated testosterone levels compared to non-violent offenders**.

One reason testosterone is linked to crime is its effect on **impulse control and threat perception**. High levels of testosterone **increase sensitivity to perceived threats and lower the threshold for aggressive responses**. This means that individuals with elevated testosterone may be more likely to react violently in situations where others would de-escalate. This is particularly relevant in crimes involving rage, territorial disputes, and violent confrontations. However, not everyone with high testosterone becomes aggressive. Socialization, upbringing, and environmental stressors are important in determining how testosterone influences behavior.

Testosterone also affects **risk-taking behavior**. People with **higher levels of this hormone are more likely to engage in sensation-seeking activities, including reckless criminal behavior.** This can manifest in crimes like robbery, drug trafficking, and fraud, where offenders take significant risks for potential rewards. Testosterone's role in risk assessment helps explain why most violent crimes are committed by men, who naturally have higher testosterone levels than women. However, studies show that in both men and women, testosterone fluctuations influence competitiveness, aggression, and decision-making, reinforcing its connection to antisocial behavior.

Another hormone that has a role in criminal behavior is **cortisol, the body's primary stress hormone**. Cortisol regulates **fear responses and emotional regulation**, affecting how individuals react to stress and punishment. Low cortisol levels are linked to a reduced fear response, making individuals less sensitive to punishment and social consequences. This explains why some offenders repeatedly engage in criminal behavior despite facing severe legal penalties. If an individual does not experience stress or fear in response to punishment, they are more likely to continue engaging in risky or antisocial behavior.

Studies on juvenile offenders and repeat criminals show that many have lower baseline cortisol levels than individuals who do not engage in criminal activity. This suggests that their bodies do not experience the same stress-related deterrents that discourage most people from engaging in crime. In contrast, individuals with higher cortisol levels tend to avoid risky behaviors due to their stronger stress responses. This has implications for criminal justice policies, as punishment-based deterrents may be **less effective for individuals with naturally low cortisol levels.**

Oxytocin and vasopressin, hormones linked to social bonding and trust, also influence criminal behavior. Oxytocin promotes **prosocial behaviors like empathy, cooperation, and emotional bonding**, while vasopressin is associated with **territorial aggression and social dominance.** Studies suggest that low oxytocin levels are linked to increased aggression and antisocial tendencies, making it harder for individuals to form emotional connections with others. This is particularly relevant in psychopathy, where offenders lack empathy and emotional engagement with their victims.

In contrast, **higher levels of vasopressin are linked to increased aggression, particularly in males.** Research on prisoners convicted of violent crimes shows that many have higher vasopressin activity than non-violent offenders. This hormone reinforces territorial aggression and dominance-seeking behavior, which can contribute to violent confrontations, gang activity, and crimes motivated by power struggles.

Another hormone implicated in criminal behavior is dopamine, a neurotransmitter and hormone involved in pleasure and reward-seeking. While dopamine is primarily a brain chemical, it also functions as a hormone that affects motivation, impulsivity, and risk-taking. Individuals with high dopamine levels are more prone to sensation-seeking behavior, which can lead to impulsive crimes, thrill-seeking offenses, and addiction-related crimes.

Dopamine imbalances are commonly observed in offenders who engage in impulsive and addictive behaviors. Substance abuse, gambling-related crimes, and high-risk fraud schemes are often driven by an overactive dopamine system that reinforces risk-taking and reward-seeking. This helps explain why drug addicts often engage in theft or other crimes to sustain their addiction, as their dopamine-driven reward system prioritizes short-term pleasure over long-term consequences.

Hormonal influences on criminal behavior also vary across **different life stages.** During adolescence, testosterone levels surge, increasing **risk-taking, impulsivity, and aggression.** This explains why **juvenile crime rates are significantly higher than adult crime rates**, particularly for violent offenses. The combination of **high testosterone, immature impulse control, and underdeveloped decision-making abilities makes adolescents more prone to engaging in criminal activity.**

Hormonal imbalances can also contribute to **temporary aggression and criminal behavior in adults.** For example, steroid abuse significantly increases testosterone levels, leading to heightened aggression, mood swings, and increased risk-taking. Many athletes and bodybuilders who use anabolic steroids report increased irritability and violent outbursts, sometimes resulting in criminal behavior.

The interaction between hormones and environmental factors is critical in determining how these biological influences manifest in behavior. Not everyone with high testosterone, low cortisol, or dopamine imbalances engages in crime. Family stability, education, social support, and access to positive role models can counteract biological risk factors by reinforcing self-control and prosocial behavior.

Neuroscientists and criminal psychologists are exploring **how hormonal regulation could be used in rehabilitation programs.** Some studies suggest that medications that stabilize hormone levels, combined with behavioral therapy, could help reduce aggression and impulsivity in violent offenders. For example, selective serotonin reuptake inhibitors (SSRIs) can help regulate mood and impulse control by balancing serotonin and dopamine levels. Similarly, stress-management techniques that reduce cortisol fluctuations may help offenders develop stronger emotional regulation skills.

Understanding the role of hormones in criminal behavior provides insight into **why some individuals are more prone to aggression and poor decision-making.** While hormones do not determine criminality, they influence behavior in ways that make some individuals more vulnerable to antisocial tendencies, particularly in high-stress or unstable environments. Future research in this field may lead to new approaches for reducing recidivism by addressing both biological and environmental risk factors in criminal behavior.

Chapter 4: Personality, Psychopathology, and Crime

Personality Traits Predisposing Individuals to Criminality

Criminal behavior is influenced by personality traits that shape how individuals think, react to stress, and interact with others. Certain traits increase the likelihood of engaging in crime, particularly when combined with environmental risk factors such as neglect, trauma, or peer influence. Personality traits do not determine criminality on their own, but they create tendencies that make some individuals more prone to aggression, manipulation, impulsivity, or risk-taking.

One of the most common personality traits linked to criminal behavior is impulsivity. People who act without thinking about consequences are more likely to engage in crime, especially offenses that involve **immediate gratification, such as theft, assault, or substance abuse-related crimes**. Impulsivity is often tied to poor emotional regulation, where individuals struggle to control anger, frustration, or excitement. Studies on offenders show that many have lower impulse control compared to non-offenders, making them more likely to engage in unplanned, reckless, or violent acts.

Low conscientiousness is another personality factor associated with criminality. Conscientiousness involves **self-discipline, responsibility, and goal-oriented behavior**. People with low conscientiousness tend to be careless, unreliable, and indifferent to long-term consequences. They are more likely to engage in delinquent behavior, avoid responsibilities, and disregard social norms. In criminal settings, this trait contributes to chronic lawbreaking, repeated offenses, and failure to comply with rehabilitation efforts.

Aggression and hostility are strongly linked to violent crime. Some individuals have naturally high levels of aggression, making them more prone to physical violence, intimidation, and revenge-seeking behavior. Aggressive individuals often react excessively to provocation, escalating minor conflicts into serious offenses. This is common in cases of domestic violence, gang violence, and impulsive homicides. Research on violent criminals shows increased activity in brain regions responsible for aggression, combined with lower inhibition from the prefrontal cortex, making them more likely to act on violent impulses.

Callousness and lack of empathy contribute to crimes involving **exploitation, fraud, and violent offenses**. People who lack empathy do not experience guilt, shame, or concern for their victims, making them more likely to harm others for personal gain.

Many financial criminals, serial offenders, and violent criminals **display emotional detachment, manipulative tendencies, and an inability to understand or care about the pain they cause**. Studies on offenders with high levels of callousness show that they are less likely to respond to punishment or rehabilitation, as they do not feel remorse or recognize the need for change.

Sensation-seeking and thrill-seeking behavior are also linked to crime, particularly among young offenders and those involved in high-risk criminal activities. Individuals who seek excitement often engage in reckless behavior, including drug use, dangerous driving, and violent acts. Crime provides an adrenaline rush for some individuals, reinforcing their desire for risk-taking. Research on juvenile delinquents and repeat offenders shows that they often describe crime as exciting or fun, rather than dangerous or harmful. This pattern is common in individuals involved in street racing, gang activity, and violent robberies.

Defiance and resistance to authority are personality traits commonly found in **repeat offenders and career criminals**. Some individuals **actively reject rules, laws, and social expectations**, seeing them as **unfair or restrictive**. This mindset contributes to rebellion, anti-social behavior, and resistance to legal consequences. Many offenders with this trait rationalize their crimes as acts of defiance rather than wrongdoing. They may believe that laws do not apply to them, that the system is corrupt, or that they are justified in breaking rules.

Narcissistic traits, including **grandiosity, entitlement, and arrogance**, are linked to **financial crimes, fraud, and violent offenses**. Narcissistic individuals believe they deserve special treatment and should not be bound by laws or moral standards. They often commit crimes to prove superiority, gain control, or maintain power over others. Some violent offenders with narcissistic traits engage in revenge crimes, domestic abuse, or public acts of aggression when their ego is threatened.

Emotional instability and difficulty managing stress also contribute to criminal behavior. Individuals who lack coping mechanisms for frustration, rejection, or failure are more likely to react with aggression, substance abuse, or impulsive crime. This is particularly relevant in domestic violence cases, where offenders lash out due to emotional instability rather than calculated intent. Many crimes of passion occur because individuals cannot regulate their emotions under stress.

While personality traits increase the likelihood of criminal behavior, they do not act in isolation. Many individuals with **high impulsivity, aggression, or narcissism do not become criminals**. However, when these traits are combined with poor social support, exposure to violence, or economic hardship, the risk of offending increases significantly. Recognizing these personality patterns helps criminal psychologists assess offender risk, predict recidivism, and develop intervention strategies tailored to individual psychological profiles.

Antisocial Personality Disorder: Diagnostic Criteria and Manifestations

Antisocial Personality Disorder (ASPD) is one of the most commonly associated psychiatric conditions with criminal behavior. It is characterized by **a persistent pattern of disregard for the rights of others, impulsivity, and lack of remorse**. Individuals with ASPD often engage in **manipulative, deceitful, and aggressive behavior**, making them more prone to criminal activities ranging from fraud and theft to violent offenses. While not all individuals with ASPD become criminals, studies show that **a significant percentage of prison populations meet the diagnostic criteria for this disorder**.

The Diagnostic and Statistical Manual of Mental Disorders (DSM-5) outlines specific criteria for ASPD. To receive a diagnosis, an individual must show **a pattern of antisocial behavior since the age of 15**, with evidence of **conduct disorder in childhood**. Conduct disorder includes behaviors such as **lying, stealing, aggression, property destruction, and rule violations**. Adults with ASPD display **consistent irresponsibility, reckless disregard for others, repeated legal problems, and an inability to maintain stable relationships**.

One of the core traits of ASPD is **lack of empathy and remorse**. People with this disorder **do not experience guilt or emotional distress over harming others**. They often rationalize their actions, blame their victims, or fail to recognize the moral implications of their behavior. This makes them **less likely to respond to rehabilitation efforts**, as they do not see their behavior as problematic.

Another defining feature is **impulsivity and poor risk assessment**. Individuals with ASPD often engage in **reckless decision-making, thrill-seeking, and disregard for consequences**. This is seen in crimes such as **violent assaults, substance abuse-related offenses, and dangerous driving**. Their inability to delay gratification or consider long-term repercussions makes them more likely to reoffend.

Manipulation and deceit are also common characteristics. Many individuals with ASPD **engage in fraud, con artistry, and deceptive behavior for personal gain**. They are skilled at **lying, exploiting others, and using charm to manipulate situations in their favor**. This is particularly common in white-collar criminals and habitual offenders who deceive others for financial or social advantage.

Research on ASPD shows that genetics and environment both are influential in its development. Studies on twins suggest a strong genetic component, but childhood experiences—such as abuse, neglect, and unstable home environments—also contribute. Many individuals diagnosed with ASPD **grew up in dysfunctional families, where violence, crime, or parental neglect were common**. These conditions reinforce antisocial behaviors, making them more likely to persist into adulthood.

Brain imaging studies reveal **structural differences in the prefrontal cortex and amygdala** of individuals with ASPD. These areas regulate impulse control, decision-making, and emotional processing. Reduced activity in the prefrontal cortex is linked to **poor judgment and lack of inhibition**, while abnormalities in the amygdala contribute to **low emotional responsiveness and reduced fear of punishment**. This neurological profile explains why individuals with ASPD often **fail to learn from past mistakes or modify their behavior based on consequences**.

Not all individuals with ASPD are violent, but **many engage in chronic lawbreaking and disregard social norms**. Some become **con artists, corporate fraudsters, or exploitative business leaders**, using deception instead of physical aggression. Others, particularly those with additional risk factors such as substance abuse or exposure to criminal networks, are more likely to engage in **violent or high-risk offenses**.

In criminal justice settings, ASPD presents challenges for rehabilitation and risk management. Traditional approaches based on **remorse, guilt, or moral reasoning** are often ineffective, as individuals with ASPD do not respond to these emotional appeals. Instead, structured programs focusing on **behavioral incentives, strict rule enforcement, and risk reduction strategies** tend to be more effective. Cognitive-behavioral interventions that focus on **impulse control, risk assessment, and long-term planning** show some promise in managing criminal behaviors associated with ASPD.

While ASPD is prevalent among offenders, not all individuals with this disorder engage in serious crimes. Some develop alternative strategies to satisfy their need for control, power, or risk-taking without breaking the law. Understanding the traits and behaviors associated with ASPD helps criminal psychologists assess risk factors, predict recidivism, and design intervention strategies that account for the unique cognitive and emotional profile of these individuals.

Psychopathy: Emotional Deficits and Behavioral Patterns

Psychopathy is one of the most studied personality disorders in relation to criminal behavior. Unlike Antisocial Personality Disorder (ASPD), which primarily focuses on rule-breaking and impulsivity, **psychopathy is characterized by a profound lack of empathy, emotional detachment, and manipulative tendencies**. Many of the most dangerous and predatory criminals—serial killers, con artists, and violent offenders—display psychopathic traits. However, not all psychopaths engage in criminal behavior; some function in society without ever breaking the law. The key to understanding psychopathy lies in recognizing **the way these individuals process emotions, interact with others, and pursue their own interests with little regard for consequences**.

One of the defining traits of psychopathy is **emotional detachment**. Psychopaths **do not experience emotions the same way non-psychopathic individuals do**. While most people feel guilt, remorse, or empathy, psychopaths remain emotionally indifferent, even when their actions cause significant harm. Brain imaging studies show that psychopaths have **reduced activity in the amygdala**, the brain region responsible for processing emotions like fear and empathy. This explains why they often appear cold, unbothered by distress, and unable to connect emotionally with others.

Psychopaths also **lack a normal fear response**. Most people feel anxiety when facing punishment or negative consequences, but psychopaths do not. Research using startle reflex tests shows that while non-psychopathic individuals react strongly to disturbing images or fearful situations, **psychopaths show little to no physiological response**. This makes them more likely to take extreme risks, engage in violent acts without hesitation, and repeatedly break laws despite facing penalties. Their ability to remain calm under high-pressure situations also makes them **effective manipulators, liars, and deceivers**.

A key behavioral pattern among psychopaths is **superficial charm and manipulation**. Many psychopaths **excel at mimicking emotions** they do not actually feel, allowing them to deceive others and gain their trust. They use charm strategically, **exploiting social interactions for personal gain**. This is why psychopaths are often found in positions of power, such as corporate leadership, politics, or high-risk professions like law enforcement and military service. In the criminal world, this ability makes them highly effective **con artists, fraudsters, and serial offenders** who can manipulate their victims without remorse.

Grandiosity and entitlement are also central to psychopathy. Psychopaths believe they are superior to others and **entitled to take what they want, regardless of laws or social norms**. This belief fuels their **manipulative and predatory behavior**, as they see others as tools to be used rather than individuals with their own rights and feelings. Many **white-collar criminals, financial fraudsters, and corporate executives** exhibit psychopathic traits, using deception and manipulation to achieve their goals without concern for ethical considerations.

Unlike individuals with ASPD, who often act impulsively, **many psychopaths engage in premeditated, calculated criminal acts**. They do not commit crimes in the heat of the moment but rather **plan their actions carefully, ensuring they benefit with minimal risk**. This makes psychopathic criminals **harder to detect and more difficult to apprehend**. Many serial killers, for example, display high levels of psychopathy, meticulously planning their crimes and maintaining an outward appearance of normalcy.

Another important characteristic of psychopathy is **the inability to form deep emotional connections**. While psychopaths may engage in relationships, these connections are purely **surface-level and self-serving**.

They **manipulate partners, family members, and colleagues** for personal benefit but do not experience genuine affection or attachment. In cases of domestic abuse and intimate partner violence, **psychopathic individuals often use charm to lure victims in before engaging in psychological or physical abuse**.

The neurological basis of psychopathy further distinguishes it from other personality disorders. Research shows that **psychopaths have reduced connectivity between the prefrontal cortex (responsible for impulse control and ethical reasoning) and the limbic system (which processes emotions)**. This disconnect explains why psychopaths **can commit violent crimes without emotional distress**. Unlike typical violent offenders, who may act out of anger, jealousy, or desperation, **psychopaths commit crimes out of cold calculation or for personal amusement**.

Psychopathy is commonly measured using the Hare Psychopathy Checklist-Revised (PCL-R), a tool developed by psychologist Robert Hare. This checklist assesses **key psychopathic traits such as superficial charm, lack of remorse, manipulativeness, impulsivity, and parasitic lifestyle**. A score of **30 or higher on the PCL-R indicates a strong likelihood of psychopathy**, while lower scores may suggest **antisocial traits without full psychopathy**.

Although psychopathy is strongly linked to violent crime, not all psychopaths are violent. Many function in society without engaging in overt criminal behavior. These individuals are often referred to as **"successful psychopaths"**—people who use their traits to **gain power, wealth, or social influence through manipulation rather than physical violence**. Some CEOs, politicians, and high-ranking military officers exhibit psychopathic traits, allowing them to navigate competitive environments without emotional interference. However, in cases where **successful psychopaths do engage in crime, their offenses tend to involve fraud, corruption, and corporate exploitation rather than physical aggression**.

The distinction between **primary and secondary psychopathy** also helps explain behavioral differences. **Primary psychopaths are naturally unemotional and manipulative, showing little distress even under extreme circumstances**. These individuals are generally **highly calculated and self-controlled**, making them **more dangerous in strategic criminal activities** such as fraud, organized crime, and serial offenses. **Secondary psychopaths, on the other hand, exhibit high impulsivity and emotional instability**, often engaging in reckless, violent, or drug-related crimes. While both types lack empathy, primary psychopaths operate with a clear, rational mindset, whereas secondary psychopaths act out due to poor impulse control.

Efforts to rehabilitate psychopathic offenders have proven largely ineffective. Unlike individuals with ASPD, who may respond to structured interventions, **psychopaths do not experience emotional regret or moral reasoning, making traditional therapy approaches unsuccessful**. Studies on prison-based rehabilitation programs show that psychopathic offenders are more likely to reoffend than other criminals, even after completing treatment. Some researchers suggest that psychopathy is a neurological condition rather than a treatable disorder, meaning interventions should focus more on risk management rather than rehabilitation.

The legal system struggles with **how to handle psychopathic criminals**, as they **do not respond to deterrence in the same way as other offenders**. While most criminals fear punishment, psychopaths often view incarceration as an inconvenience rather than a deterrent. This creates challenges in sentencing and parole decisions, as psychopaths can easily deceive legal professionals, manipulate parole boards, and fake remorse to gain early release.

Future research on psychopathy continues to explore its genetic, neurological, and behavioral origins. Advances in brain imaging, neurochemistry, and early childhood intervention may help **identify risk factors for psychopathy before individuals engage in criminal behavior**. While psychopathy remains **one of the most difficult disorders to treat**, understanding its neurological and psychological mechanisms provides **important insights into criminal behavior, legal policy, and risk assessment**.

The Influence of Narcissistic and Borderline Traits

Narcissistic and borderline personality traits both influence criminal behavior, but in different ways. While narcissism is characterized by **grandiosity, entitlement, and lack of empathy**, borderline personality traits are associated with **emotional instability, impulsivity, and intense interpersonal conflicts**. People with these traits do not always engage in criminal activity, but when they do, their motivations and methods often reflect their underlying psychological patterns.

Narcissistic traits in criminals often manifest through **exploitation, manipulation, and a belief in personal superiority**. Individuals with high narcissism see themselves as more important than others and may feel **justified in breaking laws if it benefits them**. Many white-collar criminals and fraudsters exhibit narcissistic traits, as they are willing to **deceive, exploit, and manipulate others without remorse**. Narcissists often engage in financial crimes, corporate corruption, and political scandals because they believe they deserve special privileges.

One of the most dangerous aspects of narcissism in criminal behavior is the **inability to accept failure or criticism**. Narcissistic individuals **react aggressively to perceived slights** and may seek revenge against those who challenge their authority or damage their self-image. This is particularly relevant in **domestic violence cases, workplace retaliation, and revenge crimes**, where the offender seeks to restore their perceived dominance. When a narcissist feels humiliated, they may respond with calculated aggression, whether through physical violence or legal and financial retribution.

Some narcissistic offenders **crave admiration and recognition**, which can lead to crimes designed for attention. Serial criminals who enjoy media coverage, con artists who craft elaborate scams, and political figures who engage in corruption often have **high levels of grandiosity and a need for validation**. Unlike impulsive criminals, narcissistic offenders tend to **plan their crimes carefully, ensuring they receive maximum benefit and recognition**.

While narcissistic traits drive **manipulation and control**, borderline traits often lead to reckless, emotionally-driven crimes. Borderline individuals struggle with intense emotional swings, fear of abandonment, and impulsivity, which can result in violent or self-destructive behavior. Many crimes committed by individuals with borderline traits are unplanned, fueled by extreme emotions, and often regretted afterward.

One of the hallmarks of borderline personality traits is **intense and unstable relationships**, which can lead to **domestic violence, stalking, and crimes of passion**. When a borderline individual experiences rejection or abandonment, they may react with explosive anger or desperate attempts to regain control. This is why many homicides and assaults linked to jealousy or relationship conflicts involve individuals with borderline traits.

Borderline traits also contribute to **substance abuse-related crimes and reckless behavior**. Many individuals with borderline tendencies engage in **drug use, shoplifting, or reckless driving** as a way to cope with emotional distress. These actions are not necessarily premeditated crimes but rather **self-destructive behaviors that spiral into legal trouble**.

Another key issue with borderline traits in criminality is **difficulty regulating emotions under stress**. Unlike narcissists, who plan and manipulate, borderline individuals often **lash out without thinking**. This makes them more likely to engage in assault, public disturbances, or crimes committed in the heat of the moment. Studies show that many incarcerated individuals with histories of impulsive violence score high on measures of borderline traits, reflecting a pattern of unstable emotions leading to poor decision-making.

While both narcissistic and borderline traits contribute to criminal behavior, **their motivations and criminal patterns differ significantly**. Narcissists commit crimes **to assert power, control, or superiority**, often in a **calculated and manipulative way**. Borderline individuals, on the other hand, are **more likely to commit crimes impulsively, driven by emotional distress or fear of abandonment**.

Understanding these personality traits helps criminal psychologists and law enforcement professionals **differentiate between calculated, predatory offenders and emotionally reactive criminals**. While narcissistic offenders may require long-term monitoring due to their manipulative nature, those with borderline traits may benefit more from emotional regulation therapies and crisis intervention strategies. Recognizing these distinctions allows for more effective risk assessment, legal decision-making, and rehabilitation approaches in criminal psychology.

Mental Illness: Intersection of Psychopathology and Criminal Behavior

Mental illness and criminal behavior are deeply intertwined, though the relationship is complex and often misunderstood. While most individuals with mental disorders do not commit crimes, research shows that some mental health conditions increase the likelihood of offending. The criminal justice system frequently encounters individuals with psychiatric disorders, and understanding how mental illness contributes to criminality is crucial for both law enforcement and rehabilitation efforts.

One of the primary challenges in studying mental illness and crime is distinguishing between **correlation and causation**. Many offenders with mental illnesses have also experienced **childhood trauma, substance abuse, poverty, and lack of access to treatment**, all of which contribute to criminal behavior. Mental illness alone does not make someone a criminal, but in combination with other risk factors, it can increase the likelihood of violent or impulsive actions.

Schizophrenia is one of the most studied mental disorders in relation to violent crime. Individuals with schizophrenia experience **delusions, hallucinations, and disorganized thinking**, which can sometimes lead to dangerous behavior. Research indicates that **untreated schizophrenia, particularly cases involving paranoid delusions or command hallucinations, increases the risk of violence**. Some offenders with schizophrenia believe they are **acting in self-defense against imagined threats or following the orders of auditory**

hallucinations. However, the vast majority of individuals with schizophrenia are **not violent**, and when they receive proper treatment, their risk of offending drops significantly.

Bipolar disorder is another mental illness associated with criminal behavior, primarily due to **extreme mood swings, impulsivity, and episodes of mania or depression**. During manic episodes, individuals may exhibit **reckless behavior, aggression, or poor judgment**, leading to impulsive crimes such as **assault, theft, or drug-related offenses**. In depressive episodes, they may engage in self-destructive behaviors that lead to legal trouble, such as substance abuse, suicide attempts in public spaces, or neglect of responsibilities. Studies show that offenders with bipolar disorder often commit crimes impulsively rather than as part of a long-term pattern of antisocial behavior.

Personality disorders, particularly **borderline, narcissistic, and antisocial personality disorders**, are strongly linked to criminal behavior. Unlike mood disorders, which fluctuate over time, personality disorders involve **long-term patterns of maladaptive thinking and behavior. Antisocial Personality Disorder (ASPD)** is the most directly linked to crime, with characteristics such as **manipulativeness, lack of remorse, impulsivity, and disregard for others**. Many repeat offenders and career criminals exhibit **ASPD traits**, making them **resistant to rehabilitation and more likely to reoffend**.

Borderline Personality Disorder (BPD) is associated with **intense emotional instability, impulsive aggression, and difficulties in maintaining relationships**. Unlike individuals with ASPD, who commit crimes for **power or material gain**, those with BPD are more likely to engage in emotionally-driven offenses. Crimes of passion, domestic violence, and self-destructive behaviors are common among individuals with borderline traits, as they struggle with emotional regulation and react impulsively to perceived abandonment or rejection.

Narcissistic Personality Disorder (NPD) contributes to criminal behavior when individuals feel **entitled to break the law or seek revenge for perceived slights**. Narcissistic offenders often commit **fraud, financial crimes, and acts of retaliation against perceived enemies**. Unlike borderline offenders, who act out of emotional distress, **narcissistic criminals carefully plan their actions, often deceiving and exploiting others for personal gain**.

Depression is not typically associated with violent crime, but it can lead to **self-destructive or negligent behaviors that result in legal consequences**. Individuals with severe depression may engage in **substance abuse, reckless driving, or suicidal actions that endanger others**. Some violent crimes committed by individuals with depression are driven by desperation, feelings of hopelessness, or a desire for revenge against those they believe have wronged them. Mass shootings and murder-suicides are sometimes linked to severe depression combined with underlying personality disorders or psychotic symptoms.

Substance use disorders significantly increase the risk of criminal behavior, both directly and indirectly. Many offenses are committed under the influence of drugs or alcohol, as substances impair **judgment, impulse control, and aggression regulation**. Individuals with **alcohol dependence are more likely to engage in domestic violence, reckless driving, and disorderly conduct**, while those addicted to **stimulants like methamphetamine or cocaine are at higher risk for violent outbursts and paranoid behavior**.

Substance abuse also contributes to crime through **economic necessity and criminal association**. Many drug users engage in **theft, fraud, or prostitution to support their addiction**. Drug trafficking and gang-related violence often involve individuals with co-occurring substance use disorders and antisocial traits. The cycle of addiction and crime is difficult to break, as incarceration often worsens substance dependence without providing effective treatment.

Dissociative disorders, including **Dissociative Identity Disorder (DID), formerly known as multiple personality disorder**, are sometimes linked to criminal behavior, though these cases are rare. In legal settings, **claims of dissociation are often met with skepticism**, as many individuals attempt to use dissociative symptoms as a defense to avoid responsibility. However, genuine cases of DID can involve **memory gaps, identity confusion, and difficulty distinguishing reality from past trauma**, which may lead to criminal actions without conscious intent.

Obsessive-Compulsive Disorder (OCD) and anxiety disorders are not commonly associated with crime, but in some cases, **severe OCD symptoms can lead to compulsive behaviors that result in legal trouble**. For example, individuals with hoarding disorder may violate health and safety laws, and those with compulsive checking behaviors may be accused of stalking or trespassing. In extreme cases, **anxiety-driven paranoia can lead to violent self-defense against imagined threats**.

Psychosis, which can occur in **schizophrenia, bipolar disorder, or severe depression**, sometimes leads to **bizarre or irrational crimes**. Individuals experiencing psychotic episodes may believe they are acting on divine orders, protecting themselves from an imagined enemy, or fulfilling a delusional prophecy. Some of the most high-profile cases of violent crime involve offenders experiencing untreated psychosis, highlighting the importance of early psychiatric intervention.

The criminal justice system faces significant challenges in handling mentally ill offenders. Many individuals with psychiatric disorders do not receive adequate mental health care before committing crimes, leading them into a legal system that is not designed to treat complex psychiatric conditions. Prisons often lack **proper psychiatric care, leading to worsening symptoms and higher rates of recidivism**.

Efforts to improve mental health diversion programs, specialized psychiatric courts, and rehabilitation services have shown promise in reducing the number of mentally ill individuals in prison. Studies indicate that offenders who receive proper psychiatric treatment are less likely to reoffend, emphasizing the need for integrated approaches that combine mental health care with legal accountability.

Understanding the relationship between mental illness and crime is critical for developing fair sentencing policies, improving rehabilitation efforts, and reducing recidivism among mentally ill offenders. While mental disorders do not absolve individuals of responsibility, recognizing the role of psychopathology in criminal behavior allows for more effective intervention strategies. Future advancements in neuroscience, psychology, and forensic psychiatry may offer better tools for early detection, risk assessment, and treatment, ultimately leading to a more just and effective criminal justice system.

Impact of Trauma and Adverse Childhood Experiences

Trauma and adverse childhood experiences (ACEs) have profound effects on brain development, emotional regulation, and behavior. Research consistently shows that individuals who experience **early-life abuse, neglect, domestic violence, parental substance abuse, or unstable environments** are at higher risk for developing criminal tendencies later in life. Childhood trauma does not directly cause criminal behavior, but it **disrupts normal psychological and neurological development**, increasing the likelihood of impulsivity, aggression, substance abuse, and antisocial behavior.

The brain is highly sensitive to stress in early childhood. When children are exposed to **chronic fear, instability, or violence**, their developing brains become wired to anticipate threats. The amygdala, the part of the brain that processes fear and aggression, becomes hyperactive, making them more prone to reactive aggression and heightened emotional responses. At the same time, the prefrontal cortex, responsible for impulse control, rational decision-making, and emotional regulation, often develops abnormally, leading to **poor self-regulation and increased impulsivity**. This neurological imbalance creates a **higher risk for violent and antisocial behavior**, as individuals struggle to regulate emotions and consider long-term consequences.

Attachment theory provides additional insight into how trauma influences behavior. Early childhood relationships shape emotional development, and children who **lack stable, supportive caregivers** often develop **insecure or disorganized attachment styles**. Those with **insecure attachment may struggle with trust, emotional regulation, and forming healthy relationships**, leading to increased **hostility, manipulation, and social withdrawal**. Disorganized attachment, often seen in children who experience both **abuse and neglect**, is linked to **erratic behavior, heightened aggression, and difficulty processing emotions in a healthy way**.

Neglect can be just as damaging as physical or emotional abuse. Children who grow up in **environments without structure, guidance, or emotional warmth** often struggle with **self-discipline, empathy, and impulse control**. Without positive role models or reinforcement of social norms, they may **gravitate toward delinquent peer groups** that offer a sense of belonging and validation. Many studies on incarcerated individuals reveal **high rates of childhood neglect**, indicating that **a lack of proper emotional and moral development increases the likelihood of criminal behavior**.

Domestic violence exposure in childhood also is influential in shaping future behavior. Children who **witness violent conflict between parents or experience physical abuse themselves** may internalize aggression as a normal response to stress or conflict. **Boys who observe their fathers abusing their mothers are more likely to become violent toward their own partners**, while girls who experience childhood abuse are at higher risk for **engaging in criminal activity, substance abuse, and entering abusive relationships**.

Sexual abuse is one of the strongest predictors of later criminal behavior. Victims of childhood sexual abuse are significantly more likely to develop substance abuse problems, engage in self-harm, and commit violent or sexual offenses. Some survivors develop **deep-seated rage, leading to aggressive behavior**, while others engage in **self-destructive patterns that result in legal trouble**. The psychological effects of sexual abuse, including **shame, dissociation, and emotional dysregulation**, contribute to criminal behavior as individuals struggle to **cope with unresolved trauma**.

Substance abuse is a common outcome of childhood trauma and is a **major risk factor for criminal behavior**. Many individuals with histories of abuse or neglect **turn to drugs or alcohol as a coping mechanism**, increasing their likelihood of engaging in theft, drug-related offenses, and violent crime. Studies show that juvenile offenders with histories of trauma are more likely to develop substance dependence, which further entrenches them in the criminal justice system.

The cycle of trauma and crime is often intergenerational. Children who grow up in violent or criminal households are **more likely to repeat these patterns in adulthood**, not necessarily due to genetics, but because **crime and violence become normalized as problem-solving strategies**. Some individuals with traumatic backgrounds end up involved in gang activity, organized crime, or repeat offending, as these environments provide the **structure and identity they lacked in childhood**.

Resilience is important in determining whether trauma leads to criminal behavior. Some individuals with severe childhood trauma **develop strong coping skills, positive relationships, or receive early intervention**, allowing them to **break the cycle of violence and crime**. Protective factors such as positive mentorship, therapy, stable schooling, and supportive communities help reduce the effects of trauma and provide alternative paths for at-risk youth.

Early intervention programs have shown success in reducing the long-term impact of childhood trauma. Programs that **focus on emotional regulation, social skills, and conflict resolution** help young individuals develop **non-violent coping mechanisms**. Trauma-informed care in juvenile detention centers and prison rehabilitation programs has also been shown to **reduce recidivism by addressing the root causes of criminal behavior**.

Understanding the relationship between trauma and crime is essential for **developing more effective prevention and rehabilitation strategies**. While not all individuals with traumatic backgrounds become criminals, those who do often require trauma-informed approaches rather than purely punitive measures.

Addressing the underlying psychological damage caused by adverse childhood experiences can help break cycles of crime and improve rehabilitation outcomes for those within the criminal justice system.

Chapter 5: Environmental and Social Influences

Family Dynamics and Early Socialization in Offending

Family is the first and most influential environment a child experiences. It shapes how a person views authority, discipline, morality, and social relationships. Criminal behavior does not emerge in isolation; it is often the result of dysfunctional family dynamics, poor socialization, and learned behaviors that normalize deviance.

Children who grow up in environments where crime, violence, neglect, or instability are present are more likely to develop antisocial tendencies and delinquent behavior. Understanding how family structures contribute to offending requires looking at parenting styles, early discipline, exposure to crime, family criminal history, and overall household stability.

Parenting styles influence a child's development in ways that either encourage prosocial behavior or create conditions that increase the likelihood of criminal tendencies. Authoritative parenting, which balances discipline with warmth, produces children who understand boundaries and respect rules. In contrast, authoritarian parenting, which relies on excessive control and harsh punishment, often leads to resentment, defiance, and secretive behavior in children. Many offenders come from households where discipline was inconsistent —where rules were either too harsh or entirely absent. Permissive or neglectful parenting leads to poor impulse control, lack of respect for authority, and difficulty in understanding consequences.

Attachment theory explains why some individuals engage in criminal behavior as a response to unstable relationships with caregivers. A secure attachment to parents or guardians provides a child with emotional stability and a framework for healthy relationships.

In contrast, children with insecure attachments—especially those who have been neglected, abandoned, or abused—are more likely to develop antisocial traits. Many violent offenders describe childhoods where they felt emotionally rejected, leading to aggression as a way to gain control or assert dominance.

Exposure to violence within the home creates a direct pathway to criminal behavior. Children who witness domestic violence between parents or caregivers internalize aggression as a normal response to conflict.

Research shows that boys who observe their fathers abusing their mothers are more likely to become violent toward women in adulthood. Girls who experience abuse or witness domestic violence are at higher risk for substance abuse, criminal activity, and involvement in violent relationships later in life. The normalization of violence during childhood makes it more likely that individuals will repeat these patterns rather than break away from them.

A family history of crime significantly increases the likelihood of offending. Studies on intergenerational criminality show that children of incarcerated parents are far more likely to enter the criminal justice system themselves. **This is not solely due to genetics but rather the environment in which these children grow up**. Many are raised in households where criminal activity is common, whether through parental involvement in drug trafficking, gang affiliations, or financial fraud. When a child's role models engage in crime without facing serious consequences, they internalize the belief that illegal activity is a viable option.

Neglect and emotional detachment are just as damaging as physical abuse. Children raised in environments where their emotional needs are ignored often develop difficulty in regulating emotions and managing relationships. They are more likely to act out, seek negative attention, or turn to delinquent peer groups for validation. Many juvenile offenders report growing up in homes where their basic needs—food, stability, safety—were unmet. In the absence of parental guidance, these children seek out belonging in gangs or engage in criminal activity for survival.

Substance abuse within the household further disrupts early socialization. Parents struggling with addiction often expose their children to chaotic environments, financial instability, and criminal activity. Children of substance abusers are more likely to engage in underage drinking, drug use, and crime.

The lack of consistent supervision means they are often left to their own devices, increasing the likelihood of delinquency. Research shows that children who grow up in households where substance abuse is present are at a higher risk of becoming involved in criminal activity themselves.

Sibling influence also has a role in early criminal behavior. If an older sibling engages in delinquent activities, the younger sibling is more likely to follow the same path. This is especially true in households where parents are either absent or unable to intervene. In some cases, younger siblings are actively recruited into criminal behavior by older family members, reinforcing the cycle of crime within families. The presence of a criminal sibling increases exposure to illegal activities and reduces deterrence, as crime becomes normalized within the home.

Economic stress within families contributes to criminal behavior by creating conditions where crime appears to be the only solution. Children who grow up in extreme poverty often experience food insecurity, inadequate housing, and lack of access to education. In these conditions, **survival becomes the primary focus, and criminal activities like theft, drug dealing, or gang involvement become more appealing**. Single-parent households, particularly those in low-income neighborhoods, are at a greater risk for producing delinquent children, not because single parents are ineffective, but because economic hardship reduces parental supervision and increases exposure to negative influences.

Educational neglect is another critical factor in the relationship between family dynamics and crime. Children who experience early school failure, truancy, or expulsion are far more likely to engage in delinquency. Many offenders have histories of dropping out of school or chronic absenteeism. When families don't prioritize education or fail to provide support for struggling children, the likelihood of criminal behavior increases. Schools often serve as a stabilizing force in a child's life, but without family reinforcement, academic failure can lead to increased association with delinquent peers and engagement in criminal activity.

Early intervention can reduce the long-term effects of negative family environments. Programs that focus on parent education, family therapy, and community-based mentorship help prevent criminal behavior in at-risk children. Studies show that children who receive early intervention, particularly those from high-risk families, are less likely to engage in crime.

Effective strategies include teaching parents how to implement consistent discipline, providing support for substance-abusing households, and offering social services for children exposed to violence or neglect.

Family-based interventions in the juvenile justice system have shown success in reducing recidivism. Rather than focusing solely on punitive measures, these programs address the **root causes of criminal behavior**, such as parental neglect, household instability, and lack of supervision. When families are actively involved in the rehabilitation process, juvenile offenders are more likely to reintegrate into society without reoffending.

Family dynamics are central to understanding early criminal behavior. Whether through exposure to violence, lack of parental guidance, substance abuse, or economic hardship, the home environment **shapes how individuals develop moral reasoning, impulse control, and emotional regulation**. Recognizing the impact of family structures on crime provides opportunities for early intervention, breaking cycles of delinquency before they escalate into lifelong criminal patterns.

Socioeconomic Disparities and Crime Correlation

Crime does not occur in a vacuum. It is deeply connected to **economic conditions, social inequality, and systemic disadvantages** that shape people's choices and opportunities. Individuals living in poverty-stricken neighborhoods, with limited access to education, healthcare, and employment, are significantly more likely to engage in criminal activity. While crime is not exclusive to the poor, economic hardship increases the risk of offending due to limited legal avenues for financial stability, heightened stress, and social marginalization.

One of the strongest correlations between socioeconomic status and crime is the **strain theory**, which suggests that individuals commit crimes when they feel unable to achieve socially approved goals through legitimate means. In societies where **success is measured by material wealth and economic power, those who lack financial opportunities may resort to illegal activities such as theft, fraud, drug dealing, or robbery**. When legal employment does not provide a living wage, or when jobs are scarce, crime becomes an alternative means of survival.

Unemployment is a key factor in crime rates. Studies consistently show that regions with high unemployment also have higher rates of property crime and violent offenses. When individuals are unable to find work, financial desperation sets in, making illegal activities such as burglary, drug trafficking, or scams more attractive.

For many offenders, crime is not a deliberate choice but a response to the lack of legal means to secure housing, food, or financial security.

Economic disparities also create **social resentment and frustration**, which can lead to violent crime. The **relative deprivation theory** explains that **people do not just react to poverty itself, but to the gap between their expectations and their reality**. If individuals see others in their community living comfortably while they struggle with economic hardship, feelings of injustice and resentment can turn into anger, leading to violent confrontations, riots, or retaliatory crimes. Many gang conflicts, violent robberies, and homicides stem from perceived inequalities and the belief that crime is the only way to gain respect or financial power.

The lack of quality education in low-income communities is another major contributor to crime. Schools in economically disadvantaged areas often suffer from **underfunding, overcrowding, and a lack of resources**, making it difficult for students to succeed academically. **High school dropout rates are strongly linked to criminal behavior**, as individuals without a diploma have fewer legal employment options and are more likely to be drawn into illegal economies such as drug trade, prostitution, or organized crime. Without education to provide structure and future opportunities, many young people in struggling neighborhoods see crime as the only viable path forward.

Urban crime rates are often higher in high-density, economically depressed neighborhoods, where social services are minimal, law enforcement is inconsistent, and poverty is generational.

Broken windows theory suggests that visible signs of disorder—graffiti, vandalism, abandoned buildings—signal to residents that crime is tolerated, leading to more lawlessness. If people believe that the police do not respond to crime in their area or that the legal system is biased against them, they are less likely to obey laws.

Systemic discrimination and racial disparities further complicate the relationship between **poverty and crime**. Minority communities in many countries face higher rates of unemployment, lower wages, and reduced access to education, increasing their risk of involvement in crime. In some cases, the criminal justice system disproportionately targets these communities, leading to cycles of incarceration that make it even harder for individuals to reintegrate into society. A criminal record limits employment opportunities, leading many ex-offenders back into illegal activities for survival.

Gentrification and economic displacement have also been linked to crime trends. When **wealthy investors develop low-income neighborhoods, longtime residents are often pushed out due to rising rents and property values**. This economic displacement leads to increased homelessness, financial strain, and resentment, sometimes resulting in theft, vandalism, or protest-related crime. The loss of stable communities also weakens social bonds that previously helped reduce crime, such as neighborhood watch programs or community support networks.

Gender disparities in economic opportunity influence crime patterns as well. **Men in low-income communities are more likely to engage in violent crime**, partly due to **societal expectations of masculinity and the pressure to provide financially**. When legal job opportunities are unavailable, some men turn to gang activity, drug dealing, or robbery as a way to gain respect and financial independence. In contrast, women in economically deprived situations are more likely to be involved in survival crimes, such as shoplifting, prostitution, or welfare fraud.

Substance abuse is both a cause and consequence of economic hardship. Drug-related offenses are more common in impoverished areas, where addiction is often linked to stress, unemployment, and hopelessness. Many individuals who struggle with substance abuse commit theft, burglary, or fraud to support their addiction, creating a cycle of crime and incarceration that is difficult to escape. Drug markets themselves also drive violent crime, as conflicts between dealers and law enforcement responses create an unstable and dangerous environment.

Economic inequality between regions also affects crime rates. Countries with **extreme wealth gaps tend to have higher levels of violent crime**, particularly in cities where **rich and poor communities exist side by side**. When individuals feel that **society is rigged against them, they are more likely to engage in lawbreaking activities**. Nations with stronger social safety nets—providing universal healthcare, affordable education, and employment support—tend to have lower crime rates than those with high levels of inequality.

While poverty and crime are strongly correlated, not all individuals in poverty turn to crime. The presence of community programs, social support systems, and positive role models can reduce criminal behavior even in high-risk environments. Research shows that individuals who have strong family ties, mentorship, or access to vocational training are less likely to engage in criminal activity, even if they experience economic hardship. Addressing socioeconomic disparities through education, employment programs, and criminal justice reform is a critical step in reducing long-term crime rates.

Many modern crime prevention strategies focus on **economic empowerment rather than just law enforcement crackdowns**. Providing job training, improving education in low-income areas, and ensuring access to stable housing are all strategies that have been proven to lower crime rates. Long-term economic solutions offer individuals an alternative to crime, reducing the likelihood of repeat offending and breaking cycles of generational poverty.

Crime does not exist in isolation from social and economic conditions. When individuals **lack access to stable employment, quality education, and social mobility, they become more vulnerable to criminal influences**. Addressing the root causes of economic disparity not only reduces crime but also creates stronger, more stable communities where individuals feel they have a future outside of illegal activities.

Peer Group Influence and the Formation of Gang Culture

Criminal behavior is not always a solitary act. Many offenders are introduced to crime through **peer groups that reinforce deviant behavior, create a sense of identity, and offer social rewards for participation in illegal activities**. While family and economic factors shape early development, **peers become highly influential in adolescence and young adulthood**, particularly in environments where traditional social institutions, such as schools and families, fail to provide structure and support.

One of the primary reasons individuals become involved in criminal activity through peer influence is the need for **acceptance and belonging**. Adolescence is a period when individuals **seek approval and validation from their peers**, often prioritizing peer opinions over those of parents or authority figures. In disadvantaged communities, where opportunities for legitimate social mobility are limited, young people may gravitate toward groups that provide a sense of loyalty, respect, and power. In many cases, criminal behavior begins with small acts of delinquency—skipping school, shoplifting, vandalism—before escalating to more serious offenses.

Gangs represent the most extreme form of **peer group influence on criminal behavior**. They operate as **structured organizations with their own codes, hierarchies, and initiation rituals**. Young individuals often join gangs because they offer protection, financial opportunities, and social status, especially in communities where traditional paths to success appear blocked. Many gang members view their gang as a surrogate family, providing emotional support and a sense of purpose that may be lacking in their home environments.

The process of **gang recruitment and initiation** reinforces criminal behavior. Many gangs require new members to **prove their loyalty through illegal acts**, such as committing assaults, drug trafficking, or robbery. This process not only serves as an entry test but also creates **a psychological commitment to the group**, making it harder for individuals to walk away. Once someone has committed a crime in the name of the gang, **they may feel trapped—both by the legal consequences of their actions and by the fear of retaliation if they try to leave**.

Gang culture thrives on **a strict code of loyalty and respect**, which can lead to violent confrontations over perceived slights. Many gang-related homicides and assaults stem from disrespect, territorial disputes, or revenge killings. The idea that members must "defend their reputation" or retaliate against perceived threats fuels cycles of violence that are difficult to break.

Economic incentives also are influential in gang involvement. Many young people join gangs because **they provide financial opportunities that legitimate employment cannot**. In communities with high unemployment, few educational opportunities, and little economic mobility, gang-related drug sales, extortion, and theft become lucrative alternatives. While the risks of gang life—imprisonment, injury, death—are high, they are often perceived as no worse than the struggles of poverty and social exclusion.

The psychological effects of gang membership are long-lasting. Many gang members **internalize criminal behavior as part of their identity**, making desistance from crime difficult even when they want to leave. The longer an individual stays involved, the harder it becomes to break away. Former members often **struggle with reintegration into society, facing stigma, limited job opportunities, and threats from former associates**.

While peer influence can encourage criminal behavior, it can also **serve as a protective factor against crime**. When young people associate with **peers who prioritize education, employment, and positive social interactions, they are less likely to engage in delinquent activity**. Programs that introduce mentorship, structured after-school activities, and job training have been successful in diverting at-risk youth away from gangs and criminal networks.

Law enforcement strategies aimed at breaking gang cycles often focus on **community intervention, social services, and education rather than just suppression tactics**. Suppression efforts, such as mass arrests and gang injunctions, often fail because they do not address the root causes of gang involvement. Effective anti-gang programs work by providing alternative social structures, offering pathways to legal employment, and addressing the systemic conditions that make gangs appealing in the first place.

Understanding the role of peer groups in shaping criminal behavior highlights the importance of **early intervention, social support systems, and community-based prevention efforts**. When young individuals find belonging, structure, and opportunity in positive social settings, they are far less likely to seek those things in criminal circles.

Cultural Norms and Deviance in Varying Societal Contexts

Crime does not exist in a vacuum. What one society defines as criminal, another may see as acceptable or even honorable. Cultural norms dictate which behaviors are acceptable, tolerated, or punished, and these norms influence the types of crime that emerge within a society. The concept of deviance is not universal—**what is considered criminal in one culture may be legal or even encouraged in another**. Understanding how cultural values shape criminal behavior is essential for analyzing crime patterns across different regions and historical periods.

Deviance is largely defined by **social expectations and legal frameworks**, both of which are shaped by cultural traditions, religious beliefs, political structures, and economic conditions.

Some acts are considered universally criminal—murder, rape, and theft—but even these offenses are interpreted differently depending on the **social context and the cultural justifications surrounding them**. In many societies, killing in self-defense is considered justifiable, but in others, honor killings, state executions, or revenge killings may be widely accepted despite their violent nature.

Crime is often linked to **shifts in cultural norms**, particularly during periods of rapid social change. When traditional values clash with modern influences, new forms of deviance emerge. Societies that undergo **economic upheaval, political instability, or technological advancement** often see shifts in their legal and moral codes. For example, actions that were once seen as deviant—homosexuality, interracial marriage, divorce—have become socially accepted in many parts of the world, while other behaviors—corporate fraud, cybercrime, and environmental destruction—are increasingly criminalized.

Cultural perceptions of crime influence **which offenses are heavily policed and which are ignored or tolerated**. In some authoritarian societies, political dissent is treated as a crime, while in democratic nations, freedom of speech is protected. In some regions, financial crimes such as tax evasion and bribery are seen as **minor offenses or even necessary for doing business**, while in others, they are aggressively prosecuted. **The extent to which corruption is tolerated varies significantly between cultures**, shaping economic crime patterns worldwide.

Honor-based violence provides a striking example of **how cultural norms shape criminal behavior**. In some parts of the world, honor killings—where family members kill a relative, usually a woman, for bringing perceived shame to the family—are still practiced, even if legally prohibited. These crimes stem from **deeply ingrained social beliefs about family honor, gender roles, and control over female autonomy**. While legally classified as murder, honor killings may receive lenient punishments or be ignored by authorities in societies where they are culturally accepted.

Gang culture is another example of **culturally influenced crime**, with different regions producing different gang structures and behaviors. In some parts of Latin America, drug cartels operate as parallel governments, enforcing their own laws and punishing members who disobey. In the United States, urban street gangs are often linked to territorial disputes, drug trafficking, and organized violence, while in parts of Asia, secretive criminal organizations like the Triads and Yakuza operate with a mix of legality and underground influence, often maintaining close ties to legitimate businesses and political figures.

Religious influence on crime and punishment also varies across cultures. In some theocratic societies, crimes such as **blasphemy, apostasy, and adultery** carry **severe penalties, including death sentences, despite being legally insignificant in secular nations**. In other cases, religious institutions act as rehabilitative forces, advocating for restorative justice and offering alternatives to incarceration. The role of religion in shaping criminal justice policies can determine whether an offender is sentenced to harsh punishment, rehabilitated through faith-based programs, or provided with legal leniency based on religious interpretation.

Cultural attitudes toward drug use provide another lens for examining crime differences across societies. In some countries, **drug possession and use are treated as public health issues rather than criminal offenses**, leading to decriminalization and harm reduction policies. Portugal, for example, decriminalized drug use and focused on treatment, resulting in a decline in drug-related crime and addiction rates. In contrast, nations with strict drug laws, such as Singapore or the Philippines, impose severe penalties, including the death sentence, for drug-related offenses. These differences reflect broader cultural views on **individual responsibility, state control, and the perceived dangers of substance use**.

Economic crime, such as fraud and financial deception, is viewed differently depending on cultural norms regarding wealth accumulation and business ethics. In some societies, **tax evasion and corporate misconduct are accepted as part of economic life**, while in others, they are met with strict legal consequences. White-collar crime is often overlooked in cultures where financial success is valued over ethical conduct, allowing business elites to engage in corruption with minimal repercussions. This explains why corporate fraud is more widespread in some regions than others, as legal enforcement often reflects cultural tolerance for economic manipulation.

Technological advancement has introduced **new forms of crime that challenge traditional legal systems**. Cybercrime, for example, is a **global issue, but responses to it vary widely**. Some nations heavily police online fraud, hacking, and digital piracy, while others turn a blind eye to intellectual property theft and online criminal markets. Cybercriminal networks often exploit legal loopholes in nations with weaker enforcement, leading to international crime syndicates that operate across borders.

Even violent crime rates are influenced by **cultural attitudes toward conflict resolution and personal honor**. In societies where **individual retaliation is normalized or where law enforcement is weak, personal disputes are more likely to result in violence**.

The presence of strong legal institutions, social trust, and cultural emphasis on peaceful conflict resolution reduces violent crime rates. In contrast, cultures with a high tolerance for interpersonal violence—whether through dueling traditions, blood feuds, or revenge-based justice—tend to have higher rates of violent crime.

Migration and globalization have further complicated cultural views on crime. As people move across borders, **they bring different cultural attitudes toward law, authority, and deviance**. This sometimes leads to **clashes between immigrant communities and host countries**, particularly when legal expectations differ. Criminal organizations often take advantage of these cultural differences by **smuggling illicit goods across jurisdictions with different enforcement priorities**. For example, human trafficking networks thrive in regions where **law enforcement is weak, bribery is common, or legal definitions of forced labor are unclear**.

Understanding crime from a cultural perspective requires acknowledging that **laws are not purely objective but are shaped by social norms, historical legacies, and moral beliefs**. Criminal justice policies that **fail to consider cultural attitudes may be ineffective or counterproductive**, as seen in cases where legal crackdowns create more underground criminal activity rather than reducing crime itself. Addressing culturally driven crime requires **a mix of legal enforcement, social reform, and public education to shift attitudes toward deviant behavior**.

Crime is not just about breaking laws—it is about **how societies define wrongdoing, enforce justice, and determine who gets punished and who gets protected**. Cultural differences shape everything from gang structures to corporate fraud, from honor-based violence to cybercrime, making crime a reflection of deeper social values and historical forces rather than just individual choices.

Chapter 6: The Psychology of Crime in Various Categories

Crimes Against Persons (Violent Crimes)

Violent crimes are the most physically destructive and psychologically damaging forms of criminal behavior. Unlike property or financial crimes, these offenses directly harm victims through physical aggression, coercion, or lethal force. Crimes against persons include homicide, assault, sexual violence, kidnapping, and robbery, with each offense varying in intent, severity, and impact. Understanding the psychological mechanisms behind violent crime provides insight into **why offenders act, how they select victims, and what environmental and biological factors contribute to their behavior**.

Homicide is the **most extreme form of violent crime**, involving the deliberate or reckless killing of another person. The psychology of homicide varies depending on **motive, premeditation, and emotional state at the time of the crime**. Some homicides are **coldly calculated**, while others are **reactive and impulsive**. Premeditated murder, often committed by serial killers, contract killers, or revenge-driven offenders, involves careful planning and emotional detachment. These individuals frequently display antisocial traits, lack empathy, and have a history of manipulation and control-seeking behavior. On the other hand, impulsive homicides—often occurring in domestic disputes, bar fights, or moments of uncontrolled rage—result from poor emotional regulation and high levels of aggression. In these cases, offenders may act in the heat of the moment, later expressing remorse, confusion, or justification for their actions.

Psychopaths and serial killers commit **homicide with a different psychological framework**. Unlike crimes of passion, these individuals lack emotional connections to their victims. Many serial offenders exhibit narcissistic and sadistic traits, enjoying the power and control that comes with taking a life.

Some kill for sexual gratification, dominance, or ritualistic pleasure, while others view their victims as expendable objects, dehumanizing them to avoid guilt. Neuroscientific studies show that many psychopathic killers have reduced amygdala activity, which is linked to diminished fear responses and emotional processing.

Assault is a violent offense that ranges from **simple battery to aggravated physical attacks with weapons**. Unlike homicide, assault does not necessarily result in death, but it inflicts bodily harm and psychological trauma on victims. Many assaults are driven by anger, substance abuse, or disputes that escalate beyond control. Domestic violence is a common form of assault, where intimate partners exert control through physical harm and intimidation. Perpetrators in abusive relationships often display possessiveness, jealousy, and a deep-seated need to dominate their victims. Studies show that many repeat domestic abusers were raised in violent households, where aggression was normalized as a method of conflict resolution.

Sexual violence, including rape and sexual assault, is a uniquely devastating crime that blends **physical harm with psychological trauma**. The motives behind sexual violence differ among offenders. Some **seek power and dominance, using sexual assault as a weapon to degrade and control their victims**. Others act out of impulse and lack of self-regulation, taking advantage of vulnerable situations or overpowering their victims without premeditation. Many sexual offenders rationalize their behavior, convincing themselves that the victim consented, provoked the act, or deserved punishment. Studies on rapists and repeat offenders show that many exhibit cognitive distortions, poor impulse control, and in some cases, sadistic tendencies that make sexual violence an extension of their need for control.

Kidnapping involves **the forceful or coercive abduction of an individual, often for ransom, exploitation, or personal vendetta**. The psychology of kidnappers varies based on their motives and the duration of captivity. Some abduct victims for financial gain, using them as bargaining chips for ransom payments.

Others, particularly child abductors and human traffickers, target victims for long-term control, exploitation, or enslavement. In cases of parental abductions, a parent may take a child illegally, believing they are protecting them from the other parent. Long-term captivity cases, such as those involving **hostage situations or forced servitude, often result in psychological conditions like Stockholm syndrome, where victims develop emotional bonds with their captors as a survival mechanism**.

Robbery is a unique violent crime because it **combines property theft with physical aggression or intimidation**. Unlike burglary, which involves stealth and property invasion, robbery is a direct confrontation where force, threats, or weapons are used to obtain valuables. The psychological profile of robbers varies—some are opportunistic criminals seeking fast cash, while others commit violent holdups as part of gang culture or organized crime.

Many robbers justify their actions as necessity-based, believing that financial desperation leaves them with no other options. Others, particularly those involved in armed robberies, display heightened aggression, thrill-seeking tendencies, and a willingness to escalate violence when challenged.

Substance abuse is a major contributing factor in violent crime. Alcohol and drugs **lower inhibitions, impair judgment, and increase aggression**, making conflicts more likely to turn violent. Studies show that a significant percentage of homicides, assaults, and domestic violence incidents involve intoxicated offenders. Stimulants like methamphetamine and cocaine increase paranoia and aggression, while depressants like alcohol reduce impulse control, leading to reckless and violent outbursts. Many violent criminals use substances to numb their guilt or enhance their confidence before committing crimes, further entrenching them in cycles of violence and addiction.

Environmental and social factors also have a role in violent crime. Individuals raised in **high-crime neighborhoods, where gang activity and violence are common, are more likely to engage in aggression as a learned behavior**. The cycle of violence hypothesis suggests that children exposed to abuse, neglect, or violent role models internalize aggression as a legitimate means of problem-solving. This is particularly evident in gang-affiliated youth, who view violence as a necessity for survival and respect.

Mental illness is frequently debated in discussions of violent crime. While most individuals with mental health disorders **do not commit violent acts**, some conditions—particularly **schizophrenia, bipolar disorder, and psychotic episodes**—can lead to **violent outbursts in untreated individuals**. Studies show that individuals experiencing psychotic breaks, particularly those with paranoia or delusions, are at higher risk for committing homicide or assault.

However, many violent offenders do not have a diagnosed mental illness but instead exhibit personality disorders such as antisocial personality disorder (ASPD) or psychopathy, which involve a lack of empathy, disregard for others, and a willingness to use violence for personal gain.

Social dynamics and group psychology influence violent crime as well. Mob violence, riots, and gang-related attacks often involve individuals who, under normal circumstances, would not commit violent acts. The deindividuation effect explains how people lose their sense of personal responsibility when acting as part of a group, leading to escalated violence, destruction, and moral disengagement. This phenomenon is seen in hate crimes, political uprisings, and organized assaults, where group loyalty overrides ethical considerations.

Understanding the psychology of violent crime is essential for both prevention and intervention. Many violent offenders **follow predictable patterns of escalation, starting with minor aggressive acts before progressing to more severe violence**. Early intervention—through **anger management programs, therapy, and conflict resolution training—can prevent impulsive violence from becoming a lifelong pattern**. Legal systems that emphasize rehabilitation for non-habitual violent offenders, rather than strict punitive measures, have shown success in reducing recidivism.

Despite the many factors influencing violent crime, human aggression is not inevitable. With the right social structures, psychological interventions, and preventive measures, many violent offenders can be redirected away from crime and toward productive, nonviolent behaviors. By understanding the biological, psychological, and social roots of violent crime, criminal psychologists and law enforcement can develop strategies to mitigate its occurrence and protect potential victims from harm.

Crimes Against Property

Crimes against property involve the **theft, destruction, or unlawful use of someone else's possessions**. Unlike violent crimes, these offenses do not typically result in physical harm to victims, but they can cause **significant financial loss, emotional distress, and social consequences**. Many property crimes stem from **economic desperation, thrill-seeking behavior, or a rational decision to exploit weaknesses in security or enforcement**. While some offenders commit these crimes opportunistically, others engage in them systematically as part of organized criminal networks.

Theft, or larceny, is the most common type of property crime. It involves taking someone else's belongings without permission and with no intention of returning them. Theft can be petty, involving low-value items like shoplifting, or grand, involving high-value goods such as automobiles, jewelry, or electronics. Many thefts are opportunistic, occurring when an offender sees an easy target with minimal risk of getting caught. Shoplifters, for example, often steal items that are easy to conceal and resell, while pickpockets target crowded areas where they can operate unnoticed.

Some thefts are premeditated and involve careful planning. High-level fraud, embezzlement, and organized retail theft rings operate with structured methods, often targeting businesses or wealthy individuals who are less likely to notice missing assets immediately. These offenders rationalize their crimes as victimless, believing that large corporations or insurance companies can absorb the loss without serious consequences.

Burglary is a more **invasive form of property crime**, as it involves **breaking into a home, business, or other structure to commit theft or another crime**. Unlike simple theft, burglary often requires forced entry or trespassing, making it a more serious offense. Some burglars scout locations in advance, looking for vulnerabilities such as unlocked doors, unmonitored properties, or weak security systems. Others act impulsively, breaking into homes or businesses without much planning, often under the influence of drugs or alcohol.

The psychological profile of burglars varies. Some are career criminals who specialize in breaking and entering, while others commit burglaries out of financial desperation. Drug addiction is a common factor, as many offenders steal to fund their substance use. Research on repeat offenders shows that burglars often return to locations they deem easy targets, reinforcing the need for stronger security measures and community awareness programs to reduce property crime.

Arson is one of the **most destructive forms of property crime**, involving the **intentional setting of fire to buildings, vehicles, or land**. While some arsonists act out of revenge, vandalism, or financial motives (such as insurance fraud), others commit arson for psychological gratification. Some offenders experience a compulsive need to start fires, linked to thrill-seeking behavior or underlying mental health disorders. Pyromania, a rare psychological condition, involves an obsessive urge to set fires with no clear financial or personal gain.

Insurance fraud is a major motivator behind intentional arson, where property owners destroy their own assets to collect payouts from insurance companies. These crimes can be sophisticated, involving staged accidents, falsified records, and attempts to make the fire appear accidental. Law enforcement agencies use fire pattern analysis, forensic investigation, and insurance record reviews to distinguish between genuine accidents and deliberate acts of destruction.

Vandalism involves deliberate destruction or defacement of property and is often driven by anger, rebellion, or the desire for recognition. Many vandals **target public spaces, schools, businesses, or government buildings, viewing their**

actions as statements of defiance against authority. Graffiti, while sometimes seen as an art form, is considered a crime when it **damages public or private property without consent.**

Some acts of vandalism are **linked to gang culture**, where tagging buildings with gang symbols **establishes territorial dominance**. In other cases, vandalism is purely destructive, committed by individuals seeking excitement, revenge, or retaliation against perceived injustices. Alcohol and peer influence often contribute to reckless acts of property destruction, particularly among juvenile offenders who engage in thrill-seeking behaviors.

Auto theft, or motor vehicle theft, ranges from joyriding to organized vehicle theft operations. Joyriding offenders, often teenagers or young adults, steal cars for short-term use, either for excitement or convenience. In contrast, professional car thieves target vehicles for resale, parts stripping, or export to international markets.

Advancements in vehicle security, such as GPS tracking, immobilizers, and keyless entry systems, have reduced car theft rates in many developed nations.

However, organized auto theft rings have adapted, using sophisticated hacking tools and key cloning devices to bypass security features. Some stolen vehicles are shipped overseas, repainted, or re-registered under false identities, making recovery difficult.

Financial crime is an **increasingly prevalent form of property crime**, particularly in the digital age. Fraud, identity theft, and cybercrime have replaced traditional burglary and theft in many criminal enterprises. Unlike violent crime, financial criminals often operate anonymously, using hacking techniques, data breaches, and online scams to steal money and personal information from victims.

Identity theft involves **stealing someone's personal information—such as Social Security numbers, credit card details, or banking credentials—to commit fraud.** Victims may not realize they have been targeted until unauthorized transactions, fraudulent loans, or tax filings appear in their name. Cybercriminals often use phishing scams, malware, and social engineering tactics to gain access to sensitive information.

Embezzlement is a white-collar crime that occurs **when individuals in positions of financial trust steal money or assets from businesses, organizations, or employers**. Unlike common theft, embezzlement typically involves deception over a long period, with offenders covering their tracks through falsified records and financial manipulation. Many embezzlers justify their actions by believing they are owed money, underpaid, or unfairly treated by their employers.

The rise of digital transactions and cryptocurrency has **created new opportunities for financial crime**. Online fraud schemes, including **Ponzi schemes, investment scams, and unauthorized account takeovers**, allow criminals to **steal millions without ever making direct contact with their victims**. Law enforcement agencies face growing challenges in tracking and prosecuting cybercriminals, as many operate from jurisdictions with weak enforcement or legal loopholes.

Property crimes have **lasting psychological and financial effects on victims**. While they may not involve direct physical harm, the emotional impact of burglary, identity theft, or financial fraud can be severe. Victims often experience feelings of violation, loss of trust, and long-term financial difficulties. The trauma of having one's home invaded or personal information stolen can lead to paranoia, stress, and changes in daily habits.

Prevention strategies for property crime involve **a combination of security measures, legal deterrents, and social interventions**. Surveillance cameras, alarm systems, and neighborhood watch programs help deter burglary and theft, while consumer education on cybersecurity reduces the risk of digital fraud. In cases where economic hardship fuels property crime, rehabilitation programs, employment assistance, and social services can provide alternatives to criminal behavior.

While property crime does not carry the same level of physical violence as other offenses, it **represents a significant burden on individuals, businesses, and law enforcement**. Understanding why offenders commit these crimes and how they justify their actions provides important insight into preventing and reducing economic-driven criminal activity.

Inchoate Crimes

Inchoate crimes, also known as incomplete or preparatory offenses, involve **actions taken toward committing a crime, even if the crime itself is never completed**. These offenses exist because the legal system recognizes that attempting or planning a crime poses a serious enough threat to warrant punishment. Common inchoate crimes include attempt, conspiracy, and solicitation. While they do not always result in harm or loss, they are prosecuted to prevent greater crimes from occurring.

Attempt occurs when an individual takes substantial steps toward committing a crime but ultimately fails or is stopped before completion. The law distinguishes between mere preparation and an actual attempt—for an act to qualify as an attempt, the offender must have moved beyond planning and taken concrete steps toward execution. Courts assess intent, actions taken, and how close the offender came to completing the crime.

For example, **if someone breaks into a house intending to commit burglary but is caught before stealing anything, they can still be charged with attempted burglary**. Similarly, if an individual fires a gun at someone but misses, they can be charged with attempted murder. Attempt laws exist because waiting until a crime is fully completed would put victims at greater risk and make law enforcement less effective at preventing harm.

One key legal debate surrounding attempt is the issue of **"impossibility."** In some cases, an offender may **attempt a crime that is impossible to complete**—for example, trying to pickpocket someone who has no money in their wallet or trying to shoot someone with an unloaded gun. Courts often distinguish between **factual**

impossibility (where external circumstances prevent the crime from succeeding) and **legal impossibility** (where the intended act is not actually a crime). In most jurisdictions, **factual impossibility is not a defense**, meaning offenders can still be prosecuted for attempting an impossible crime.

Conspiracy involves **two or more people agreeing to commit a crime, even if they never follow through with the plan**. The reasoning behind conspiracy laws is that group efforts to break the law pose a greater threat to society than individual actions. Criminal organizations, drug trafficking rings, and terrorist groups rely on coordinated efforts, making conspiracy laws an essential tool for law enforcement to disrupt criminal networks before they act.

One challenge in prosecuting conspiracy is proving that an agreement existed and that the individuals involved intended to commit a crime. Courts often look for evidence such as written communications, financial transactions, or recorded conversations that show a clear intent to commit an illegal act.

In some cases, a single overt act—such as purchasing weapons, scouting a target, or transferring money—can be enough to establish conspiracy, even if the main crime is never committed.

Solicitation occurs when one person **encourages, hires, or persuades another person to commit a crime**. Unlike conspiracy, solicitation does not require an agreement between multiple parties—one person can be guilty even if the other person refuses to go through with the crime. Common examples of solicitation include hiring a hitman, encouraging someone to commit fraud, or persuading another person to sell drugs. The crime is based on the intent and effort to involve another person in illegal activity.

A unique aspect of solicitation laws is that **the solicitor can be punished even if the crime never takes place**. If someone tries to hire a killer but the hitman is actually an undercover officer, the person making the request can still be charged. Courts recognize that the act of trying to involve others in criminal behavior is dangerous in itself, even if no direct harm occurs.

Many inchoate crimes **carry the same or nearly the same penalties as the completed offense**. Attempted murder, for example, often carries a prison sentence similar to that of actual murder, reflecting the intent and danger posed by the offender. The reasoning is that if law enforcement intervenes early enough to stop a crime, the perpetrator should not escape serious punishment simply because they were unsuccessful.

However, **not all inchoate crimes result in equal sentencing to the completed act**. Courts take into account factors such as the degree of completion, the level of planning, and the likelihood that the crime would have succeeded if left uninterrupted. Someone who makes vague statements about committing a crime but takes no real action may receive a lesser sentence than someone who actively takes steps toward committing a major offense.

Defenses for inchoate crimes vary depending on the circumstances. Some defendants argue they abandoned the crime before it could be completed, showing a change of heart or voluntary withdrawal. However, for abandonment to serve as a legal defense, the decision to stop must be truly voluntary—not just due to external factors like getting caught or facing unexpected obstacles.

Law enforcement agencies **use inchoate crime laws as tools for crime prevention**, allowing them to intervene before major offenses occur. Many arrests for conspiracy or solicitation come from undercover operations, surveillance, and informant testimony, where police monitor and disrupt criminal plans before they escalate into full-scale offenses.

Inchoate crimes highlight **the legal system's approach to intent, preparation, and risk prevention**. By criminalizing the steps leading up to a crime, authorities aim to reduce harm, dismantle criminal organizations, and deter individuals from engaging in dangerous behavior before it results in real damage. Understanding these offenses provides insight into how law enforcement and the courts balance crime prevention with individual accountability.

Statutory Crimes

Statutory crimes are offenses that are illegal **because laws specifically prohibit them**, even if they do not directly harm another person or property. Unlike violent or property crimes, which have clear victims, statutory crimes often involve **acts that society deems harmful, unsafe, or morally unacceptable**. These offenses vary widely across jurisdictions, reflecting cultural values, political priorities, and historical legal traditions. Common examples include drug crimes, alcohol-related offenses, traffic violations, and white-collar crimes.

Drug-related offenses make up a significant portion of statutory crimes, with laws regulating possession, distribution, manufacturing, and trafficking of controlled substances.

Drug laws are often controversial, as different countries and even states disagree on what should be criminalized. Some places treat drug use as a public health issue, focusing on rehabilitation, while others enforce harsh penalties, including life sentences and the death penalty for drug trafficking.

The psychology of drug offenders varies based on their role in the drug trade. **Casual users** may face possession charges but **do not typically see themselves as criminals**, while **dealers and traffickers often operate within organized networks, engaging in calculated risk-taking and financial motivations**. Some drug traffickers rationalize their actions by believing they are fulfilling a demand, much like any other business. Others, particularly those in impoverished regions, see drug selling as a necessity for survival.

Alcohol-related crimes include offenses such as public intoxication, underage drinking, and driving under the influence (DUI). While alcohol is legal in most societies, laws exist to prevent reckless and dangerous behavior linked to excessive consumption. DUI laws are among the most strictly enforced because alcohol impairment increases the risk of fatal accidents. Research shows that alcohol lowers inhibition, impairs judgment, and increases aggression, leading to more violent confrontations and risky decision-making.

In many cultures, underage drinking is **socially tolerated but legally prohibited**, creating a **gray area where law enforcement may or may not intervene**. Some countries impose strict minimum drinking ages, while others have more relaxed regulations, allowing alcohol consumption at home under parental supervision. The enforcement of these laws often reflects broader societal attitudes toward youth responsibility and substance use.

Traffic violations are another major category of statutory crime, encompassing offenses such as speeding, reckless driving, and driving without a license or insurance. While these crimes might seem minor, serious traffic offenses can result in fatalities, injuries, and significant property damage. Reckless drivers often exhibit poor impulse control, overconfidence in their abilities, or disregard for safety regulations. Some traffic offenders engage in habitual risky driving, while others violate laws due to distraction, stress, or poor decision-making.

Certain traffic offenses, such as hit-and-run incidents or vehicular manslaughter, blur the line between statutory and violent crimes, as they involve direct harm or endangerment of others. Courts take these cases seriously, often imposing severe penalties when negligence or reckless behavior leads to injury or death.

White-collar crimes are a unique subset of statutory offenses involving **fraud, embezzlement, insider trading, and corporate misconduct**. Unlike violent crimes, these offenses **rely on deception, exploitation, and manipulation rather than physical force**. Many white-collar criminals rationalize their actions, viewing them as bending the rules rather than outright criminal behavior. They often exploit legal loopholes, trusting that their wealth or influence will protect them from severe consequences.

Psychological studies show that **white-collar offenders often exhibit traits associated with narcissism, entitlement, and moral disengagement**. Some believe that their crimes do not truly harm anyone, especially when victims are large corporations or government institutions. Others see financial fraud as a game of strategy, where the goal is to maximize personal gain while avoiding detection. Unlike impulsive street criminals, white-collar offenders tend to be methodical, calculating risks, and weighing potential rewards against the likelihood of punishment.

One of the challenges of prosecuting white-collar crime is **public perception and legal enforcement**. While drug-related offenses and violent crimes receive heavy police attention and harsh sentencing, financial crimes often go under-prosecuted due to their complexity and the difficulty of proving intent. Many perpetrators receive lighter sentences, even when their crimes result in massive financial losses for victims.

Public morality laws, such as those banning prostitution, gambling, and indecent exposure, reflect social attitudes about acceptable behavior. While these offenses do not always involve clear victims, they are often regulated to prevent broader societal harms. Some places criminalize prostitution to combat human trafficking, while others legalize and regulate it to reduce exploitation and violence. Similarly, gambling laws vary—some countries ban all forms of betting, while others allow it under strict government oversight.

The enforcement of morality laws often raises **ethical questions about personal freedom versus societal control**. Some argue that criminalizing personal choices leads to unnecessary government intrusion, while others believe these laws protect individuals from exploitation and harmful consequences. In many cases, morality laws evolve over time as social values change, leading to legal debates over issues such as same-sex marriage, reproductive rights, and drug legalization.

Statutory crimes are a **constantly shifting area of law**, reflecting **changes in cultural norms, economic priorities, and political landscapes**. Understanding the motivations behind these offenses helps explain why individuals break laws that do not involve direct harm to others. Whether through economic desperation, social pressure, addiction, or calculated risk-taking, statutory offenders engage in illegal activity for a variety of reasons that extend beyond simple criminal intent.

Financial Crimes (White-Collar Crimes)

Financial crimes involve deception, fraud, and manipulation for financial gain. Unlike violent or street crimes, these offenses are committed by individuals who abuse positions of trust or exploit financial systems.

White-collar criminals often operate in corporate, political, or financial settings, using their knowledge of laws and regulations to engage in fraud, embezzlement, and money laundering. These crimes can devastate economies, destroy businesses, and leave thousands of victims in financial ruin.

Despite their severity, financial crimes are often perceived as less harmful than violent offenses, leading to lighter punishments and more lenient legal treatment.

Fraud is one of the most common financial crimes. It occurs when an individual or organization deliberately deceives another for financial benefit. This can take many forms, including securities fraud, mortgage fraud, healthcare fraud, and consumer fraud.

Investment scams, such as Ponzi schemes, lure victims in with promises of high returns, only to collapse when the fraudster can no longer recruit new investors. The psychology of fraudsters varies—**some believe they can outsmart the system indefinitely, while others justify their actions by claiming their victims were greedy or careless**.

Embezzlement is another widespread white-collar crime. It involves an individual in a position of financial trust siphoning money or assets for personal use. Unlike simple theft, embezzlement is often gradual and hidden through false accounting or financial manipulation. **Many embezzlers do not start with the intention to steal large amounts but begin by taking small sums, rationalizing that they will repay the money later**. Over time, as financial pressures increase or they grow bolder, the theft escalates. Embezzlers are often well-respected employees, making their crimes difficult to detect until massive sums have been lost.

Money laundering is the process of concealing the origins of illegally obtained money, making it appear legitimate. Criminal organizations, drug cartels, and corrupt politicians use money laundering to hide illicit profits. This crime often involves multiple financial institutions, offshore accounts, and shell companies, making it difficult for authorities to track.

Many financial criminals rely on weak regulatory oversight in certain countries to funnel money through legal businesses, real estate, or fake transactions. The increasing use of cryptocurrency has added new layers of complexity, allowing criminals to move large sums across borders with minimal detection.

Corporate fraud involves executives and business leaders manipulating financial reports, misleading investors, or engaging in insider trading. Some executives inflate stock prices by falsifying earnings reports, while others exploit legal loopholes to avoid taxes or mislead shareholders. The 2008 financial crisis exposed numerous instances of corporate fraud, where banks and financial institutions misrepresented risky investments, leading to global economic collapse. Many perpetrators walked free or received minimal sentences, fueling public outrage over the perceived double standard in the justice system.

Cybercrime has become a dominant form of financial crime, as criminals exploit digital vulnerabilities to commit fraud, identity theft, and financial scams. Hackers steal sensitive financial data, compromise bank accounts, and engage in large-scale financial fraud using phishing schemes and ransomware attacks. As businesses and individuals rely more on digital transactions, financial criminals are constantly adapting, developing new ways to exploit security flaws. Governments and financial institutions struggle to keep pace, creating a constant arms race between cybersecurity experts and cybercriminals.

Financial crime is often considered a crime of opportunity rather than necessity. Many offenders are not driven by poverty or desperation but by ambition, greed, or a belief that they are smarter than the system. **White-collar criminals often minimize their wrongdoing, believing that they are simply bending rules rather than committing serious offenses**.

Unlike violent criminals, **they don't see their victims directly, making it easier to detach from the harm they cause**. Some financial criminals even rationalize their actions as victimless, despite the fact that fraud and financial deception ruin lives, destroy businesses, and destabilize entire economies.

The legal system has historically treated financial criminals with more leniency than violent offenders. Many white-collar criminals receive short prison sentences, fines, or are allowed to settle out of court, particularly if they have political connections or the means to hire powerful defense attorneys. Some financial crimes result in penalties that amount to a fraction of the money stolen, making crime financially worthwhile for some offenders. **The difficulty in prosecuting financial crimes lies in the complexity of these cases**—proving intent, tracking money, and navigating international financial regulations create significant legal obstacles.

Efforts to combat financial crime include stricter regulations, enhanced corporate oversight, and increased enforcement of anti-money laundering laws. Some governments have imposed harsher penalties for financial criminals, recognizing that economic crimes can be just as destructive as violent offenses.

However, loopholes remain, and **as long as financial rewards outweigh the risks, white-collar crime will continue to thrive**. Preventing financial crime requires stronger regulatory bodies, ethical corporate leadership, and improved public awareness to recognize and avoid scams.

Crimes Against Morality (Victimless Crimes)

Crimes against morality, sometimes called victimless crimes, involve behaviors that are prohibited by law but do not directly harm another person or their property. These offenses are criminalized based on social, religious, or ethical standards rather than direct harm to others. Common examples include prostitution, gambling, drug use, and public indecency. The legal and social perception of these crimes varies across cultures, with some jurisdictions enforcing strict prohibitions and others legalizing or regulating them to reduce harm.

Prostitution is one of the oldest forms of morality-based crime. While some societies consider it a legitimate profession, others criminalize it entirely. Many laws surrounding prostitution aim to combat **human trafficking, exploitation, and public health concerns**, but they also push sex work into underground markets where regulation is nearly impossible. Some countries, like the Netherlands, have legalized and regulated prostitution, creating legal frameworks that prioritize **worker safety, health screenings, and consumer protections**. Other nations impose **harsh penalties, arguing that criminalization is necessary to prevent coercion and abuse**.

The psychology of sex work varies. Some individuals engage in prostitution due to economic necessity, coercion, or substance addiction, while others view it as a personal choice and a means of financial independence. Criminalization often makes sex workers more vulnerable to violence, exploitation, and unsafe working conditions because they fear seeking help from law enforcement. In contrast, legalized or decriminalized models provide **medical and legal protections, reducing the risks associated with underground sex work**.

Gambling is another morality-based crime that is regulated differently across societies. Some cultures embrace gambling as entertainment, while others view it as **a destructive force that leads to addiction, financial ruin, and organized crime involvement**. Legalized gambling industries generate **billions in revenue through casinos, sports betting, and lotteries**, but illegal gambling remains a major source of crime, particularly in areas where betting is banned.

Psychological studies show that gambling addiction functions similarly to drug dependency, with individuals experiencing compulsive urges, dopamine-driven reward cycles, and financial recklessness. Problem gamblers may resort to **fraud, theft, or embezzlement to fund their addiction**, leading to broader criminal consequences. Governments that permit gambling often implement **responsible gaming initiatives, addiction treatment programs, and strict regulatory oversight** to balance revenue generation with social responsibility.

Drug use and possession laws represent one of the most controversial aspects of morality-based crime. Some countries **decriminalize or legalize drug use, focusing on harm reduction and rehabilitation**, while others enforce **strict penalties, including long prison sentences or even the death penalty**. The war on drugs, particularly in countries like the United States, has resulted in **mass incarceration, disproportionately affecting low-income and minority communities**.

The motivations behind drug use vary widely. Some individuals use substances recreationally, while others self-medicate for mental health issues or escape from trauma. Many drug offenders in prison are non-violent users rather than traffickers or manufacturers, leading to debates over whether incarceration is an effective approach or whether treatment and education would be more beneficial. Studies show that decriminalization and public health approaches reduce addiction rates and drug-related crime, as seen in Portugal, where drug decriminalization led to lower overdose deaths and reduced drug-related incarcerations.

Public indecency laws, including **nudity bans, obscenity laws, and restrictions on lewd behavior**, reflect cultural attitudes toward morality and decency. What is considered **offensive or inappropriate varies widely across societies**. In some places, topless sunbathing or public displays of affection are **socially accepted**, while in others, they **result in fines or legal consequences**.

Hate speech laws also fall into the category of morality-based crime, aiming to **protect individuals from discrimination and incitement to violence**. However, they also raise concerns about freedom of expression, censorship, and the line between offensive speech and criminal behavior. Some governments use hate speech laws to silence political dissent or suppress controversial opinions, leading to further debates about how morality should be enforced through legal measures.

Crimes against morality challenge the legal system to **balance personal freedoms with social order**. The debate over these laws often centers on whether the government should regulate personal behavior when there is no direct harm to others. While some argue that prohibiting certain actions maintains societal values and protects the vulnerable, others believe that criminalizing personal choices creates more harm by pushing these activities into unsafe, unregulated spaces. Understanding the motivations and consequences of morality-based crimes provides insight into how laws shape society and how legal systems evolve alongside changing cultural norms.

Chapter 7: Criminal Behavior Analysis and Profiling

Crime Scene Analysis: From Evidence Collection to Interpretation

Crime scene analysis is the foundation of criminal investigations. Every crime leaves behind **physical evidence, behavioral clues, and forensic data** that can be used to reconstruct events and identify offenders. Properly analyzing a crime scene requires **a systematic approach, attention to detail, and knowledge of forensic science**. A misstep in evidence collection or interpretation can lead to wrongful arrests, missed leads, or even case dismissals in court. Investigators must work methodically, ensuring that every piece of evidence is preserved, documented, and analyzed correctly.

The process begins with **securing the crime scene**. The first officers on the scene must ensure **no one contaminates evidence, removes objects, or interferes with forensic examination**. Any changes—such as moving a body, stepping in blood, or touching objects—can alter the crime scene, potentially destroying crucial evidence. Once the area is secured, investigators document the scene through photographs, video recordings, sketches, and written reports. These records capture the original condition of the crime scene before forensic teams begin collecting evidence.

Physical evidence is the backbone of crime scene analysis. Investigators search for **fingerprints, footprints, bloodstains, hair, fibers, DNA, weapons, and any trace materials that might link a suspect to the crime**. Each type of evidence tells a different story. Blood spatter patterns can indicate the type of weapon used, the force of impact, and the position of the victim and offender at the time of the attack. Bullet trajectories help reconstruct the shooter's position and angle of fire. Fingerprints and DNA establish direct connections between individuals and crime scenes.

Forensic specialists analyze **biological, chemical, and trace evidence** to uncover details about the crime. **Toxicology reports** determine if a victim or suspect was under the influence of drugs or poison. **Ballistics experts** match bullets to specific firearms, helping determine if a gun recovered at the scene was the murder weapon. Hair and fiber analysis link suspects to crime scenes when direct DNA evidence is unavailable. Even microscopic particles, such as pollen or soil samples, can reveal where a suspect has been before or after committing a crime.

Investigators also look for **behavioral evidence, which helps reconstruct the sequence of events and the offender's psychological profile**. The arrangement of objects at the scene—such as whether valuables were taken or left behind, if forced entry occurred, or if the victim's body was posed in a specific way—offers insight into the offender's mindset. A carefully staged crime scene suggests premeditation, control, and an attempt to mislead investigators. A chaotic, disorganized scene often indicates an impulsive crime, possibly fueled by rage or panic.

Detecting **staged crime scenes** is a critical aspect of analysis. Some offenders attempt to **manipulate evidence to mislead law enforcement**. For example, a suspect might try to make a murder appear like a suicide by placing a weapon in the victim's hand or stage a burglary to cover up a personal attack. Investigators identify inconsistencies by examining blood flow patterns, injury consistency, and signs of forced entry. If the evidence does not match the expected outcome, further investigation is needed.

Crime scene analysts also study **body positioning and postmortem clues. Rigor mortis, livor mortis, and algor mortis** help determine the time of death and whether the body was moved. Entomological analysis, which studies insect activity on the body, can narrow down time-of-death estimates. These forensic details provide critical timelines for investigators, helping them confirm or disprove alibis.

Bloodstain pattern analysis is often used to reconstruct violent crimes. The shape, size, and distribution of blood drops reveal **the type of attack, number of blows, and movement of the victim and offender. Cast-off blood patterns, created when an object like a knife or bat is swung repeatedly, show how many times a victim was struck and in which direction**. High-velocity blood spatter, common in gunshot wounds, helps determine firing distance and weapon type. Analysts compare bloodstains to witness statements and suspect confessions to identify inconsistencies in their accounts.

Crime scene reconstruction combines **physical and forensic evidence with behavioral analysis**. Investigators must answer **key questions about the sequence of events**—who arrived first, what actions took place, how long the crime lasted, and whether the offender acted alone or with accomplices. By cross-referencing witness statements, forensic findings, and surveillance footage, analysts piece together an accurate timeline of events.

Forensic technology has significantly improved the accuracy and speed of crime scene analysis. 3D laser scanning allows investigators to create digital reconstructions of crime scenes, preserving details that can be re-examined later. Advanced DNA analysis techniques, such as familial DNA matching, help identify suspects even when direct DNA evidence is unavailable. Facial recognition and digital forensic tools assist in tracking suspects using security footage and online activity.

Crime scene analysis extends beyond detecting offenders—it also aids in exonerating the innocent. Wrongful convictions often result from misinterpreted evidence, forced confessions, or flawed eyewitness testimony. Proper forensic procedures ensure that suspects are charged based on physical proof rather than assumptions or biases.

Investigators must remain **objective, methodical, and open to all possibilities** when analyzing crime scenes. Assumptions can lead to **confirmation bias, where investigators focus on evidence that supports their initial theory while ignoring contradictory findings**. A careful, evidence-based approach ensures that every possible lead is considered before drawing conclusions.

Every crime scene tells a story. The challenge lies in interpreting the evidence accurately, identifying patterns, and ensuring that nothing is overlooked. By combining forensic science, behavioral analysis, and investigative techniques, crime scene analysts work toward uncovering the truth and delivering justice for victims and their families.

Behavioral Profiling: Methods and Applications

Behavioral profiling is a method used in criminal investigations to analyze patterns in an offender's actions, personality, and decision-making. It helps law enforcement narrow down suspect lists, predict future behaviors, and understand the psychological motivations behind crimes. Profiling is based on the idea that criminal behavior is not random; it follows patterns that reveal details about the offender's background, emotional state, and reasoning. While profiling does not provide an exact identity, it helps investigators focus their search and develop leads.

There are two primary types of profiling: inductive and deductive. **Inductive profiling relies on statistical patterns drawn from past criminal cases**. It assumes that offenders with similar characteristics will behave in similar ways.

For example, data on serial killers might reveal that many have a history of childhood abuse, unstable employment, and difficulty maintaining relationships. If a new case matches these patterns, investigators might look for suspects who fit the same profile. While this method is useful for identifying trends, it is not always precise since individual criminals do not always conform to broad patterns.

Deductive profiling, on the other hand, **focuses on analyzing the specific details of a crime scene and the behaviors displayed during the offense**. Instead of applying general statistics, it builds a profile based on unique aspects of the case. A profiler examines how the offender approached the crime, interacted with the victim, and attempted to conceal evidence. This method relies heavily on forensic evidence, witness statements, and crime scene analysis to reconstruct the offender's mindset.

A key aspect of profiling is distinguishing between organized and disorganized offenders. Organized offenders plan their crimes carefully, select victims deliberately, and take measures to avoid leaving evidence. They often have above-average intelligence, stable employment, and social skills that allow them to blend into society. Their crime scenes are controlled, showing signs of forethought and strategic decision-making. Disorganized offenders, by contrast, act impulsively, leaving behind chaotic crime scenes with clear evidence. They may attack victims randomly, lack a coherent escape plan, and act out of emotional distress or psychological instability.

Investigators also examine modus operandi and signature behaviors when building a profile. Modus operandi refers to the techniques an offender uses to commit a crime. This can include the tools they use, how they approach their victims, and how they escape. Modus operandi can change over time as criminals refine their methods or adapt to law enforcement pressure. Signature behaviors, however, remain consistent. These are personal touches that have no practical purpose but fulfill a psychological need for the offender. A serial killer who leaves a specific mark on their victims, arranges bodies in a particular way, or takes trophies is displaying signature behaviors. Identifying these unique traits helps link crimes to a single perpetrator.

Behavioral profiling is particularly useful in cases involving serial crimes. When an offender commits multiple offenses, patterns emerge that provide insight into their psychology. Investigators look at victimology—analyzing the characteristics of the victims—to determine why they were chosen. Some offenders target victims based on physical traits, while others select them based on opportunity or symbolic significance. Understanding the victim-offender relationship helps profilers predict future targets and determine how the offender perceives their victims.

Geographic profiling is another component of behavioral analysis. It studies the locations of crimes to identify patterns in offender movement. Most criminals operate within a familiar area, and their crime locations can reveal details about their home, workplace, or areas they frequently visit. Geographic profiling software uses data on crime locations to generate probability maps, guiding law enforcement in their searches.

While profiling is valuable, one major issue is confirmation bias, where **investigators may become fixated on a specific type of suspect while ignoring other possibilities**. Misinterpretations of behavioral patterns can lead to false accusations or overlooking real suspects. Additionally, profiling is not an exact science; human behavior is complex, and not all offenders fit neatly into categories.

Despite its limitations, behavioral profiling has been instrumental in solving many high-profile cases. It provides investigators with psychological insight into offenders, helping to anticipate their next move and prevent further crimes. As forensic psychology and criminal analysis evolve, profiling techniques continue to improve, making them more reliable and effective in modern investigations.

Victimology: Understanding the Victim-Offender Dynamic

Victimology is the study of victims, their relationships with offenders, and the role they play in the crime itself. While criminal investigations often focus on offenders, understanding victims provides critical insight into why crimes occur, how offenders select their targets, and how legal systems should address victim rights and support. Victimology helps law enforcement refine their suspect lists, assists forensic psychologists in assessing offender motivations, and informs policies aimed at preventing future victimization.

One of the first steps in victimology is analyzing victim characteristics. Investigators examine details such as age, gender, occupation, lifestyle, routines, and personal history to determine whether the victim was targeted deliberately or chosen at random. Certain victims may be at higher risk due to their circumstances —those who live alone, work late hours, or engage in high-risk behaviors are often more vulnerable to crime. Some offenders carefully select victims based on specific traits, while others strike based on opportunity.

Victim-offender relationships vary significantly across different crimes. In many cases, victims and offenders know each other. Domestic violence, workplace harassment, and financial fraud frequently involve close relationships between victim and perpetrator. In contrast, some violent crimes, such as serial killings and mass shootings, involve offenders selecting victims randomly or based on a perceived symbolic meaning. Understanding whether an offender knew the victim can influence how investigators approach a case.

Victim precipitation theory suggests that some victims, knowingly or unknowingly, contribute to the events leading up to the crime. This doesn't mean victims are responsible for their victimization but rather that their actions or behaviors may have influenced the offender's decision to act.

This is particularly examined in cases of self-defense killings, bar fights, and fraud schemes where victims may have engaged in risky behaviors or interactions that escalated into criminal acts. However, this theory is controversial, as it risks shifting blame away from offenders and onto victims, particularly in cases of sexual violence or abuse.

Serial offenders often have specific victim preferences. Some choose victims based on appearance, such as a particular age group or gender. Others select victims based on symbolic reasons—certain serial killers target individuals who remind them of someone from their past, while hate crimes often involve victims attacked for their ethnicity, religion, or sexual orientation. Understanding these patterns helps profilers predict future targets and assess an offender's underlying motivations.

Routine activity theory explains how the absence of capable guardians, the presence of a motivated offender, and a suitable target create the conditions for crime. Victims who find themselves in isolated areas, poorly lit streets, or situations where security measures are lacking are more likely to be targeted. This theory is widely used in crime prevention strategies, encouraging environmental design changes such as better lighting, surveillance cameras, and neighborhood patrols to reduce victimization opportunities.

Psychological effects on victims vary based on the severity and nature of the crime. Many experience post-traumatic stress disorder, anxiety, depression, and difficulties re-engaging with daily life. Some victims develop hyper-vigilance, avoiding certain places or situations similar to where the crime occurred. Others struggle with guilt, particularly in cases where they survived but others did not. Understanding these effects is crucial for victim advocacy and support services, ensuring survivors receive proper mental health care and legal assistance.

Victim blaming remains a major issue in many legal systems and social discussions. Certain crimes, such as sexual assault, often lead to public scrutiny of the victim's actions rather than the offender's. Questions like what the victim was wearing, whether they had been drinking, or why they were in a certain location shift responsibility away from the perpetrator. This type of thinking discourages victims from reporting crimes, fearing they will not be believed or will be held accountable for their own victimization. Legal reforms and education efforts continue to challenge these biases, emphasizing that the focus should remain on offender actions rather than victim behavior.

The study of repeat victimization reveals that some individuals or groups are more frequently targeted for crime. Victims of domestic violence, for example, often endure multiple incidents before seeking help or escaping abusive relationships. Businesses that experience burglaries once are statistically more likely to be targeted again. Criminals recognize weak points in security or vulnerable individuals and may return to exploit them multiple times. Identifying repeat victimization patterns helps law enforcement allocate resources to better protect those at risk.

Victimology is also essential in wrongful convictions. Many cases of mistaken identity or coerced confessions stem from poor victim or witness recall. **The stress and trauma of being a crime victim often distort memory, leading to inaccurate testimonies**. Understanding how trauma affects recall can prevent false accusations and improve the accuracy of investigations. Some victims, due to fear or influence from others, may intentionally misidentify a suspect, making it critical for legal professionals to scrutinize victim statements carefully.

The legal system has evolved to give victims a greater voice in criminal proceedings. Victim impact statements allow survivors or their families to address the court directly, describing how the crime affected them. These statements can influence sentencing decisions, particularly in cases where victims demand harsher penalties or seek rehabilitative justice approaches. Many jurisdictions now have victim compensation programs, offering financial and emotional support to help survivors recover from their experiences.

Victimology is not just about understanding past crimes—it's important in preventing future victimization. Crime prevention programs focus on teaching individuals how to recognize risks, improve personal safety, and report suspicious behavior. Schools, workplaces, and communities incorporate training on recognizing warning signs of domestic violence, fraud schemes, and online exploitation to reduce the number of victims.

Understanding the victim-offender dynamic is essential for both solving crimes and improving justice system responses. Victims are not just incidental figures in a crime —they provide crucial evidence, shape legal outcomes, and reveal patterns that help law enforcement prevent similar offenses. Their experiences offer insight into the nature of crime itself, influencing policies and strategies aimed at making society safer for everyone.

Geographic Profiling: Mapping Offense Patterns

Geographic profiling is a method used in criminal investigations to analyze the spatial patterns of an offender's crimes. It helps law enforcement identify **where an offender is likely to live, work, or travel based on crime locations**. Most criminals do not act randomly; their offenses are influenced by familiarity with an area, comfort levels, and strategic decision-making. By studying these patterns, investigators can narrow down search areas, predict future crimes, and allocate resources more efficiently.

The foundation of geographic profiling is based on **criminal mobility patterns**. Most offenders operate within a comfort zone—a region where they feel confident enough to commit crimes while minimizing the risk of getting caught. However, they also tend to avoid committing offenses too close to home, where they might be recognized. This creates a **buffer zone**, an area surrounding their residence where crimes are less likely to occur. By mapping crime locations, investigators can identify **hot spots** that reveal an offender's movement patterns.

One of the earliest theories related to geographic profiling is **routine activity theory**, which explains that crime occurs when a motivated offender encounters a suitable target in the absence of effective guardianship. Offenders do not usually travel great distances to commit crimes; instead, they select locations that are **easily accessible and provide opportunities with minimal risk**. Serial offenders, for example, often choose areas that are **close enough to be familiar but far enough to avoid immediate suspicion**.

The **distance decay function** is another key principle in geographic profiling. It states that the likelihood of committing a crime decreases the farther an offender moves from their home base. Most criminals operate within **five to ten miles of their residence**, though this varies depending on the type of offense. Property crimes, such as burglary, tend to occur closer to home because they require **quick escapes and local knowledge of security weaknesses**. Violent crimes, such as homicide or sexual assault, may occur at greater distances, particularly if the offender is attempting to **avoid detection or separate themselves from the crime scene**.

Criminals fall into two broad categories based on their movement patterns: **marauders and commuters**. Marauders commit crimes within a set range around their home or workplace, gradually expanding outward over time. Commuters, on the other hand, travel to a different location to commit crimes, deliberately avoiding areas they are connected to. Geographic profiling helps determine which category an offender belongs to, influencing how police conduct their search.

A key tool in geographic profiling is computerized mapping technology. Geographic Information Systems (GIS) allow investigators to enter crime scene data and generate maps that highlight patterns, clusters, and potential base locations. These systems use algorithms to calculate the most probable areas where an offender may live based on the distribution of their crimes. Software such as Criminal Geographic Targeting (CGT) assigns probability scores to different areas, guiding law enforcement toward the most likely locations of a suspect.

One of the most successful applications of geographic profiling was in the case of the "Railway Rapist" in London. In the 1980s, serial rapist and murderer John Duffy targeted women near railway stations, committing multiple assaults across different locations. Investigators used geographic profiling techniques to analyze **the pattern of attacks, distance between crime scenes, and locations of railway stops**. The analysis led them to **a small region of London where Duffy lived**, significantly narrowing down the suspect pool.

Geographic profiling is particularly useful in **serial crimes**, where offenders strike multiple times in different locations. Patterns emerge when comparing **the distances between crime scenes, the method of approach, and the surrounding geography**. By analyzing environmental factors, such as **road networks, public transportation, and secluded areas**, profilers can determine how an offender moves through their environment and **where they are most likely to strike again**.

Environmental criminology has a major role in geographic profiling. Factors such as **urban layout, crime density, and accessibility of targets** influence where offenders choose to commit crimes. Areas with low police presence, poor lighting, and easy escape routes are prime locations for crime. Offenders take advantage of routine public spaces like shopping centers, parks, or transit hubs, where they can blend in and observe potential victims before acting.

Geographic profiling also helps eliminate false leads. Investigators often receive tips and suspect lists that include **hundreds or even thousands of names**. By applying geographic analysis, police can **focus on individuals who live within a high-probability zone**, reducing time and resources spent investigating unlikely suspects.

While geographic profiling is effective, it is not a standalone method. It works best when combined with **behavioral profiling, forensic evidence, and investigative leads**. A major limitation is that it requires **a sufficient number of crimes to establish a pattern**. If an offender has only committed one or two crimes, there may not be enough data to generate an accurate geographic profile.

Criminals adapt their behavior in response to law enforcement efforts. Some offenders deliberately change locations, target different types of victims, or alter their methods to disrupt profiling efforts. In cases where geographic profiling is less effective, investigators rely on witness accounts, surveillance footage, and forensic evidence to track offender movements.

Advancements in technology continue to improve geographic profiling. The rise of **predictive policing**, which uses historical crime data to forecast where future crimes may occur, has given law enforcement new tools to anticipate criminal activity. Machine learning algorithms analyze **past crime trends, suspect movements, and social patterns** to provide **real-time intelligence on emerging crime hotspots**.

Geographic profiling is particularly relevant in cases involving **human trafficking, organized crime, and cybercrime**. Traffickers use established routes and locations to move victims, creating identifiable patterns that investigators can track. Cybercriminals leave digital footprints linked to their geographic locations, allowing law enforcement to trace hacking activity back to specific regions or networks.

Despite its challenges, geographic profiling remains one of the most effective tools for narrowing down suspect pools and understanding criminal behavior. It allows investigators to **move beyond random searches and focus their efforts on the most likely areas where an offender operates**. The ability to **map crime patterns and predict future activity gives law enforcement a strategic advantage in solving complex cases** and preventing further offenses.

Identifying Signature Behaviors and Ritualistic Patterns

Signature behaviors and ritualistic patterns in criminal offenses provide crucial insights into an offender's psychological motivations. Unlike modus operandi (MO), which refers to the practical techniques used to commit a crime, signature behaviors are the unique, personal elements that an offender includes, even when they serve no functional purpose. These behaviors offer a psychological fingerprint, revealing the offender's emotional and cognitive state, personality traits, and underlying compulsions.

Signature behaviors often emerge in cases involving **serial offenders, particularly serial killers, rapists, and arsonists**, who commit crimes driven by psychological gratification rather than material gain. These offenders **repeat specific behaviors across multiple crime scenes**, allowing investigators to link cases even when physical evidence is lacking. Some signatures are overt and easily recognizable, while others are subtle and require careful forensic and behavioral analysis.

A signature can include **how a victim is positioned after death, personal messages left at the crime scene, specific injuries inflicted, or unique post-mortem actions**. Some offenders take trophies—items from victims such as jewelry, clothing, or personal belongings—to relive the crime later. Others leave behind taunting messages, symbols, or cryptic notes meant to confuse law enforcement or assert dominance.

Ritualistic patterns differ from signatures in that they are often **compulsive and driven by deep-seated psychological needs**. Rituals follow a consistent sequence of actions that are psychologically necessary for the offender, even if they do not contribute directly to the crime itself. Some offenders engage in pre-crime rituals, such as stalking a victim for days or dressing in specific clothing before an attack. Others have post-crime rituals, such as revisiting crime scenes, arranging objects in a specific way, or even communicating with law enforcement through letters or coded messages.

Forensic psychologists analyze signature behaviors and rituals to **build a psychological profile of the offender**. If an offender poses a victim's body in a particular way, binds them in a specific fashion, or leaves behind a consistent symbol, investigators can infer aspects of their personality, background, and potential motives. For example, an offender who washes a victim's body after a murder may have compulsive tendencies or feelings of guilt, while one who inflicts specific post-mortem injuries might be acting out a deep-seated fantasy or rage toward a particular type of person.

Understanding the difference between MO, signature, and ritual is crucial in criminal profiling. **MO evolves over time as offenders refine their techniques or respond to law enforcement pressure**, but signature behaviors remain psychologically significant and do not change. A burglar may adjust their approach based on security measures, but a serial offender will continue expressing their psychological needs through consistent crime scene patterns.

One of the most well-documented cases of signature behavior is that of **Ted Bundy**, who targeted young women with similar physical characteristics and often **posed their bodies in a specific way post-mortem**. His crimes followed **a repetitive psychological script**, suggesting a deep-rooted need for control and reenactment of previous fantasies. Similarly, the **Zodiac Killer's cryptic letters and symbolic messages** became a signature that defined his crimes, creating a distinct behavioral pattern that separated him from other serial offenders.

Arsonists often display signature behaviors through **fire-setting patterns, choice of accelerants, and locations targeted**. Some arsonists return to the scene to watch the destruction unfold, experiencing psychological satisfaction from witnessing their crime. Others follow a specific ignition pattern, such as using symbolic materials or setting multiple fires in a geometric arrangement. These behaviors can help investigators distinguish between revenge-driven arsonists, thrill-seekers, and compulsive fire-setters.

Sexual offenders frequently exhibit **ritualistic behaviors related to power, humiliation, or dominance**. Some rapists force victims to say specific words, dress a certain way, or perform particular acts, indicating a compulsive need to control and script their crimes. In cases of serial sexual assault, identifying common elements in victim accounts can reveal a perpetrator's deep-seated psychological needs, allowing profilers to anticipate future offenses.

The presence of a signature does not always mean an offender is conscious of their patterns. Many serial offenders act on subconscious impulses, driven by compulsions they do not fully understand. However, some criminals **deliberately craft a signature to mislead investigators or gain notoriety**. This is particularly common in **media-driven cases**, where offenders crave attention and attempt to manipulate the public narrative.

One of the challenges in identifying signature behaviors is distinguishing them from staged crime scenes. Some offenders **attempt to create false patterns to mislead law enforcement** or **copy aspects of well-known crimes to obscure their true motivations**. Investigators carefully analyze whether a behavioral element is genuine or an intentional misdirection, using forensic evidence and psychological profiling to determine authenticity.

Advancements in forensic psychology and behavioral analysis continue to improve **law enforcement's ability to identify signature behaviors and rituals,** helping connect crimes that might otherwise seem unrelated. By understanding the **psychological needs and compulsions that drive offenders**, investigators can better anticipate **future behavior, refine suspect lists, and develop interrogation strategies tailored to an offender's specific mindset**.

Technological Advances in Behavioral Profiling

Advancements in technology have transformed behavioral profiling, allowing investigators to analyze criminal behavior with greater precision, efficiency, and accuracy. Traditional profiling relied heavily on psychological theory, case studies, and experience-based intuition, but modern tools now integrate forensic science, artificial intelligence, and big data analysis. These innovations have helped law enforcement predict offender behavior, track criminal activity, and identify patterns that might otherwise go unnoticed.

One of the most significant technological breakthroughs in behavioral profiling is **predictive analytics**, which uses algorithms and historical crime data to forecast where and when offenses are likely to occur. By analyzing past criminal activity, predictive models generate risk assessments for certain locations, helping law enforcement allocate resources more effectively. These systems consider variables such as crime type, geographic location, time of day, and offender movement patterns, producing heat maps that indicate high-risk areas for specific types of crime.

Artificial intelligence (AI) and machine learning have further revolutionized profiling by automating pattern recognition. Traditional criminal profiling required human analysts to manually examine crime scene details, behavioral traits, and forensic evidence. AI-based systems can now process vast amounts of data **at speeds far beyond human capability**, detecting connections across different cases, identifying common offender traits, and even predicting escalation patterns in serial crimes. AI-driven analysis is especially useful for identifying modus operandi and signature behaviors in large criminal databases, helping connect offenses that might have otherwise seemed unrelated.

Facial recognition technology has enhanced **suspect identification and behavioral tracking**, particularly in urban areas with extensive surveillance networks. Law enforcement agencies use facial recognition software to match **CCTV footage, social media images, and other digital records with known offenders or persons of interest**. While controversial due to privacy concerns, facial recognition has been instrumental in identifying suspects who operate across multiple locations or who attempt to conceal their identities.

Digital forensics has become an integral part of modern behavioral profiling, as many crimes now leave **digital footprints** that reveal offender behavior. Investigators analyze **search history, social media activity, chat logs, and location data** to understand a suspect's psychological state, interests, and potential motivations. For example, a serial offender might conduct online searches about forensic countermeasures, stalk potential victims through social media, or participate in dark web forums that discuss violent fantasies. This information provides **behavioral clues that complement traditional psychological profiling**.

Geospatial analysis software has refined **geographic profiling**, allowing investigators to track **movement patterns, likely offender home bases, and travel behaviors**. By mapping out crime locations and using algorithmic models, geospatial tools calculate the most probable areas where an offender resides or frequently visits. This method has been particularly effective in tracking serial offenders who commit crimes across different regions but follow predictable movement patterns.

The rise of **behavioral biometrics** has introduced new ways to profile offenders based on how they interact with digital devices. Behavioral biometric systems analyze keystroke dynamics, mouse movement patterns, touchscreen pressure, and gait recognition to determine unique identifiers for individuals. This technology is used in cybercrime investigations, helping law enforcement distinguish between different hackers or fraudsters based on how they type, navigate, or manipulate digital platforms.

Sentiment analysis tools, which use **natural language processing (NLP)** to assess text-based communication, have enhanced law enforcement's ability to detect threats, extremist behavior, and criminal intent in online interactions. These tools scan emails, social media posts, and private messages for linguistic patterns associated with violent ideation, deception, or radicalization. By identifying early warning signs, sentiment analysis helps prevent crimes before they occur.

Forensic linguistics, a field that has benefited from technological advancements, examines **speech patterns, writing styles, and linguistic markers** to profile unknown offenders. Criminals often reveal subconscious aspects of their personality, background, and level of education through their writing. Linguistic analysis has been instrumental in **identifying anonymous criminals, verifying suspect statements, and detecting deceptive language in interrogations**.

Another major development in behavioral profiling is **neurological and psychological assessment technology**, including fMRI (functional magnetic resonance imaging) and polygraph advancements. These tools allow researchers to analyze brain activity associated with deception, aggression, and impulse control. While not yet admissible as standalone legal evidence, neuropsychological assessments help distinguish between different types of offenders and evaluate their capacity for criminal responsibility.

While technology has greatly improved behavioral profiling, it also presents challenges. Many advanced profiling techniques raise ethical concerns regarding privacy, data collection, and potential bias in AI-driven systems. Additionally, criminals are adapting to technological surveillance, using encryption, anonymization tools, and digital countermeasures to evade detection. As profiling techniques evolve, so too must law enforcement strategies to anticipate and counteract emerging methods of criminal activity.

Despite these challenges, technological advancements continue to refine and enhance behavioral profiling, making investigations **more precise, data-driven, and capable of handling complex criminal patterns**. By integrating **AI, forensic science, digital analysis, and geospatial mapping**, modern profiling has become very important in understanding offender behavior, preventing crimes, and delivering justice.

Cybercrime Profiling: New Frontiers in Digital Offenses

Cybercrime profiling has become essential as digital offenses have grown in complexity, frequency, and impact. Traditional profiling methods focused on physical evidence, geographic patterns, and behavioral traits observable at crime scenes. Cybercriminals, however, leave **digital footprints rather than physical**

ones, requiring law enforcement to adapt profiling techniques to a world where crimes are committed remotely, often across international borders. Understanding how cybercriminals operate, what motivates them, and how they evolve their tactics is critical for effective cybercrime investigations.

Cybercriminals vary widely in skill, motivation, and behavior. Unlike violent criminals, who may be driven by impulse, emotional disturbances, or power dynamics, cybercriminals often exhibit **high cognitive abilities, technical expertise, and an ability to work methodically**. Many offenders begin engaging in cybercrimes as **hobbyists, testing their technical skills on minor hacking challenges before progressing to more serious offenses**. Others are **financially motivated criminals who exploit security weaknesses for profit**, engaging in identity theft, credit card fraud, ransomware attacks, or financial scams.

Law enforcement categorizes cybercriminals into different profiles based on their behavior and intent. **Script kiddies** are individuals with limited technical skills who rely on prewritten hacking tools or exploit kits. They often engage in cybercrime for **thrill-seeking, social recognition, or minor financial gain**. While they may not develop their own malware, they can still cause significant disruption, particularly if they access sensitive data or compromise personal accounts.

More advanced cybercriminals, often referred to as **black hat hackers**, have a deep understanding of programming, network security, and cryptographic weaknesses. These individuals are responsible for **high-profile data breaches, sophisticated phishing campaigns, and financial fraud at a large scale**. Unlike impulsive criminals, black hat hackers are strategic, taking careful steps to **cover their digital tracks, use anonymization tools, and exploit zero-day vulnerabilities before they are patched**.

Cybercrime profiling also distinguishes between **lone actors and organized cybercriminal networks**. Some hackers operate independently, testing their abilities, seeking financial gain, or engaging in politically motivated cyberattacks. Others work as part of **coordinated cybercrime syndicates that function similarly to traditional organized crime groups**, complete with hierarchies, specialized roles, and underground markets for stolen data, hacking tools, and illicit services.

Dark web marketplaces have facilitated the growth of cybercrime, creating a **hidden economy for stolen credit card numbers, hacking software, counterfeit documents, and illegal goods**. Many cybercriminals interact anonymously using **cryptocurrencies, encryption tools, and proxy servers to evade detection**. Profilers analyze **transaction patterns, user behavior on darknet forums, and linguistic markers in communication** to identify potential offenders.

Another major category of cybercriminals includes **nation-state hackers**, who engage in cyberespionage, infrastructure sabotage, and disinformation campaigns on behalf of governments. Unlike financially motivated criminals, these actors are driven by **political objectives, intelligence gathering, or efforts to destabilize geopolitical adversaries**. Their attacks often target government agencies, critical infrastructure, military databases, and corporate intellectual property. Cybercrime profiling in these cases involves tracking malware signatures, analyzing attack vectors, and linking digital fingerprints to known state-sponsored hacking groups.

Cybercriminals exhibit unique psychological traits compared to traditional offenders. Many are **introverted, highly analytical, and adept at problem-solving**. They often thrive in online communities where they share hacking techniques, collaborate on cyberattacks, and test new exploits. Unlike violent criminals, cybercriminals may not perceive their actions as harmful, particularly when engaging in fraud or data theft. Some believe large corporations, government agencies, or financial institutions are fair game, rationalizing their crimes as acts of rebellion, social justice, or digital warfare.

Profiling cybercriminals requires analyzing their attack patterns, choice of tools, and level of operational security. Some hackers leave distinct signatures in their code—reused encryption techniques, specific programming languages, or patterns in how they structure their attacks. Others make mistakes, such as reusing usernames, forgetting to mask their IP addresses, or leaving identifiable metadata in malware samples. Digital forensic analysts exploit these errors to trace offenders, link attacks, and dismantle cybercrime networks.

The evolution of cybercrime profiling has led to the development of AI-driven threat intelligence systems, which monitor network traffic, detect anomalies, and identify emerging cyber threats in real time. Machine learning algorithms can recognize patterns in hacking attempts, track login credential theft, and flag suspicious financial transactions, helping companies and law enforcement respond before major breaches occur.

Cybercrime profiling is also crucial for identifying **insider threats**, where employees, contractors, or business partners engage in **data leaks, financial fraud, or corporate espionage**. Unlike external hackers, insider threats exploit **their legitimate access to secure networks**, making detection more difficult. Behavioral analysis techniques monitor sudden access to restricted files, abnormal data transfers, and irregular login behavior to identify potential internal risks.

The use of social engineering in cybercrime presents another challenge for profilers. Many cybercriminals exploit psychological vulnerabilities rather than technical ones, tricking individuals into revealing passwords, granting access to sensitive systems, or transferring money through well-crafted deception tactics. Phishing emails, impersonation scams, and deepfake technology have made it easier for attackers to manipulate victims into compliance. Profiling these offenders requires examining **how they craft their messages, who they target, and how they adapt their tactics based on past successes**.

While cybercrime profiling has made significant advancements, it faces major obstacles. Cybercriminals continuously evolve their methods, developing **new encryption techniques, using decentralized networks, and leveraging artificial intelligence to automate attacks**. Unlike traditional criminals, cyber offenders can operate globally with minimal risk of physical capture, making international cooperation essential in cybercrime investigations. Law enforcement agencies must collaborate across borders, share intelligence, and adapt to the constantly shifting landscape of digital crime.

Chapter 8: Motivations and Triggers for Criminal Acts

Intrinsic vs. Extrinsic Motivational Factors

Criminal behavior is driven by different types of motivation, broadly categorized as intrinsic or extrinsic. Intrinsic motivations come from within the individual, often rooted in personal desires, psychological needs, or emotional states. Extrinsic motivations, on the other hand, are shaped by external factors such as financial gain, social pressure, or environmental circumstances. Understanding the difference between these two categories helps explain why people commit crimes, how motivations vary between offenders, and what influences long-term criminal behavior.

Intrinsic motivation is often psychological or emotional. Some offenders commit crimes for **the thrill, sense of power, or emotional satisfaction they derive from the act itself**. Serial offenders, particularly those with psychopathic tendencies, often engage in crime because they find personal gratification in exerting control, inflicting harm, or manipulating others. These individuals are not necessarily seeking financial gain or external rewards but are instead driven by internal compulsions, deep-seated anger, or personal ideologies.

Some crimes are intrinsically motivated by **revenge, hatred, or personal grudges**. A person who kills their spouse's lover, an employee who sabotages their workplace out of resentment, or a bullied individual who seeks violent retribution is acting based on **internal emotional forces rather than external incentives**. These crimes are often **highly emotional and personal**, distinguishing them from **financially or materially motivated offenses**.

Sadistic offenders commit crimes purely for **the psychological pleasure of watching others suffer**. They are not motivated by profit, personal defense, or necessity—rather, they experience emotional or sexual gratification from inflicting pain. These individuals are often **resistant to rehabilitation** because their motivation is deeply ingrained in their psychological makeup. Unlike material criminals, who may be deterred by loss of income or stricter laws, offenders driven by sadism or personal satisfaction are **less likely to be influenced by external punishments**.

Intrinsically motivated offenders may also be driven by **compulsions or mental health disorders**. Some crimes stem from **obsessive behavior, delusions, or psychotic episodes**. Kleptomaniacs, for example, do not steal because they need the items they take, but rather because they feel an overwhelming internal urge to do so.

Similarly, individuals with severe impulse control disorders may commit violent or destructive acts not for any tangible gain, but because they feel an uncontrollable need to release pent-up emotions.

Extrinsic motivations, in contrast, involve external rewards, pressures, or circumstances that push someone toward crime. Financial incentives are among the most common extrinsic motivators. Many criminals engage in fraud, burglary, robbery, or organized crime because **they seek money, luxury, or a higher standard of living**. These individuals may not have any deep-seated psychological desire to harm others but see crime as a means to an end.

Economic necessity can drive extrinsically motivated crime. In high-poverty areas, individuals may turn to **theft, drug dealing, or scams** as a survival strategy. Unlike intrinsically motivated criminals, who commit crimes regardless of circumstances, extrinsically motivated criminals often respond to changes in **economic opportunities, social support, or legal consequences**. If they find stable employment or face harsher law enforcement crackdowns, they may abandon crime.

Social pressure is another major extrinsic factor. Gang involvement, for example, is often driven by peer influence, community expectations, and the need for protection or status. Many young offenders join criminal organizations not because they have an internal desire to harm others, but because they feel pressured by their social environment. They may view crime as a requirement for acceptance, a path to financial stability, or a means of survival in dangerous neighborhoods.

Political and ideological motivations are also extrinsic. Terrorists, extremists, and cult members may commit crimes **not for personal psychological satisfaction, but because they believe in a cause that demands violence or destruction**. These individuals often do not exhibit traditional criminal psychology but instead are **driven by external propaganda, group dynamics, or ideological brainwashing**. Their motivation does not come from personal thrill-seeking but from **a perceived duty to a larger mission**.

Extrinsic motivations can also come from opportunism and ease of access. If someone sees a wallet left unattended, finds a security loophole in a financial system, or realizes they can falsify documents without being caught, they may commit a crime purely because the opportunity presents itself. These crimes are often unplanned and situational, distinguishing them from intrinsically driven crimes that stem from deep-seated needs or compulsions.

Understanding whether a criminal is **intrinsically or extrinsically motivated influences legal consequences, rehabilitation efforts, and crime prevention strategies**. Intrinsically driven offenders, particularly those with sadistic or compulsive tendencies, are harder to rehabilitate because their crimes are linked to personal psychological fulfillment rather than external factors. In contrast, extrinsically motivated criminals are more likely to respond to economic opportunities, social interventions, and deterrents.

Some criminals exhibit **a blend of intrinsic and extrinsic motivations**. A person who commits fraud may initially do so **for financial gain (extrinsic motivation)** but later develop a **thrill for deception and power over victims (intrinsic motivation)**. A gang member may start engaging in crime **due to peer pressure (extrinsic)** but later begin to enjoy the authority, status, and violence associated with their role (intrinsic).

Profilers and forensic psychologists analyze motivation to predict **recidivism rates, criminal escalation, and likelihood of rehabilitation**. Someone who steals due to **financial hardship is more likely to stop if given economic support**, whereas **someone who finds emotional satisfaction in crime is more likely to continue even when circumstances change**.

Criminal motivation is complex, with no single factor explaining all offenses. Some crimes are driven purely by **internal desires**, others by **external pressures**, and many by **a combination of both**. Recognizing what pushes individuals toward crime helps shape **preventive policies, legal responses, and correctional strategies**, ensuring that interventions are tailored to the specific drivers behind criminal behavior.

Emotional and Psychological Triggers in the Build-Up to Crime

Criminal acts are often the result of a series of emotional and psychological triggers that push an individual toward breaking the law. These triggers may build up over time, creating internal pressure that eventually explodes into action, or they may be sudden, overwhelming impulses that drive immediate behavior. Understanding what sparks criminal activity requires analyzing the **emotions, thought patterns, and psychological stressors that lead to crime**.

One of the most significant emotional triggers is **anger and resentment**. Many violent crimes occur when an individual loses control in a fit of rage. Domestic violence, assaults, and even homicides often stem from **long-standing grievances, personal betrayals, or humiliations**. A man who feels disrespected in a public argument, an employee who is repeatedly mistreated by a supervisor, or a spouse who feels emotionally abandoned may act impulsively in an outburst of frustration. The key factor is not just anger itself but the **inability to process and manage it constructively**.

Some offenders hold onto their anger for long periods, allowing it to turn into **deep-seated resentment and obsessive thoughts of revenge**. Crimes driven by revenge are often premeditated rather than impulsive. The offender may spend days, weeks, or even years **fantasizing about retaliation, waiting for the right moment to act**. Unlike a spontaneous violent outburst, revenge crimes involve **careful planning, manipulation, and strategic execution**, making them particularly dangerous.

Humiliation and shame are also powerful triggers. Some individuals commit crimes **not out of anger, but to restore a sense of self-worth after experiencing deep embarrassment or failure**. Workplace shooters, for example, are often individuals who have been publicly humiliated, fired, or rejected by colleagues. School shooters frequently target peers who they believe have bullied or excluded them. These crimes are often motivated by a desire to **assert dominance, regain lost power, or erase feelings of inadequacy**.

Fear can drive criminal behavior as well. Individuals facing **financial ruin, physical threats, or social disgrace** may resort to illegal acts to **protect themselves or**

escape a situation they believe they cannot endure. A person caught embezzling money might commit further fraud or even violent acts to cover their tracks. A gang member who fears retaliation from a rival group may strike preemptively, killing someone not out of malice, but to avoid being a victim themselves.

Anxiety and paranoia contribute to crimes that appear **irrational or disproportionate to the situation**. Some individuals, particularly those suffering from severe mental illnesses such as schizophrenia, delusional disorders, or extreme anxiety, commit crimes because they believe they are in imminent danger.

A paranoid individual might attack someone they mistakenly believe is spying on them or destroy property under the belief that hidden cameras or tracking devices are inside. Their actions may appear senseless to outsiders, but in their minds, they are acting in self-defense against perceived threats.

Depression and despair can also lead to crime. While depression is often associated with withdrawal and passivity, in some cases, it results in self-destructive acts that harm others. Some individuals who feel hopeless about their future commit murder-suicides, where they kill family members, coworkers, or even strangers before ending their own lives. Others engage in **reckless criminal activity—such as drug abuse, vandalism, or arson—not because they desire harm, but because they no longer care about consequences**.

Another major psychological trigger is **a sense of powerlessness or loss of control**. Many crimes stem from an individual trying to regain a sense of dominance in a world where they feel insignificant or overlooked. Domestic abusers often escalate violence when they feel they are losing control over their partner. Serial killers frequently describe a need to assert power over victims, making them feel helpless as a way of compensating for their own past experiences of being powerless.

Boredom and thrill-seeking behavior can also drive individuals to crime, particularly **younger offenders and those with antisocial traits**. Crimes such as vandalism, car theft, and robbery are sometimes committed **not out of necessity or anger, but because the offender craves excitement and risk**. Many criminals describe the **"rush" they feel when engaging in illegal activity**, likening it to an addiction. For some, committing crimes provides an emotional high, reinforcing **repeat offenses even when the risks are clear**.

Social rejection is another key emotional trigger. Individuals who feel excluded from family, friends, or their community may turn to crime as a means of gaining recognition or belonging. Gangs capitalize on this, offering a sense of identity, loyalty, and status to young individuals who feel ignored or alienated. Similarly, some mass shooters are individuals who feel completely cut off from society and seek recognition through violence. In these cases, the crime is a way to make themselves known, even if only through destruction and chaos.

Substance abuse is a well-documented factor that amplifies emotional and psychological triggers. Alcohol and drugs lower inhibitions, making individuals **more likely to act on violent impulses, engage in risky behavior, or misinterpret situations as threats**. A person who might normally walk away from a fight when sober may **lash out aggressively under the influence of alcohol**. A struggling addict, desperate for money to fund their habit, may rob, steal, or engage in prostitution—not because they inherently wish to break the law, but because the withdrawal symptoms override rational decision-making.

Crimes influenced by psychological and emotional triggers are often **highly situational**, meaning the right combination of stressors, emotions, and environmental factors must align for an individual to act. Some individuals may go years without committing a crime, only to break under **specific pressures such as financial ruin, marital breakdown, or workplace conflicts**. Others may **escalate their behavior gradually**, with minor offenses eventually building toward more serious crimes.

Law enforcement and forensic psychologists analyze emotional and psychological triggers to understand which individuals are at risk of escalating from minor offenses to serious crimes. By recognizing patterns—such as **unresolved anger, obsessive revenge fantasies, or increasing paranoia**—intervention strategies can be developed to **prevent violent acts before they occur**.

Understanding what pushes someone over the edge from **thought to action, from frustration to criminal behavior**, is one of the most critical aspects of criminal psychology. While not everyone who experiences anger, rejection, or despair turns to crime, those who do often follow **recognizable psychological pathways**. Recognizing these warning signs can help in **crime prevention, rehabilitation, and reducing recidivism rates**.

Substance Abuse as a Catalyst for Criminal Behavior

Substance abuse is one of the most significant factors in criminal behavior, influencing everything from petty theft to violent crime. Drugs and alcohol impair judgment, lower inhibitions, and alter decision-making processes, leading individuals to engage in actions they might otherwise avoid. While not all substance users become criminals, a strong connection exists between addiction and criminal activity, particularly when individuals turn to illegal means to sustain their drug use or when intoxication leads to violent or reckless behavior.

Alcohol-related crimes are among the most common offenses linked to substance use. Alcohol is a central nervous system depressant that lowers impulse control and increases aggression, making intoxicated individuals more likely to engage in fights, domestic violence, sexual assaults, and reckless driving. Studies show that **a significant percentage of violent crimes, including homicides and assaults, involve alcohol consumption by either the offender, the victim, or both**. Drunk driving, one of the leading causes of vehicular deaths worldwide, occurs because alcohol impairs motor coordination, reaction time, and judgment, leading drivers to miscalculate risks and overestimate their ability to control a vehicle.

Drugs such as cocaine, methamphetamine, and PCP contribute to violent and erratic behavior. Stimulants like cocaine and methamphetamine heighten aggression, paranoia, and impulsivity, making users more prone to violent outbursts, unpredictable actions, and confrontations with law enforcement. PCP (phencyclidine), known for causing hallucinations and psychotic episodes, has been linked to violent crimes where offenders display extreme aggression and resistance to pain, making them difficult to subdue.

Opioids, including heroin and prescription painkillers, are less commonly associated with violent behavior but contribute heavily to property crimes. Opioid addiction creates **intense physical and psychological dependence**, leading users to engage in theft, fraud, and burglary to finance their drug use.

Many opioid addicts steal from family members, employers, or strangers to obtain money for their next dose, and some engage in prostitution or drug dealing to support their addiction. The economic burden of maintaining a heroin habit often forces users into a cycle of crime, arrest, and incarceration.

Crack cocaine, a cheaper and more addictive form of cocaine, was notoriously linked to crime waves in the 1980s and 1990s, when its use surged in urban communities. Crack users often displayed erratic behavior, engaged in violent altercations, and committed robberies or burglaries to sustain their addiction. The crack epidemic also fueled gang violence, as rival groups fought over territory and distribution networks, increasing homicide rates in major cities.

Methamphetamine has similarly devastating effects on crime. Chronic meth use **leads to severe paranoia, hallucinations, and compulsive behaviors**, increasing the likelihood of violent encounters with police, domestic violence incidents, and property crimes. Meth labs, where the drug is illegally produced, pose additional risks of explosions, chemical exposure, and environmental contamination, leading to broader public safety concerns.

Marijuana is often considered a nonviolent drug, but its involvement in crime stems from illegal distribution, trafficking, and conflicts between dealers. While marijuana use itself does not typically lead to violent behavior, the black market economy surrounding it has historically contributed to organized crime, smuggling operations, and territorial disputes among drug distributors. In regions where marijuana remains illegal, users still face **arrests and legal consequences that can impact employment, housing, and future opportunities, contributing to cycles of crime and incarceration**.

One of the strongest links between substance abuse and crime is seen in **drug trafficking and organized crime networks**. The global drug trade generates billions of dollars annually, fueling cartel violence, corruption, and cross-border smuggling operations. Drug cartels use intimidation, murder, and bribery to control territories and eliminate competition, making drug-related crime one of the most violent sectors of organized criminal activity.

Prescription drug abuse has also contributed to an increase in **white-collar crimes such as prescription fraud, doctor shopping, and pharmacy robberies**. Many individuals addicted to opioids, benzodiazepines, or ADHD medications engage in fraudulent activities to obtain prescriptions, forging documents or deceiving medical professionals to access controlled substances. Some become involved in illegal distribution networks, selling prescription pills on the black market for profit.

The impact of substance abuse on domestic violence is another critical area of concern. Studies have found that a high percentage of domestic violence cases involve alcohol or drug use by the perpetrator. Substance abuse intensifies mood swings, aggression, and impaired decision-making, leading to repeated cycles of abuse. Victims of domestic violence who also struggle with addiction may find it **even harder to leave abusive relationships, as dependency on substances can create psychological and financial barriers to escaping violence**.

Sexual crimes, particularly rape and sexual assault, are often committed under the influence of alcohol or drugs. Intoxicated offenders **misjudge social cues, engage in reckless behavior, and may become more aggressive or coercive**. Alcohol is a common factor in date rape cases, where victims are either incapacitated by their own consumption or deliberately drugged by the offender.

Substance abuse also has a role in **gang culture and juvenile crime**. Many gang members engage in **drug distribution as a primary source of income**, exposing them to violent turf wars, retaliatory shootings, and law enforcement crackdowns. Young offenders who grow up in environments where substance use is normalized are more likely to engage in drug-related offenses, including dealing, theft, and violent crime.

The relationship between substance abuse and mental illness complicates criminal behavior. Individuals suffering from schizophrenia, bipolar disorder, or severe depression often self-medicate with drugs or alcohol, leading to increased impulsivity, risk-taking, and unpredictable actions.

Law enforcement officers frequently encounter mentally ill individuals who are intoxicated, making de-escalation more challenging and increasing the likelihood of violent altercations.

Rehabilitation efforts for substance-abusing offenders vary in effectiveness. Some programs focus on detoxification, therapy, and relapse prevention, while others combine treatment with vocational training, education, and social reintegration programs. Studies show that comprehensive drug treatment reduces recidivism, particularly for offenders whose crimes are directly linked to addiction rather than intentional criminal behavior.

Substance abuse continues to be a major driver of criminal activity, with its effects rippling through **families, communities, and entire criminal justice systems**. Whether through **violent acts committed under the influence, financial crimes driven by addiction, or organized drug trafficking networks**, the connection between substance abuse and crime remains one of the most significant challenges in modern law enforcement. Addressing addiction through **prevention, treatment, and rehabilitation** is essential in breaking the cycle of drug-fueled criminal behavior.

Economic Pressures and Material Incentives

Economic hardship has long been a driving force behind criminal activity. Many individuals who engage in crime do so out of financial necessity, seeing illegal means as the only way to survive or improve their quality of life. Others, even those not in desperate situations, commit crimes due to the allure of wealth, status, and material success. Economic motivations influence a wide range of offenses, from petty theft and fraud to large-scale corporate corruption and organized crime.

Poverty and financial desperation are among the most common reasons individuals turn to crime. People living in economically disadvantaged communities often face **limited job opportunities, inadequate education, and systemic barriers to financial stability**. When legal avenues fail, crime can seem like the only viable alternative. Property crimes such as shoplifting, burglary, and robbery are frequently committed by individuals struggling to meet basic needs. A person who steals food or shoplifts essential items is motivated not by greed but by sheer survival.

The relationship between poverty and crime is complex. Not everyone in financial distress resorts to illegal activity, but **statistical data consistently shows higher crime rates in areas with high unemployment, income inequality, and economic instability**. These conditions **create frustration, resentment, and a sense of hopelessness**, particularly among individuals who feel that society has left them behind. Some turn to crime out of necessity, while others do so as an act of defiance against a system they believe has failed them.

However, economic pressure does not only push people into low-level crime. It also influences more sophisticated financial offenses such as **fraud, embezzlement, and insider trading**. White-collar criminals are often individuals with stable jobs and financial security but feel compelled to commit crimes **due to greed, opportunity, or a desire to maintain a certain lifestyle**. Many corporate executives convicted of financial crimes were already wealthy but committed fraud to amass even greater power and influence.

One of the most studied economic drivers of crime is **relative deprivation**, the idea that individuals who perceive themselves as worse off than others around them are more likely to engage in crime.

People living in poor neighborhoods may feel economic distress, but if everyone around them is in a similar financial situation, they may be less likely to resort to illegal activity. However, when individuals see **wealth and privilege in close proximity—through social media, luxury advertising, or gentrification in their communities—it increases frustration and the desire to achieve financial success by any means necessary**.

The illicit drug trade is one of the most profitable illegal industries, offering financial incentives that far exceed what many legal jobs provide. For individuals growing up in neighborhoods with few job prospects, selling drugs can appear as **the only way to achieve economic independence**. Young people recruited into drug trafficking often come from single-parent households, struggling communities, or educationally disadvantaged backgrounds, making them vulnerable to promises of quick money and status within criminal organizations.

Organized crime groups thrive on economic incentives, building sophisticated networks of illegal activity to generate massive profits. **Human trafficking, arms**

smuggling, illegal gambling, and counterfeit goods are all industries fueled by financial gain. Many individuals who participate in organized crime do not see themselves as traditional criminals but as entrepreneurs in an underground economy. They justify their actions by claiming they are simply providing services that people demand—whether it's drugs, illegal loans, or counterfeit luxury items.

Fraud and financial scams often target those who are economically vulnerable. Ponzi schemes, identity theft, and online financial fraud disproportionately affect individuals who are **desperate for financial relief, investment opportunities, or quick returns on their money**. Many financial criminals take advantage of economic downturns and recessions, knowing that people are more likely to take risks or fall for deceptive financial offers when they are struggling.

Economic pressures also drive labor-related crimes, such as wage theft, human trafficking, and illegal employment practices. Some business owners engage in exploiting workers, failing to pay fair wages, or engaging in illegal subcontracting to cut costs. On the other end, financially desperate workers may engage in off-the-books employment, identity fraud, or illegal immigration to secure jobs in places where they would not otherwise be able to work legally.

Materialism and the pursuit of wealth often push individuals toward crime, even when they are not facing economic hardship. Many high-profile criminals, from corporate executives to celebrities, have engaged in illegal activity despite already having financial success. Some individuals commit crimes because they **feel entitled to wealth, status, and luxury, regardless of whether they can attain it through legal means**.

The psychology of greed-driven crime differs from necessity-driven crime. Individuals who steal food or shoplift clothing for their children are acting out of **immediate survival needs**, whereas someone who embezzles millions from a corporation is doing so out of **a desire for excess, power, or social dominance**. White-collar criminals often convince themselves that **they are not harming anyone directly**, making it easier to justify fraudulent schemes, financial manipulation, or insider trading.

Technology has created new economic incentives for crime. Cybercriminals steal **millions through hacking, identity theft, and digital fraud**, often targeting banks, corporations, and unsuspecting individuals through sophisticated online scams. These crimes require little physical risk but offer potentially massive financial rewards, making them appealing to individuals with technical skills who want to exploit digital systems for economic gain.

The global nature of financial crime means that **law enforcement faces significant challenges in tracking and prosecuting offenders**. Many economic crimes cross international borders, involve offshore accounts, and are hidden through complex financial transactions, making prosecution difficult. While street-level crimes are often aggressively policed, many financial criminals escape severe consequences due to weak regulatory enforcement or legal loopholes that allow them to manipulate financial systems without direct criminal charges.

Prisons are filled with economically motivated offenders, yet rehabilitation programs often fail to address the root causes of why these individuals turn to crime in the first place. Many incarcerated individuals convicted of property crimes, drug offenses, or fraud committed their crimes because they saw no viable economic alternative. When released, they often face the same financial struggles they had before incarceration, increasing the likelihood of recidivism.

Economic crime prevention requires **addressing structural inequalities, increasing access to education and job training, and providing economic alternatives to at-risk populations**. Research shows that when individuals have stable jobs, access to financial resources, and legitimate paths to success, crime rates decrease. Many countries have experimented with social programs, minimum income guarantees, and community investment strategies to reduce economically motivated crime.

Economic pressures and material incentives drive crime at every level of society, from **impoverished individuals engaging in survival-based offenses to wealthy elites manipulating financial markets for personal gain**. While the motivations may differ, the underlying factor remains the same: money and the pursuit of financial security or wealth create opportunities and temptations that push individuals toward criminal activity. Addressing these economic drivers is essential in understanding, preventing, and reducing crime in both low-income and high-income communities.

Ideological, Political, and Hate-Driven Motivations

Crime is not always committed for personal gain, revenge, or survival. Some offenders act based on deeply held beliefs, ideological convictions, or political motivations that drive them to commit acts of violence, sabotage, or disruption. These crimes are often calculated, planned, and justified by the offender as serving a greater cause. Whether rooted in religious extremism, political radicalization, or hate-based ideologies, these crimes present significant challenges for law enforcement and society, as they are often committed by individuals or groups who see themselves as righteous warriors rather than criminals.

One of the most well-known forms of ideologically driven crime is terrorism. Terrorists commit violent acts to instill fear, advance a political agenda, or force governments to change policies. Some engage in suicide bombings, mass shootings, or large-scale attacks, believing that their actions serve a religious or political cause. Groups like Al-Qaeda, ISIS, and domestic extremist organizations have used **ideological radicalization to recruit individuals who see themselves as soldiers in a larger battle against perceived enemies**. These individuals often do not view themselves as criminals but as **martyrs or revolutionaries**.

Political assassinations are another form of ideologically motivated crime. History is filled with examples of leaders, activists, and officials being **targeted for their policies, beliefs, or symbolic value**. Assassins who act on ideological beliefs often **see their victims as threats to a larger movement**. The motivations can vary— some assassins kill to **prevent political change, while others believe they are accelerating a revolution or resisting oppression**. John Wilkes Booth, who assassinated Abraham Lincoln, believed he was defending the Confederacy, while

Lee Harvey Oswald, the killer of John F. Kennedy, acted on a mix of personal and political motivations.

Hate crimes are committed **against individuals or groups based on race, religion, gender, sexual orientation, nationality, or other identity factors**. Unlike personal vendettas, hate crimes are **meant to send a message to an entire community**, reinforcing power dynamics, instilling fear, and asserting dominance over marginalized groups. Lynchings, synagogue shootings, mosque attacks, and racially motivated violence all fall under this category. Hate crime offenders often come from backgrounds where they have been exposed to extremist propaganda, social isolation, or economic resentment. Some grow up in households where racism, xenophobia, or religious bigotry are normalized, reinforcing their beliefs over time.

Religious extremism has also been a driving force behind violent crime. Some individuals interpret religious teachings as justification for acts of terror, oppression, or persecution. While all major religions promote peace, extremists twist religious doctrine to justify killing those they perceive as heretics, non-believers, or enemies of their faith.

This is seen in Islamist terrorist attacks, Christian fundamentalist anti-abortion violence, and Hindu nationalist mob killings. Religious extremists often view their crimes as acts of divine justice, believing they are fulfilling a sacred duty rather than violating the law.

Political extremists also engage in bombings, arson, kidnappings, and cyberattacks to challenge governments, corporations, or social institutions. Some are anarchists who believe that overthrowing the current system through chaos and destruction is the only way to create a fair society. Others are far-right or far-left extremists who reject democracy and seek to impose their own ideology by force. Domestic terrorism is often driven by these beliefs, with groups like eco-terrorists attacking corporations, white supremacists targeting minority communities, or militant revolutionaries planning bombings.

Radicalization is a process that transforms **ordinary individuals into extremists willing to commit crimes for their ideology**. It does not happen overnight but builds gradually through exposure to propaganda, social reinforcement, and isolation from opposing viewpoints. Many radicalized individuals start with legitimate political grievances but become increasingly consumed by extremist rhetoric, conspiracy theories, and dehumanization of their perceived enemies. Social media has accelerated radicalization, allowing extremist groups to recruit, communicate, and spread their messages to a global audience.

Conspiracy-driven violence has become more common in recent years. Some individuals commit crimes **because they believe they are uncovering hidden truths or fighting against a secret elite that controls the world**. Followers of movements like QAnon, anti-government militias, or apocalyptic cults often view their crimes as necessary acts of rebellion against oppression or tyranny. They may attack government buildings, assassinate public figures, or engage in mass shootings to "awaken" society to what they believe is a hidden reality.

Mass shootings frequently have ideological components. While some shooters act out of personal grievances, others are **inspired by white supremacist manifestos, misogynistic incel beliefs, or anti-government ideologies**. The internet has created echo chambers where these individuals find validation, encouragement, and tactical guidance from like-minded extremists, making ideological mass shootings an increasing concern.

Cyberterrorism and digital radicalization have expanded the scope of ideological crime. Extremist hackers **disrupt government infrastructure, attack financial systems, and spread propaganda through social media**. Some use deepfake technology, AI-generated misinformation, or hacked databases to manipulate public perception and incite violence. Cyber radicalization allows extremists to reach isolated individuals, providing them with ideological material, step-by-step instructions for attacks, and a sense of belonging to a virtual extremist community.

Militias and paramilitary groups blur the line between ideological crime and organized crime. Some claim to be **defending their country, religion, or race**, but engage in criminal activity such as **arms trafficking, bomb-making, and planned attacks on government institutions**. These groups often justify their actions by arguing that **the law is illegitimate, the government is corrupt, or that they are "patriots" resisting tyranny**.

The legal system struggles to handle ideological crime because **many extremists see prison as a badge of honor**. Unlike financially motivated criminals, who fear economic loss, or impulsive criminals, who regret their actions, ideological criminals view themselves as martyrs. They often use trials as platforms to spread their message, gain followers, and reinforce their belief that they are being persecuted for their cause.

Rehabilitation of ideological offenders is difficult but possible. Some former extremists **renounce their beliefs after exposure to new perspectives, personal reflection, or disillusionment with their movement**. However, many continue to hold extremist views even after serving prison sentences. Deradicalization programs focus on providing psychological counseling, reintegrating former extremists into society, and dismantling the ideological frameworks that led them to crime.

Law enforcement agencies **monitor extremist groups, track online radicalization efforts, and intervene before ideological criminals can act**. However, balancing security with civil liberties is challenging—governments must prevent attacks without violating free speech or criminalizing political dissent. The rise of hate speech laws, online content moderation, and counter-terrorism legislation reflects the need to combat ideological crime while ensuring democratic freedoms are not compromised.

Political, ideological, and hate-driven crimes are among the most dangerous offenses because they aren't **simply about personal gain but about reshaping society through violence**. These offenders **believe their crimes are justified, righteous, and necessary**, making them difficult to deter with traditional legal punishments. Understanding their psychology, tracking radicalization pathways, and countering extremist propaganda are essential to preventing violence before it occurs and breaking cycles of ideological crime.

Chapter 9: Criminal Investigation and Interrogation Techniques

Effective Interviewing Techniques for Suspects and Witnesses

Interviewing is one of the most critical aspects of criminal investigations. The ability to extract accurate, detailed, and reliable information from suspects and witnesses determines the direction of a case. A poorly conducted interview can result in misleading information, false confessions, or missed opportunities to uncover the truth. Skilled interviewers rely on psychological techniques, careful questioning, and strategic rapport-building to encourage cooperation and obtain useful statements.

The first step in any interview is **establishing rapport**. People are more likely to share information with someone they trust and feel comfortable with. This applies to both **witnesses and suspects**. A cold, aggressive approach often causes individuals to become defensive, withhold details, or even fabricate stories. A skilled interviewer begins with **small talk, casual conversation, and non-threatening body language** to create a relaxed environment. For suspects, demonstrating **understanding rather than immediate confrontation** makes them more likely to open up, even if they are guilty.

The way questions are structured impacts the quality of responses. Open-ended questions encourage **detailed and unrestricted answers**, while closed questions limit responses to simple yes/no answers. Asking, "Can you describe what you saw?" elicits more information than, "Did you see the suspect?". Leading questions, which suggest a desired answer, should be avoided because they contaminate memory and create false statements. For example, asking a witness, "Did the suspect have a gun?" may lead them to assume a weapon was present even if they were unsure. Instead, "What did the suspect have in their hands?" allows for a more reliable account.

Different approaches are required for witnesses versus suspects. Witnesses often provide critical evidence but may be **anxious, confused, or struggling to recall details accurately**. Some may exaggerate events due to **fear or social pressure**, while others may **unintentionally alter their memories based on discussions with others**. Using **the cognitive interview technique, which enhances memory recall by encouraging visualization and multiple perspectives**, helps witnesses provide more reliable information.

Suspect interviews are more complex. A guilty suspect often has **strong psychological motivation to lie, minimize, or redirect blame**. An innocent suspect may react **defensively, fearing wrongful accusation**. The **PEACE model (Preparation, Engage, Account, Closure, Evaluate)** is widely used in law enforcement as a non-confrontational approach to gathering information. Unlike the traditional accusatory Reid technique, which pressures suspects into confessions, the PEACE model **focuses on conversation, evidence presentation, and open-ended inquiry to uncover inconsistencies**.

Timing and psychological state influence interview effectiveness. If a suspect has just been arrested, they may still be **in a heightened emotional state, making them less likely to cooperate or provide clear responses**. Waiting until **they have calmed down but remain uncertain about their situation** increases the likelihood of useful information being revealed. Witnesses should be interviewed **as soon as possible** while memories are fresh. However, if a witness is traumatized, pushing them to recall details too soon can result in **incomplete or distorted memories**.

Interviewers must also consider **nonverbal cues**, including **body language, facial expressions, and speech patterns**. A suspect who avoids eye contact, shifts frequently in their chair, or hesitates before answering may be experiencing stress or deception. However, nonverbal behavior alone does not confirm guilt, as anxiety, cultural differences, and personality traits all affect how people react under pressure.

Mirroring techniques, where the interviewer subtly **matches the suspect's speech patterns and body language**, can build subconscious trust. If a suspect leans forward, the interviewer does the same. If they lower their voice, the interviewer follows. This method encourages **psychological comfort, making suspects more likely to engage in conversation**.

Strategic use of **silence** can also be an effective tool. Many people feel uncomfortable with silence and fill the gap with additional details. If a suspect gives an evasive or incomplete answer, the interviewer can pause for several seconds without responding, prompting the suspect to continue talking. This often leads to unintentional disclosures or contradictions.

Lying suspects frequently **over-explain, add unnecessary details, or repeat themselves to sound more convincing**. Their stories may lack natural pauses, seem rehearsed, or be overly chronological without deviations. Genuine memories contain some inconsistencies because human recall is imperfect, whereas fabricated stories are often too structured and free of gaps. By asking the suspect to recount the event in reverse order, interviewers can disrupt rehearsed lies, forcing the suspect to think critically about details they had previously memorized.

Theme development is a psychological tactic used to encourage suspects to confess or provide crucial details. By **offering explanations that allow the suspect to save face**, an interviewer may make it easier for them to admit wrongdoing. Instead of directly accusing them, the interviewer may say, **"It seems like this situation got out of hand, and you didn't mean for it to happen."** If the suspect agrees, they have already acknowledged involvement.

Psychological pressure can be used ethically to increase cooperation. Some suspects talk more when they believe the **evidence against them is overwhelming**. Presenting **forensic results, surveillance footage, or witness statements early in the interview** can make them feel that lying is futile, leading them to be more forthcoming. However, **fabricating evidence or making false claims** is unethical and has resulted in **false confessions in past investigations**.

Cultural and linguistic factors are influential in interviews. Some cultures encourage **direct eye contact as a sign of honesty**, while in others, avoiding eye contact is **a sign of respect rather than deception**. Misinterpretations of speech patterns and body language can lead to incorrect assumptions about truthfulness. Using trained interpreters and cultural specialists ensures that communication is clear and free of misunderstandings.

Memory recall varies among individuals, and **suggestibility is a major issue in police interviews**. Young children, for example, are highly **susceptible to suggestion** and may **unknowingly incorporate details from leading questions** into their accounts. People with cognitive disabilities or mental illnesses may struggle with linear storytelling or be prone to confabulation (filling in memory gaps with false information). Interviewers must adapt their approach based on the cognitive abilities of the person they are questioning.

Witness intimidation and fear often impact the quality of information provided. Some individuals refuse to speak due to fear of retaliation from criminals, distrust of law enforcement, or social stigma. Interviewers must ensure safety, confidentiality, and reassurance to encourage cooperation. In high-crime areas, police often **use anonymous reporting systems** or conduct interviews in **neutral locations to protect witnesses**.

Technology has changed interviewing strategies. **Video recording ensures transparency and protects against coercion claims**, making it a standard practice in many jurisdictions. Speech analysis software detects subtle verbal cues, pitch changes, and hesitation patterns, helping investigators identify signs of stress or deception. AI-driven behavioral analysis tools are also being explored to enhance investigative accuracy.

Effective interviewing is both an art and a science. It requires strategic questioning, psychological insight, and adaptability. Every suspect and witness is different, and interviewers must **adjust their techniques based on personality, emotional state, and level of cooperation**. When done correctly, interviews provide some of the **most reliable evidence in criminal investigations**, helping separate truth from deception and guiding law enforcement toward justice.

Detecting Deception: Behavioral and Verbal Cues

Detecting deception is one of the most difficult yet essential aspects of criminal investigations. People lie for many reasons—to protect themselves, to mislead investigators, to avoid embarrassment, or to manipulate a situation to their advantage. Some lies are spontaneous and poorly constructed, while others are well-planned and rehearsed. The challenge for investigators is to distinguish truth from deception without relying on assumptions or stereotypes. While no single behavior confirms deception, a combination of **verbal, nonverbal, and psychological cues** can reveal when someone is being dishonest.

Understanding Why People Lie

People lie under different circumstances, and their motivations affect how they structure their deception. Guilty suspects lie to conceal involvement in a crime, reduce their level of culpability, or shift blame onto someone else. Innocent suspects may lie out of fear, confusion, or distrust of law enforcement. Witnesses sometimes lie to protect themselves, avoid retaliation, or gain attention. Understanding these motivations helps interviewers analyze a person's statements more effectively.

Some individuals are **naturally skilled liars**—they maintain eye contact, control their emotions, and fabricate details that sound plausible. Others struggle under pressure, making obvious mistakes, contradicting themselves, or exhibiting anxiety-related behaviors. Experienced investigators recognize that deception detection is not about spotting a single "tell" but rather about identifying inconsistencies, unnatural behaviors, and speech patterns that deviate from a person's baseline responses.

Verbal Cues of Deception

One of the most effective ways to detect deception is to analyze how a person structures their responses. Deceptive individuals often exhibit **specific verbal characteristics** that distinguish lies from truthful statements.

- **Hesitation and Pauses**: A lying suspect may **pause longer than usual before answering** a direct question. This happens because deception requires extra cognitive effort—**the brain must construct a false narrative while ensuring consistency with earlier statements.**

- **Overly Formal or Distancing Language**: Deceptive individuals may use **indirect phrasing to create emotional distance from the crime.** Instead of saying, *"I took the money,"* they might say, *"The money was removed from the drawer."* Instead of *"I saw the victim,"* they might say, *"That individual was present at the time."* These subtle shifts indicate an effort to minimize personal involvement.

- **Excessive Detail or Lack of Detail**: Some liars add unnecessary details to make their story **sound more convincing.** They may include **irrelevant information** about the weather, their morning routine, or unrelated events to make their statement feel more natural. Others do the opposite— **keeping answers vague or omitting key details to avoid slipping up.**

- **Repeating the Question**: When asked a direct question, deceptive individuals often **repeat it before answering** to **buy themselves time** or to ensure they heard it correctly before committing to an answer. This behavior is common when a person is fabricating a response on the spot.

- **Avoiding Contractions**: Research shows that **deceptive individuals tend to avoid contractions in speech** because they subconsciously try to sound more formal and deliberate. Instead of saying, *"I didn't do it,"* they might say, *"I did not do it."* This effort to sound precise can be a red flag.

- **Unnatural Chronology**: Truthful individuals recall events in a **natural, flowing sequence, occasionally jumping back and forth** as memories resurface. Liars, on the other hand, **often structure their story in a rigid, overly chronological manner** because they have rehearsed it. A deceptive person may struggle if asked to **tell their story in reverse order**, as this disrupts their fabricated narrative.

- **Lack of Emotional Consistency**: When someone describes a traumatic event, their speech should reflect **genuine emotional distress**. A person falsely claiming to have been attacked might describe the event **in a cold, detached manner**, showing no emotional reaction. Conversely, a guilty suspect **might exaggerate their emotional response** to appear innocent.

Nonverbal Cues of Deception

While verbal inconsistencies provide strong evidence of deception, body language and facial expressions offer additional insight into a person's truthfulness. However, nonverbal behaviors must be interpreted cautiously—**nervousness, cultural differences, and personality traits can all affect body language.**

- **Eye Contact**: A common myth is that liars avoid eye contact. In reality, some deceptive individuals **overcompensate by making excessive eye contact** to appear confident and truthful. Others may look away frequently, especially when thinking about their response. The key is to observe **whether their eye behavior is consistent with their baseline behavior throughout the interview.**

- **Fidgeting and Gestures**: Some people become **physically restless** when lying—tapping their fingers, adjusting their clothing, or shifting in their chair. However, others **become unusually still, suppressing movement in an effort to remain composed.** Sudden changes in baseline body movement are more telling than the gestures themselves.

- **Microexpressions**: These are **brief, involuntary facial expressions** that reveal true emotions before a person has time to control them. A suspect claiming to be **sad about a victim's death may flash a slight smirk before quickly correcting their facial expression.** Detecting these fleeting emotions requires careful observation and, in some cases, video analysis.

- **Hand-to-Face Touching**: When under stress, deceptive individuals often **touch their face, rub their nose, or cover their mouth** as if subconsciously trying to block their own words. This behavior is common in **situations where a person feels guilty or uncomfortable.**

- **Defensive Postures**: Folding arms, leaning away, or turning the body slightly away from the interviewer **can indicate discomfort or an attempt to create physical distance from the situation.** However, some individuals naturally have closed-off body language, so context is important.

- **Blink Rate Changes**: A sudden increase in blinking **suggests stress or cognitive strain**, while a dramatic decrease in blinking may indicate that the person is concentrating intensely on controlling their expression.

Cognitive Load and Detecting Lies

Lying requires more mental effort than telling the truth. Investigators can use **cognitive load techniques** to make deception more difficult to sustain.

- **Asking Unexpected Questions**: Liars rehearse their main story but often fail to prepare for **secondary details**. Asking about **small, irrelevant aspects of the event** can catch them off guard. For example, instead of asking *"Where were you at 9 PM?"* an investigator might ask, *"What color was the car parked in front of the house?"* A liar may hesitate or give a vague answer.

- **Increasing the Complexity of Questions**: Since lying requires more cognitive effort, **introducing distractions**—such as asking a suspect to recall the event while completing a simple task—can make deception harder to maintain.

- **Silence as a Tool**: Long pauses make deceptive individuals **uncomfortable, prompting them to fill the silence with additional details that may reveal inconsistencies.**

Cultural Considerations in Lie Detection

Cultural background affects communication styles, body language, and perceptions of deception. In some cultures, **avoiding direct eye contact is a sign of respect rather than dishonesty**. Similarly, **certain speech patterns, such as indirect answers or polite agreement, may be cultural rather than deceptive.** Investigators must be **culturally competent** to avoid misinterpreting behavior.

Challenges in Detecting Deception

While many signs of deception exist, **there is no single "lie detector" behavior.** Some individuals—such as trained spies, career criminals, and those with certain personality disorders—lie effortlessly and show minimal emotional distress. Others may appear deceptive due to anxiety, past trauma, or social discomfort. Effective deception detection requires combining verbal analysis, body language interpretation, psychological tactics, and evidence-based investigation techniques.

The best way to catch a lie is not by looking for nervous behaviors, but by carefully analyzing inconsistencies in a person's story, comparing their statements against physical evidence, and applying cognitive stressors to disrupt fabricated narratives. Skilled interviewers know that deception is rarely revealed in a single moment—it emerges through **a pattern of contradictions, hesitation, and subtle signs that expose the truth over time.**

The Cognitive Interview: Enhancing Recall and Accuracy

Memory is not a perfect recording of events; it is reconstructive, influenced by emotions, stress, and even the way questions are asked. Witnesses often struggle to recall key details, and traditional interrogation techniques can unintentionally contaminate their memories. The **cognitive interview (CI)** was developed to address these issues, enhancing recall accuracy by aligning interview strategies with **how the human brain processes and retrieves memories**. It is widely used in law enforcement because it produces **more detailed and reliable witness accounts without increasing false information.**

The Science Behind Memory Retrieval in Investigations

Memories are not stored as complete, fixed narratives. Instead, they are **fragmented across different regions of the brain**, meaning a witness must reconstruct an event rather than simply replay it. Traditional interview methods often focus on **direct questioning and chronological recall**, but this approach **limits retrieval by restricting the way memories can be accessed**. The cognitive interview taps into multiple recall pathways, making it **more effective for retrieving complex or emotionally significant memories**.

The CI is built on **four primary techniques**:

1. **Context Reinstatement** – Mentally recreating the environment and emotions felt during the event.
2. **Report Everything** – Encouraging witnesses to share all details, even those that seem irrelevant.
3. **Recall from Different Perspectives** – Asking witnesses to consider the event from another person's point of view.
4. **Recall in Different Orders** – Changing the sequence in which the event is remembered to disrupt fabricated or misleading accounts.

Each of these techniques leverages **how the brain encodes, stores, and retrieves information**, allowing witnesses to **access memories that might otherwise remain buried**.

Step 1: Context Reinstatement—Placing Witnesses Back in the Moment

One of the most effective ways to **trigger accurate recall** is to have the witness mentally return to the scene of the crime. Context reinstatement involves **asking the witness to visualize the environment, emotions, sounds, and smells they experienced at the time of the event**.

For example, if a witness saw a robbery at a convenience store, an interviewer might say:

"Close your eyes and imagine yourself back in the store. Think about what you were doing just before the crime happened. What did the store smell like? What was the lighting like? What sounds were in the background? Were there other people around you?"

By activating **multiple sensory and emotional cues**, context reinstatement **strengthens memory associations** and helps witnesses access details that were not initially available. Studies have shown that witnesses recall **up to 30% more accurate information** when using this method compared to standard questioning.

Step 2: The "Report Everything" Approach—Encouraging Free Recall

In traditional interviews, **witnesses may withhold information** they think is unimportant. The **cognitive interview encourages them to share every detail**, even seemingly minor ones. This is crucial because **one small detail can trigger another memory, leading to a clearer picture of the event**.

For example, if a witness remembers **a suspect's distinctive smell, the music playing in the background, or the way someone walked**, this could be **linked to forensic evidence or a suspect's known habits**. Even if a detail seems irrelevant, it might **connect missing pieces of the investigation**.

Instead of asking **leading questions**, investigators use **open-ended prompts**, such as:

- "Tell me everything you remember, no matter how small."
- "Describe the suspect as best as you can, including their posture, gestures, or anything unique."
- "What did you notice about their clothing? Was anything out of place?"

By allowing free recall without interruption, investigators reduce **the risk of memory contamination** and encourage witnesses to think **beyond what they consciously focused on at the time**.

Step 3: Recall from Different Perspectives—Breaking Memory Biases

People often **experience an event from a single viewpoint**, but memory is **more complex than a fixed perspective**. This technique encourages witnesses to **reconstruct the event from another person's viewpoint**, such as **the victim, another bystander, or even the suspect**.

For instance, if a witness saw a **car accident**, the interviewer might ask:

- "Imagine you were sitting in the driver's seat of the vehicle. What would you have seen?"
- "If you were standing across the street instead of where you were, how might the scene have looked?"

This approach **forces the brain to reconstruct the event in a new way**, often revealing **hidden details**. It also helps **detect inconsistencies in dishonest witnesses**, as fabricated stories are harder to maintain from multiple viewpoints.

Step 4: Recalling in Different Orders—Disrupting Fabricated Stories

Most people recall events in a **linear, chronological order**, but memory does not always work this way. Witnesses may **remember key moments out of sequence**, and deceptive individuals **often structure their stories too neatly**. Changing the order of recall forces witnesses to **rely on actual memory rather than a rehearsed narrative**.

For example, an interviewer might say:

- "Tell me what happened, but start with the moment the suspect left."
- "Now, tell me what happened just before that."

Liars often struggle with this technique because **they rely on rehearsed storytelling rather than genuine recall**. When asked to recall **in reverse order**, inconsistencies emerge, and **details that were previously fabricated become harder to maintain**.

Why the Cognitive Interview Reduces False Memories

Traditional police interviews can accidentally implant false memories by using leading questions, suggestive phrasing, or confirmation bias. The cognitive interview minimizes these risks by allowing witnesses to reconstruct events naturally.

For example, if an interviewer asks:

* **"Was the suspect wearing a red hoodie?"** – This **introduces the idea of red** into the witness's memory, even if the suspect was wearing blue.

Instead, the CI approach would be:

* **"What was the suspect wearing?"** – Allowing the witness to **retrieve the memory without interference**.

Studies show that **witnesses questioned with cognitive interviewing techniques are less likely to develop false memories** compared to those subjected to **traditional interrogations**.

Challenges and Limitations of the Cognitive Interview

While highly effective, the cognitive interview has some limitations:

1. **Time-Consuming** – Conducting a full cognitive interview takes longer than traditional questioning, making it impractical for minor cases or time-sensitive investigations.
2. **Requires Skilled Interviewers** – Not all officers are trained to use cognitive interviewing correctly, and misuse of the technique can lead to misleading results.
3. **Varied Witness Reliability** – Some individuals, particularly children or highly traumatized witnesses, may struggle with context reinstatement or multiple-perspective recall.

Despite these challenges, research shows that cognitive interviews increase the quantity and quality of witness testimony without increasing false information.

The Future of Cognitive Interviewing: Integrating Technology

Advancements in technology are expanding the effectiveness of the cognitive interview.

* **Virtual reality (VR)** allows witnesses to re-experience a simulated crime scene, helping them recall more details.

- **AI-driven speech analysis** can **detect stress, hesitation, and inconsistencies** in a witness's recall, providing additional layers of evaluation.
- **Neuroscientific methods like fMRI scanning** are being explored to **analyze brain activity during recall, though** they are not yet widely used in investigations.

The cognitive interview remains one of the most effective, scientifically supported methods for retrieving accurate memories. By aligning questioning strategies with how the brain naturally recalls events, it improves witness reliability, reduces false information, and enhances investigative outcomes. Law enforcement agencies worldwide continue to refine and integrate cognitive interviewing techniques, ensuring that witness testimony remains powerful in solving crimes.

Behavioral Observation Methods in Interrogations

Interrogations are not just about asking questions; they involve analyzing every aspect of a suspect's behavior, from verbal responses to body language and microexpressions. Behavioral observation methods help investigators identify inconsistencies, stress reactions, and signs of deception without relying on coercive tactics. Understanding human psychology and nonverbal cues allows interrogators to assess a suspect's truthfulness, detect reluctance, and apply strategic pressure when necessary.

One of the most important aspects of behavioral observation is establishing a suspect's baseline behavior. **Every person reacts differently under stress**, so interrogators must first observe how a suspect behaves when discussing neutral topics.

Some people naturally fidget when nervous, while others remain still and controlled. By asking non-threatening questions at the start of an interview, interrogators can gauge a suspect's normal speech patterns, eye movements, and body language. Once a baseline is established, deviations from that behavior during questioning about the crime become significant. A suspect who was initially relaxed but starts shifting in their seat, avoiding eye contact, or giving clipped responses when asked about specific details might be experiencing discomfort related to deception.

Speech patterns often change when a person is lying or withholding information. Hesitation before answering, long pauses, excessive stuttering, or restarting sentences mid-thought can indicate that a suspect is fabricating details or struggling to maintain a consistent story.

Some individuals overcompensate when lying by speaking too formally, using complex language to sound more credible, or adding unnecessary details. Others may suddenly become vague, using phrases like "I don't remember" or "I guess it could have happened that way" when asked about critical aspects of the case. The way a suspect constructs their sentences can also provide insight into their mindset. Liars often distance themselves from the situation by using passive language, saying things like "the gun went off" instead of "I shot him."

Nonverbal cues are equally important in behavioral observation. While no single body language cue confirms deception, a pattern of inconsistent or unnatural behavior raises red flags. A suspect who folds their arms, leans away from the interviewer, or turns their body slightly to the side may be trying to create physical distance from an uncomfortable topic. Rapid blinking, excessive swallowing, and clenched jaw muscles often indicate stress, while sudden stillness can be a sign of internal panic. Investigators also watch for microexpressions—brief, involuntary facial movements that reveal true emotions. A suspect claiming sadness over a victim's death might unconsciously smirk for a fraction of a second, exposing a disconnect between their words and actual feelings.

Gaze aversion is often misunderstood in interrogations. While it is commonly believed that liars avoid eye contact, this is not always true. Some individuals naturally struggle with eye contact, while skilled liars may maintain steady eye contact to appear more credible. Instead of relying on eye contact alone, interrogators analyze when and how a suspect looks away. A person telling the truth often looks away to recall details, while a deceptive suspect may break eye contact at moments of fabricated statements. Rapid shifts in gaze or an unnatural staring pattern can indicate an attempt to manipulate perception.

Gestures and hand movements provide additional behavioral insights. Honest individuals tend to use open, natural gestures when explaining events, while deceptive suspects often restrict their movements, keeping their hands close to their bodies.

Some liars unconsciously touch their faces, rub their necks, or cover their mouths when answering sensitive questions. These behaviors stem from a subconscious desire to block their own words or soothe internal anxiety. Other suspects may exhibit "self-grooming" behaviors, such as adjusting their clothing or smoothing their hair, as a way to manage stress.

Speech pace and tone fluctuations reveal psychological stress. A suspect may start speaking faster when nervous, then slow down when formulating a lie. Their voice might become higher-pitched, or they might clear their throat frequently due to dryness caused by anxiety. Sudden shifts in vocal tone, such as a change from confident to hesitant speech, can indicate moments where a suspect is struggling to maintain consistency. Skilled interrogators listen for these shifts, noting when and how they occur in relation to key questions.

Observing inconsistencies between verbal statements and physical reactions is one of the strongest indicators of deception. If a suspect verbally denies involvement in a crime but nods slightly while answering, their body language contradicts their words. Similarly, if they claim to be calm but exhibit signs of agitation—such as foot tapping, clenched fists, or sudden breathing changes—this discrepancy suggests internal conflict. People generally find it difficult to control involuntary body responses, which **makes behavioral observation important when evaluating credibility**.

Stress-induced behaviors can also manifest through involuntary physiological reactions. Sweating, flushing, or trembling can signal heightened anxiety, particularly when discussing incriminating details. Some suspects develop visible muscle tension, particularly in the neck and shoulders, as they struggle to maintain composure. While stress does not automatically indicate guilt, significant changes in a suspect's physical state at key moments of questioning can be revealing.

Cognitive load is critical in behavioral observation. Lying requires more mental effort than telling the truth, as the brain must suppress reality while constructing and maintaining a false narrative. Investigators can exploit this by increasing cognitive demands on the suspect. Asking them to recount the event in reverse order or describe seemingly minor details forces them to focus on memory construction. Truthful individuals may take time to recall details but will generally remain consistent. Liars, however, often struggle with these additional cognitive tasks, leading to contradictions, pauses, or overly simplistic answers.

Detecting deception also requires an understanding of cultural differences. In some cultures, avoiding direct eye contact is a sign of respect rather than dishonesty. Similarly, individuals from high-context cultures may be more indirect in their speech patterns, leading to misunderstandings in an interrogation setting. Interrogators trained in cultural competency are less likely to misinterpret normal behaviors as deceptive. This is particularly important when interviewing individuals who are not fluent in the dominant language, as stress from communication barriers can mimic signs of deception.

The timing of an interrogation affects a suspect's behavior and ability to maintain deception. Immediately after an arrest, emotions are heightened, making it easier to observe raw, unfiltered reactions.

However, some suspects need time to adjust to their situation before revealing useful information. Extended interrogations wear down cognitive defenses, increasing the likelihood of behavioral slips. Fatigue makes it harder for liars to maintain consistency, and small contradictions begin to emerge over time.

Interrogators also use silence as a behavioral observation tool. **Many people feel uncomfortable with long pauses and will instinctively fill them with additional information. A deceptive suspect, when faced with silence, may begin over-explaining or contradicting earlier statements**. Truthful individuals, on the other hand, are more likely to sit comfortably in silence, waiting for the next question without feeling the need to justify themselves unnecessarily.

Behavioral observation methods are most effective when combined with strategic questioning. Observing a suspect's reactions to unexpected questions or evidence presentation provides key insights into their state of mind. If a suspect claims not to know a certain name or detail but visibly reacts when it is mentioned, their body language betrays their internal recognition. Law enforcement officers often introduce false but plausible details to gauge a suspect's reaction. A guilty suspect might react with immediate denial, while an innocent person might express confusion or ask for clarification.

Advances in technology are expanding behavioral observation capabilities. AI-driven analysis tools can track microexpressions, voice stress levels, and physiological responses in real-time, providing objective measurements of deception cues. Some law enforcement agencies use video analytics software to detect subtle behavioral changes that might go unnoticed by the human eye. However, while technology can enhance deception detection, human intuition and experience remain irreplaceable in interpreting behavioral cues within the broader context of an investigation.

Effective behavioral observation in interrogations is not about catching a single "tell" or assuming that nervousness equates to lying. Instead, it involves recognizing patterns, identifying inconsistencies, and assessing how a suspect's behavior changes under different questioning techniques. Trained interrogators know that deception is revealed not in one moment, but across an accumulation of subtle behavioral shifts. By combining psychology, observation, and strategic questioning, investigators can extract truthful information while avoiding coercive or unethical practices.

Legal Boundaries and Ethical Practices in Investigative Psychology

Interrogations and criminal investigations operate within strict legal and ethical boundaries to ensure justice is served without violating the rights of suspects, witnesses, or victims. Investigative psychology involves a balance between **gathering reliable information and maintaining ethical integrity**, ensuring that law enforcement does not coerce false confessions, manipulate testimony, or infringe on fundamental legal protections. Ethical considerations are especially crucial in high-stakes cases where misconduct can lead to wrongful convictions, damaged reputations, and loss of public trust in the justice system.

One of the most fundamental legal protections in criminal investigations is the **right against self-incrimination**. In many countries, suspects are granted the right to remain silent and avoid answering questions that could be used against them in court.

In the United States, this protection is outlined in the **Fifth Amendment**, while similar rights exist in other legal systems worldwide. Law enforcement officials must inform suspects of their rights before conducting interrogations, ensuring that any statement given is made voluntarily. Failing to do so can render confessions inadmissible in court.

The **right to legal counsel** is another critical safeguard. Suspects are entitled to have an attorney present during questioning, which serves to prevent coercive tactics, manipulation, or intimidation by interrogators. Defense attorneys also ensure that their clients understand the legal implications of their statements. In some cases, suspects waive this right, choosing to speak to investigators alone, but law enforcement officers must carefully document such decisions to ensure they were made voluntarily and without pressure.

One of the biggest ethical concerns in investigative psychology is the **risk of false confessions**. While it may seem counterintuitive, many innocent individuals admit to crimes they did not commit due to **psychological pressure, fear, confusion, exhaustion, or a misplaced belief that cooperating will lead to leniency**. Research has shown that **intense, prolonged interrogations increase the likelihood of false confessions**, particularly among individuals with cognitive impairments, mental illness, or high suggestibility. The infamous **Reid technique**, which relies on psychological pressure, manipulation, and confrontation, has been criticized for increasing the chances of extracting unreliable statements from suspects who are eager to end the interrogation.

To address this issue, many law enforcement agencies have shifted toward **non-coercive, evidence-based interrogation methods** such as the **PEACE model** (Preparation and Planning, Engage and Explain, Account, Closure, and Evaluate). This approach emphasizes **rapport-building, open-ended questioning, and careful assessment of inconsistencies**, rather than aggressive tactics designed to provoke emotional breakdowns. The goal is to **gather truthful information rather than force confessions**.

Ethical guidelines also apply to how **witnesses and victims** are interviewed. Investigators must ensure that interviews are conducted without leading questions, suggestive statements, or unnecessary emotional distress. In cases involving children, trauma survivors, or vulnerable individuals, specialized forensic interview techniques are required to minimize re-traumatization and maximize the accuracy of testimony. The cognitive interview, which encourages free recall and visualization, is widely used to enhance memory retrieval without contaminating the witness's account.

Police deception is a legally gray area in many jurisdictions. While law enforcement officers are often allowed to **use strategic misdirection, exaggerate evidence, or imply that they have more information than they do**, there are legal and ethical limits to this practice. Courts have ruled that certain types of deception—such as falsely promising leniency, fabricating confessions from co-defendants, or falsely claiming a suspect failed a lie detector test—can render confessions involuntary and inadmissible. Ethical concerns also arise when police interrogate minors, individuals with intellectual disabilities, or people unfamiliar with the legal system, as these groups are more susceptible to manipulation.

Surveillance and data collection methods also raise legal and ethical concerns in modern investigative psychology. With the rise of digital forensics, phone tracking, and online monitoring, law enforcement agencies must navigate privacy laws, search warrant requirements, and due process protections.

While technology is important for gathering evidence, illegally obtained data—such as warrantless phone searches or unauthorized surveillance—can be thrown out in court, undermining the investigation. Law enforcement agencies must ensure that digital evidence is collected within legal frameworks, with proper documentation and chain of custody to prevent challenges to its validity.

Racial, socioeconomic, and psychological biases in investigations present another major ethical issue. Studies have shown that **implicit bias can influence whom law enforcement officers perceive as suspects, how they interpret behavioral cues, and how interrogations are conducted**. In some cases, suspects from marginalized communities receive harsher questioning, are more likely to be presumed guilty, or face discrimination in legal proceedings. Ethical investigators must actively work to eliminate bias, approach cases objectively, and rely on factual evidence rather than personal assumptions or stereotypes.

The **use of force in interrogations and investigations** is a legally restricted area that varies by jurisdiction. While some countries prohibit any physical or psychological coercion, others still allow certain pressure tactics in terrorism cases or high-risk investigations. However, international human rights organizations, including the United Nations and Amnesty International, strongly oppose any form of coercion in interrogations, citing the high likelihood of false confessions, wrongful convictions, and violations of human dignity. Ethical investigators understand that force and intimidation are not only legally risky but also ineffective in obtaining reliable information.

False eyewitness testimony remains a major challenge in legal systems, as research has demonstrated that **memory is highly fallible and susceptible to contamination**. Ethical investigators do not pressure witnesses to confirm a particular narrative, as doing so can create false memories or reinforce inaccurate recollections. In high-profile cases, media exposure can further distort eyewitness accounts, **leading individuals to internalize false details from news reports, social media, or law enforcement suggestions**. Proper interview protocols, including sequential lineups, blind administration of suspect identifications, and careful questioning techniques, help reduce these errors.

Another ethical concern in investigative psychology is the use of informants and undercover operations. While informants provide valuable intelligence, they often have **their own motivations, including reducing their own sentences or financial incentives**. Investigators must ensure that **information provided by informants is corroborated with independent evidence** rather than taken at face value. Similarly, undercover officers must operate within ethical boundaries, avoiding entrapment or fabricating crimes to secure arrests.

The issue of **investigative misconduct** continues to plague some law enforcement agencies, with cases of **evidence tampering, coercion, and suppression of exculpatory evidence** surfacing in wrongful conviction cases. Ethical investigators recognize that the pursuit of justice does not justify unethical actions. Prosecutors and defense attorneys alike must ensure that all evidence, including potentially exonerating material, is disclosed to the court. Failing to do so not only violates legal standards but erodes public trust in the criminal justice system.

International investigations present additional challenges, as different legal systems have **varying standards for interrogation techniques, evidentiary rules, and human rights protections**. In cases involving extradition, transnational crime, or counterterrorism, investigators must navigate complex legal frameworks to ensure that evidence collected abroad is admissible in court. Cooperation between international agencies, such as Interpol and Europol, requires adherence to ethical guidelines that respect sovereignty, legal due process, and international law.

Training and oversight are essential to maintaining ethical investigative practices. Law enforcement officers, forensic psychologists, and legal professionals must receive **ongoing education on human rights laws, psychological research on false confessions, and advancements in interrogation science**. Independent review boards and civilian oversight commissions help ensure that **investigators follow legal and ethical protocols, preventing abuses of power**.

Ethical and legal boundaries in investigative psychology are not obstacles to law enforcement—they are essential safeguards that protect the innocent, preserve the integrity of the justice system, and ensure that criminal investigations remain fair, transparent, and based on reliable evidence. Investigators who operate within these frameworks are more effective, as they build stronger cases, maintain public trust, and avoid the long-term damage caused by wrongful convictions and procedural misconduct. The goal of any investigation should not be securing confessions at any cost but uncovering the truth through lawful, ethical, and scientifically sound methods.

Advanced Tools: Polygraphs, fMRI, and Emerging Technologies

Criminal investigations have increasingly relied on technology to supplement traditional interrogation and behavioral analysis techniques. Advances in neuroscience, biometrics, and artificial intelligence have led to the development of tools designed to detect deception, analyze physiological responses, and interpret cognitive processes. Among these tools, polygraphs, functional magnetic resonance imaging (fMRI), and AI-driven behavioral analysis systems have been widely studied and, in some cases, used in forensic investigations. While these technologies provide additional layers of insight, they also come with ethical concerns, reliability limitations, and legal challenges that investigators must consider.

The polygraph, commonly known as a lie detector, has been one of the most well-known deception detection tools for nearly a century. It measures **physiological responses such as heart rate, blood pressure, respiration, and galvanic skin conductance** while a subject answers questions.

The theory behind polygraph testing is that lying creates psychological stress, which in turn causes involuntary physical reactions that can be detected and analyzed. When a suspect provides a deceptive response, investigators expect to see increased sweating, changes in breathing patterns, and fluctuations in cardiovascular activity.

Despite its widespread use, the polygraph remains highly controversial. Research has shown that polygraph results are not always reliable, as anxiety, fear, and even practiced deception techniques can influence physiological readings. Some individuals experience stress even when telling the truth, while trained criminals and psychopaths have been known to control their physiological responses to pass a polygraph test. Additionally, false positives and false negatives have led to wrongful accusations and unreliable investigative leads. Due to these limitations, polygraph results are not admissible as evidence in most courts, though they are sometimes used as an investigative tool to gauge a suspect's reactions and guide further questioning.

Functional magnetic resonance imaging (fMRI) is a more recent development in deception detection. Unlike the polygraph, which measures external physiological responses, fMRI analyzes brain activity in real-time to identify patterns associated with deception. The theory is that lying requires greater cognitive effort than telling the truth, leading to increased activity in specific brain regions such as the prefrontal cortex and anterior cingulate cortex. By scanning a subject's brain while they answer questions, **researchers can observe which areas show heightened activity when deception is suspected**.

While fMRI technology has demonstrated promising results in laboratory studies, it faces several challenges in forensic applications. Brain activity is highly individualized, meaning that what constitutes deception in one person may not look the same in another. Additionally, fMRI scans require expensive equipment, controlled conditions, and expert interpretation, making them impractical for widespread law enforcement use. Ethical concerns have also emerged, as some critics argue that brain scans could be misused to invade personal thoughts, leading to violations of privacy and civil liberties. Due to these issues, fMRI-based lie detection has not been widely adopted in legal settings, though research continues to explore its potential.

Emerging AI-driven behavioral analysis technologies are gaining traction in investigative psychology. Machine learning algorithms can analyze speech patterns, microexpressions, and voice stress levels to detect subtle cues of deception that may go unnoticed by human observers. These systems use large datasets of known truthful and deceptive statements to identify common patterns, providing investigators with real-time assessments of credibility.

Voice stress analysis (VSA) is one such technology that **examines fluctuations in vocal pitch, tone, and micro tremors** to determine whether a subject is under stress while answering questions. Unlike polygraphs, which require physical sensors, VSA can be conducted **remotely using recorded speech or live conversations**. However, like the polygraph, VSA has been criticized for its high rate of false positives and susceptibility to environmental noise and individual variations.

Facial recognition and **emotion analysis software** use AI to assess **minute changes in facial muscles, eye movements, and expressions** that correlate with deceptive behavior. By comparing a suspect's facial responses to a database of emotional patterns, these systems attempt to determine whether a person is experiencing guilt, anxiety, or stress during questioning.

However, just like traditional behavioral analysis, facial expressions alone do not provide definitive proof of deception, as factors such as cultural differences, medical conditions, and emotional regulation abilities can affect results.

Thermal imaging technology has also been explored for **detecting deception through temperature changes in the face and body**. When individuals experience stress or deception-related anxiety, blood flow increases to certain areas of the face, leading to slight but measurable temperature fluctuations. Infrared cameras can detect these changes, providing another potential indicator of dishonesty. While early studies have shown promise, thermal imaging's reliability remains under debate, and it is not yet widely used in criminal investigations.

The integration of **biometric and neurophysiological monitoring tools** is expanding, with some researchers exploring the possibility of combining eye-tracking technology with AI-driven behavioral analysis. Eye-tracking systems measure pupil dilation, blink rate, and gaze patterns, as deception is often associated with increased cognitive load and involuntary eye movement changes. While some law enforcement agencies have experimented with these tools, they remain experimental and subject to further validation.

Legal and ethical considerations are critical when applying advanced interrogation technologies. Forcing suspects to undergo brain scans, AI-driven behavioral monitoring, or biometric analysis raises concerns about privacy, consent, and potential misuse of technology.

Some critics argue that these tools could be used to target innocent individuals based on faulty algorithms or biased data models, leading to wrongful accusations. Additionally, courts are reluctant to admit evidence derived from such technologies, as **scientific consensus on their accuracy is still developing**.

One of the key challenges in using technology-driven deception detection is the **lack of standardization and cross-validation across different populations**. Many existing studies focus on small, controlled samples, meaning that findings may not generalize to diverse real-world scenarios. Factors such as neurological conditions, psychological disorders, and cultural variations in stress responses can all influence results, making it difficult to establish universal deception markers.

Despite these challenges, technological advancements continue to shape the future of forensic investigations. While **no single tool has proven to be a perfect lie detector**, the integration of multiple techniques—such as combining behavioral observation, AI analysis, and physiological monitoring—may enhance law enforcement's ability to detect deception and gather more reliable information. Continued research, ethical oversight, and legal scrutiny will be essential in determining which of these technologies can be safely and effectively incorporated into the investigative process.

Ultimately, while advanced tools provide **new avenues for deception detection**, traditional investigative methods—such as careful questioning, contextual analysis, and forensic evidence evaluation—remain the foundation of reliable criminal investigations. Technology should serve as a supplement to human expertise rather than a replacement for critical thinking and investigative reasoning. The future of forensic psychology will likely involve a careful balance between leveraging new tools and ensuring ethical, scientifically sound practices that uphold justice and protect individual rights.

Chapter 10: Rehabilitation, Recidivism, and Prevention

Psychological Assessment Tools in Rehabilitation Settings

Rehabilitation programs rely on **psychological assessment tools** to evaluate offenders, understand their risks, and develop appropriate treatment plans. These assessments help determine mental health conditions, personality traits, cognitive functioning, and behavioral patterns that influence criminal behavior. A one-size-fits-all approach does not work in rehabilitation, as different offenders have varying levels of aggression, impulsivity, addiction issues, and emotional dysregulation. Psychological evaluations ensure that treatment strategies are tailored to individual needs, improving the chances of successful reintegration into society.

Risk assessment is a primary function of psychological evaluations in correctional settings. Offenders are categorized based on **their likelihood of reoffending, level of violence, and need for intervention**. Tools such as the **Level of Service Inventory-Revised (LSI-R)** and the **Hare Psychopathy Checklist-Revised (PCL-R)** provide structured frameworks for assessing risk. The LSI-R measures factors such as **criminal history, education, family environment, and substance abuse**, while the PCL-R focuses on **psychopathic traits, emotional detachment, and lack of empathy**. These tools help determine whether an offender requires intensive supervision, specialized therapy, or alternative rehabilitation programs.

The Risk-Need-Responsivity (RNR) Model is widely used to guide rehabilitation efforts. It emphasizes three key principles: risk (higher-risk offenders require more intensive interventions), need (treatment should target criminogenic factors such as substance abuse and antisocial behavior), and responsivity (interventions should match an offender's learning style and cognitive abilities). The RNR approach prevents unnecessary treatment for low-risk offenders while ensuring high-risk individuals receive the support they need.

Personality assessments such as the Minnesota Multiphasic Personality Inventory (MMPI-2) and the Personality Assessment Inventory (PAI) help identify mental health disorders, emotional instability, and behavioral tendencies that contribute to criminal activity.

Offenders with paranoid traits, mood disorders, or impulse control issues often require different treatment approaches compared to those with antisocial or narcissistic personality traits. Understanding personality profiles helps psychologists create individualized therapy plans that address emotional regulation, social skills, and behavioral modification.

Cognitive functioning is another critical area of assessment. Many offenders have neurodevelopmental disorders, learning disabilities, or low intellectual functioning, which affect their **ability to process consequences, control impulses, and engage in treatment programs**. The **Wechsler Adult Intelligence Scale**

(WAIS-IV) and the **Repeatable Battery for the Assessment of Neuropsychological Status (RBANS)** measure cognitive abilities such as memory, attention, problem-solving skills, and executive functioning. Offenders with deficits in reasoning and decision-making require specialized cognitive-behavioral interventions rather than standard correctional programs.

Substance abuse assessments are essential for offenders with addiction histories. Tools like the Alcohol Use Disorders Identification Test (AUDIT) and the Drug Abuse Screening Test (DAST) determine the severity of substance dependence and its role in criminal behavior. Many offenders engage in crimes such as theft, assault, and drug trafficking to support addiction, making substance abuse treatment a core component of rehabilitation. Without proper intervention, offenders with untreated addictions are at high risk for relapse and recidivism.

Trauma and PTSD evaluations are increasingly recognized as essential in rehabilitation settings. Many offenders have histories of childhood abuse, domestic violence, or exposure to community violence, which contribute to anger issues, dissociation, and impulsivity.

The Clinician-Administered PTSD Scale (CAPS) and the Trauma Symptom Inventory (TSI-2) assess the impact of past trauma on emotional regulation and decision-making. Trauma-informed care ensures that rehabilitation programs focus on healing rather than punishment, preventing retraumatization and promoting behavioral change.

Anger management assessments help identify triggers, coping mechanisms, and behavioral patterns related to aggression. The Novaco Anger Scale (NAS) evaluates how individuals perceive, experience, and express anger. Offenders with **high anger reactivity require interventions that teach emotional regulation, de-escalation strategies, and nonviolent conflict resolution**. Without these interventions, individuals prone to hostile thinking and aggressive outbursts are more likely to reoffend.

Sex offender risk assessments determine the likelihood of reoffending, treatment needs, and supervision requirements. Tools such as the Static-99 and the Sex Offender Risk Appraisal Guide (SORAG) analyze factors such as prior offenses, victim characteristics, and deviant sexual interests. Sex offender treatment programs rely on these assessments to implement structured cognitive-behavioral therapy, impulse control training, and relapse prevention planning.

Self-report measures are commonly used in rehabilitation but must be interpreted cautiously. Many offenders **minimize their behavior, provide socially desirable answers, or lack insight into their own actions**. Structured clinical interviews and collateral reports from family members, correctional staff, and therapists provide a more accurate picture of an offender's psychological state and rehabilitation progress.

Neuroscientific tools are emerging in offender assessments, though they remain controversial. Functional MRI (fMRI) and EEG-based assessments are being explored to analyze brain activity related to impulse control, moral reasoning, and aggression regulation. Some researchers argue that neurological markers could help predict violent tendencies, but ethical concerns about privacy, accuracy, and potential misuse of brain data limit the widespread use of these technologies in rehabilitation.

Behavioral assessments track an offender's progress in treatment programs, responsiveness to therapy, and overall attitude toward rehabilitation. Programs use tools like the Correctional Treatment Evaluation (CTE) and the Behavioral Assessment System for Criminal Offenders (BASCO) to monitor attendance, participation, and behavioral changes. Evaluations conducted at multiple points during rehabilitation ensure that interventions are adjusted to meet evolving needs.

For juvenile offenders, specialized assessments are required to account for brain development, peer influences, and environmental factors. The Youth Level of Service/Case Management Inventory (YLS/CMI) evaluates risk factors specific to adolescents, such as family instability, school engagement, and peer associations.

Since juvenile brains are still developing, rehabilitation efforts must focus on redirection rather than punishment, with interventions tailored to social skill development, mentorship, and educational support.

Cultural and demographic factors must be considered in psychological assessments. Many standardized tests are **normed on specific populations**, meaning they may **not accurately reflect cognitive abilities, personality traits, or behavioral tendencies in diverse offender groups**. Psychologists conducting assessments in rehabilitation settings must be trained in culturally competent evaluation methods, ensuring that treatment plans are tailored to each individual's background and unique experiences.

Rehabilitation settings also incorporate **dynamic risk assessment tools**, which recognize that an offender's likelihood of reoffending is not static but influenced by life circumstances, treatment progress, and external factors. Tools such as the Structured Assessment of Violence Risk in Youth (SAVRY) and the Historical Clinical Risk Management-20 (HCR-20) allow psychologists to monitor risk fluctuations over time, adapting treatment strategies based on behavioral progress.

Rehabilitation success is largely dependent on the accuracy and effectiveness of psychological assessments. Poorly conducted evaluations can lead to **misdiagnosis, improper treatment placement, and ineffective intervention strategies**. Standardized tools must be used alongside clinical judgment, observational data, and ongoing monitoring to ensure that offenders receive the support, supervision, and therapeutic interventions necessary to reduce recidivism.

Effective rehabilitation requires a holistic approach that integrates psychological assessments with targeted interventions, structured therapy, and long-term monitoring. Without proper evaluation, offenders are at risk of falling through the cracks, receiving inadequate treatment, or being placed in programs that do not match their needs.

Psychological assessments remain one of the most essential components of criminal rehabilitation, providing a scientific basis for individualized treatment plans and improving long-term outcomes for both offenders and society.

Therapeutic Interventions and Treatment Models for Offenders

Rehabilitation in the criminal justice system depends on well-structured therapeutic interventions designed to address the underlying psychological and behavioral issues contributing to criminal behavior. Offenders come from diverse backgrounds, with unique mental health conditions, cognitive deficits, trauma histories, and social influences shaping their actions.

Effective treatment models are not one-size-fits-all; they must be evidence-based, tailored to individual needs, and focused on reducing recidivism. Various therapeutic approaches, including cognitive-behavioral therapy, dialectical behavior therapy, trauma-informed care, substance abuse treatment, and restorative justice programs, are used to modify thought patterns, teach coping mechanisms, and promote long-term behavioral change.

Cognitive-behavioral therapy (CBT) is the most widely used intervention in offender rehabilitation. It is based on the principle that criminal behavior stems from distorted thinking patterns, maladaptive beliefs, and poor emotional regulation. CBT helps offenders recognize and challenge their negative thought processes, replacing them with healthier alternatives. Techniques such as cognitive restructuring, problem-solving training, and impulse control exercises teach offenders how to analyze situations more rationally and respond in non-criminal ways. CBT is particularly effective for individuals with antisocial traits, aggression issues, and histories of impulsive decision-making. Studies show that CBT-based programs significantly reduce recidivism rates when applied consistently over time.

Dialectical behavior therapy (DBT) expands on CBT by incorporating emotional regulation and interpersonal effectiveness skills. Originally developed for individuals with borderline personality disorder, DBT has been adapted for offenders with extreme mood swings, self-destructive behaviors, and chronic aggression. The therapy teaches mindfulness, distress tolerance, and emotional control techniques, helping individuals manage intense feelings without resorting to violence or manipulation. Many offenders, particularly those with histories of trauma or substance abuse, struggle with emotional dysregulation, making DBT a valuable addition to rehabilitation programs.

Substance abuse treatment programs are critical in correctional settings, as a high percentage of offenders have drug or alcohol dependencies that contribute to their criminal behavior. Addiction treatment includes detoxification, medication-assisted therapy, and behavioral interventions designed to reduce cravings and prevent relapse. The Matrix Model, a structured outpatient program, combines individual counseling, group therapy, and relapse prevention training. Motivational interviewing is also commonly used to enhance an offender's commitment to recovery by focusing on their intrinsic motivation for change rather than external pressures. Substance abuse programs that integrate CBT, medication, and peer support tend to be the most effective in reducing drug-related recidivism.

Trauma-informed therapy acknowledges that many offenders have experienced severe childhood neglect, abuse, or violence, which has shaped their behavioral patterns and emotional responses. Traditional punitive approaches often ignore these factors, leading to increased resistance and recidivism. Trauma-focused cognitive-behavioral therapy (TF-CBT) helps offenders process past trauma, reframe their narratives, and develop healthier coping mechanisms. Eye movement desensitization and reprocessing (EMDR) is also used to help individuals process traumatic memories without triggering emotional distress. By addressing the root causes of criminal behavior, trauma-informed care creates a foundation for long-term rehabilitation.

Anger management therapy focuses on teaching offenders how to recognize triggers, regulate emotions, and de-escalate conflicts before they lead to violence. Many violent offenders have difficulty controlling their temper, reacting impulsively to perceived threats or insults. Structured anger management programs teach offenders to identify physiological signs of anger, practice relaxation techniques, and apply problem-solving skills instead of resorting to aggression. These programs are especially beneficial for individuals convicted of domestic violence, assault, or gang-related crimes.

Sex offender treatment programs use specialized therapy techniques to address deviant sexual interests, impulse control deficits, and cognitive distortions. The Good Lives Model emphasizes the development of prosocial goals and adaptive coping strategies to replace harmful behaviors.

Relapse prevention techniques teach offenders how to recognize high-risk situations and implement strategies to avoid reoffending. Polygraph testing is sometimes used to assess compliance, although its reliability is debated. The success of sex offender treatment depends on the offender's willingness to engage in therapy and long-term monitoring.

Restorative justice programs focus on accountability, rehabilitation, and repairing the harm caused by criminal behavior. These programs bring offenders face-to-face with victims in controlled settings, allowing for dialogue, understanding, and reparation agreements. The goal is to help offenders develop empathy, take responsibility for their actions, and reintegrate into society with a sense of purpose. Restorative justice has been particularly effective for juvenile offenders, minor property crimes, and first-time nonviolent offenses, reducing reoffending rates by strengthening community ties and personal accountability.

Group therapy is widely used in correctional facilities as it provides offenders with peer support, shared experiences, and opportunities to develop interpersonal skills. Group-based interventions encourage participants to challenge each other's thinking, offer feedback, and reinforce prosocial behaviors.

Support groups such as Alcoholics Anonymous and Narcotics Anonymous provide ongoing recovery support and help individuals maintain sobriety after release. Group therapy can be effective for addressing criminal thinking patterns, social skill deficits, and emotional regulation issues.

Family-based interventions recognize the role of family dynamics in criminal behavior and rehabilitation. Many offenders come from dysfunctional families with histories of substance abuse, domestic violence, or neglect. Family therapy aims to rebuild trust, improve communication, and establish healthier relational patterns. Functional Family Therapy (FFT) and Multisystemic Therapy (MST) are evidence-based approaches that work with offenders and their families to prevent reoffending and strengthen community reintegration. These interventions are particularly effective for juvenile offenders, who often return to family environments that may either support or hinder their rehabilitation.

Mindfulness and meditation-based therapies are gaining attention as tools for rehabilitation, particularly for reducing stress, aggression, and impulsivity. Programs that incorporate meditation, yoga, and mindfulness training have shown promise in helping offenders develop self-awareness, emotional control, and resilience. **These approaches are especially beneficial for individuals with anxiety disorders, PTSD, and chronic stress**. By promoting mental clarity and relaxation, mindfulness practices can complement traditional therapy techniques.

Vocational and educational therapy programs provide offenders with the skills necessary for stable employment and independent living. Many offenders lack formal education, job training, or financial literacy, making reintegration into society challenging.

Rehabilitation programs that include GED preparation, vocational training, and employment counseling reduce the likelihood of reoffending by increasing access to legal employment opportunities. Cognitive-behavioral job readiness programs also address workplace conflict resolution, goal setting, and financial management, further supporting successful reintegration.

Psychoeducation is key in rehabilitation, teaching offenders about the consequences of their actions, the impact of criminal behavior on victims, and strategies for making positive life choices. Programs that educate offenders on emotional intelligence, conflict resolution, and problem-solving empower them to navigate daily challenges without resorting to crime. These educational components are often integrated into broader therapeutic interventions to reinforce learning and application.

Correctional rehabilitation programs must also consider mental health treatment for offenders with psychiatric disorders. Many incarcerated individuals suffer from depression, schizophrenia, bipolar disorder, or anxiety disorders, which contribute to criminal behavior. Without proper treatment, these conditions worsen, increasing the risk of recidivism.

Psychiatric care, including medication management, psychotherapy, and crisis intervention, is essential for stabilizing symptoms and ensuring offenders receive appropriate support. Coordination between correctional mental health professionals and community-based services is necessary for continuity of care after release.

Effective rehabilitation requires a comprehensive, individualized approach that integrates multiple therapy models, behavioral interventions, and support systems. The most successful programs recognize that criminal behavior is often the result of a combination of psychological, social, and environmental factors, rather than innate criminal tendencies. By addressing these root causes, therapeutic interventions provide offenders with the tools needed for long-term change, reducing the likelihood of reoffending and promoting safer communities.

Rehabilitation is not about excusing criminal behavior but about breaking the cycle of crime and encouraging lasting behavioral transformation.

Community-Based Programs for Reintegration

Reintegrating offenders into society after incarceration is one of the most challenging aspects of rehabilitation. Many individuals leaving prison face **significant barriers to employment, housing, social support, and mental health care**, increasing their likelihood of reoffending. Community-based programs serve as a bridge between incarceration and reintegration, providing structured support, supervision, and opportunities for rehabilitation. When implemented effectively, these programs reduce recidivism, promote social stability, and help former offenders build productive lives outside the criminal justice system.

One of the primary concerns for reintegrating offenders is **employment**. Many former inmates struggle to find jobs due to **limited work experience, gaps in employment history, and employer reluctance to hire individuals with criminal records**. Community-based job training programs provide vocational skills, resume building, interview coaching, and direct employment placement. Some programs partner with local businesses, trade unions, and government agencies to create second-chance employment opportunities. Research shows that stable employment significantly reduces recidivism rates, as financial stability discourages individuals from resorting to crime for survival.

Housing is another critical challenge. Many individuals released from prison **have no stable housing options, leading to homelessness or temporary stays in overcrowded shelters**. Without a permanent address, it becomes difficult to secure employment, access medical care, or maintain mental health treatment. Community-based reintegration programs provide transitional housing, halfway houses, and supportive housing units where individuals can live temporarily while they rebuild their lives. Some housing programs offer onsite case management, substance abuse counseling, and peer mentorship, ensuring that residents receive continuous support.

Substance abuse recovery programs are essential in reintegration efforts, particularly for individuals whose criminal behavior was linked to **drug or alcohol dependence**. Many offenders relapse shortly after release due to **the stress of reintegration, exposure to old environments, and lack of coping mechanisms**. Community-based rehabilitation centers offer outpatient substance abuse treatment, peer support groups, and relapse prevention programs to help individuals maintain sobriety. Programs like Alcoholics Anonymous (AA) and Narcotics Anonymous (NA) provide long-term peer support, reinforcing recovery and accountability.

Mental health support is a crucial component of reintegration. Many offenders suffer from **untreated psychiatric disorders, including depression, PTSD, schizophrenia, and bipolar disorder**. Without adequate treatment, these conditions can **impair decision-making, increase impulsivity, and contribute to criminal behavior**. Community mental health clinics offer therapy, psychiatric care, and medication management, ensuring that former offenders receive ongoing treatment. Peer support specialists, many of whom have lived experience with incarceration, help guide individuals through the mental health recovery process.

Probation and parole services are key in reintegration by monitoring offenders, ensuring compliance with legal conditions, and providing necessary resources. Officers work with community organizations, social workers, and treatment providers to address issues such as housing, employment, and substance abuse.

While supervision is necessary to prevent recidivism, overly strict conditions—such as frequent check-ins, travel restrictions, and limited job opportunities due to parole requirements—can create additional barriers to reintegration. A balance between accountability and support is needed to ensure that parole conditions facilitate, rather than hinder, successful reintegration.

Education and vocational training programs provide former offenders with **opportunities to gain new skills and improve their economic prospects**. Many community-based reintegration programs offer **GED preparation, literacy courses, and college enrollment assistance**. For individuals interested in **trade careers**, vocational training in **plumbing, welding, carpentry, and automotive repair** provides alternative career paths. Some programs also offer **entrepreneurship training, financial literacy workshops, and small business grants**, allowing individuals to become self-sufficient through business ownership.

Family reunification programs help former offenders **rebuild relationships with loved ones and reintegrate into family life**. Incarceration often strains parent-child relationships, romantic partnerships, and extended family bonds. Many community-based programs offer family counseling, parenting classes, and mediation services to address conflicts and rebuild trust. For individuals who have lost custody of their children due to incarceration, these programs assist in navigating legal processes, demonstrating parental stability, and working toward family reunification.

Peer mentorship programs are among the most effective community-based interventions. Formerly incarcerated individuals who have successfully reintegrated serve as **mentors, role models, and support figures for individuals recently released from prison**. These mentors help navigate the challenges of reintegration, offer guidance on avoiding high-risk situations, and provide emotional support. Research has shown that peer mentoring reduces recidivism by reinforcing positive social bonds and increasing engagement in pro-social activities.

Restorative justice initiatives focus on repairing harm caused by criminal behavior and reinforcing community accountability. Some community reintegration programs incorporate victim-offender mediation, community service projects, and conflict resolution training. By participating in these programs, former offenders develop a deeper understanding of the consequences of their actions and gain opportunities to make amends. Restorative justice approaches have been particularly successful in juvenile justice programs and first-time offender rehabilitation efforts.

Recreational and community engagement programs provide **socialization opportunities, stress relief, and positive activities** for individuals adjusting to life after incarceration. Some programs include **sports leagues, art therapy, music programs, and volunteer opportunities**, helping former offenders build

constructive hobbies and positive peer networks. Social isolation is a significant risk factor for recidivism, so participation in **structured, community-based activities** provides **a sense of belonging and purpose**.

Legal assistance programs help former offenders navigate the challenges of reintegration, particularly for those with criminal records that affect employment, housing, or custody rights.

Many community organizations provide expungement assistance, legal representation for parole hearings, and support for individuals facing discrimination based on past convictions. Access to legal aid ensures that individuals can address outstanding legal issues, reinstate driving privileges, and resolve financial obligations such as court fees and child support.

Spiritual and faith-based reintegration programs offer **moral guidance, emotional support, and a sense of purpose** for individuals seeking rehabilitation. Many community organizations, churches, and religious groups offer mentorship, housing assistance, and employment placement through faith-based initiatives. While participation is voluntary, many former offenders find that spiritual guidance provides structure, motivation, and a moral framework for rebuilding their lives.

Transportation services are often overlooked but are essential for successful reintegration. Many individuals leaving prison lack access to reliable transportation, which affects their ability to attend job interviews, probation meetings, and therapy sessions. Some community-based programs provide subsidized public transit passes, ride-sharing services, or access to bicycles and vehicle assistance to remove transportation barriers.

Community-based reintegration programs work best when they are holistic, addressing multiple needs simultaneously rather than focusing on a single aspect of rehabilitation. A former offender may require a combination of job training, housing assistance, substance abuse counseling, and mental health care to reintegrate successfully. Programs that coordinate across multiple service providers, offer long-term support, and provide case management services tend to yield the best outcomes.

Reintegration is not a **short-term process**—it requires **ongoing support, community engagement, and structured opportunities for personal growth**. Many individuals released from incarceration face **stigma, economic disadvantages, and psychological challenges that make reintegration difficult**. However, research consistently shows that when former offenders receive structured support, their chances of living crime-free lives increase dramatically.

Investing in community-based reintegration programs not only benefits former offenders but also reduces crime rates, decreases prison overcrowding, and strengthens communities. When individuals are given opportunities to rebuild their lives, contribute to society, and form healthy relationships, they are far less likely to return to criminal behavior. Rehabilitation is most effective when the focus shifts from punishment to reintegration, providing former offenders with the tools they need to succeed. The success of these programs ultimately depends on funding, public support, and a commitment to treating reintegration as a key component of criminal justice reform.

Strategies and Policies Aimed at Reducing Recidivism

Reducing recidivism—the tendency of released offenders to reoffend—is one of the most pressing concerns in criminal justice policy. High recidivism rates contribute to prison overcrowding, increased crime, and economic burdens on society. Effective strategies and policies focus on **breaking the cycle of criminal behavior by addressing the root causes of reoffending, improving rehabilitation programs, and ensuring that former offenders have the tools necessary to reintegrate successfully into society**. Research has consistently shown that evidence-based interventions, targeted policies, and a shift away from punitive models toward rehabilitative approaches lead to lower rates of reoffending.

One of the most effective ways to reduce recidivism is investing in education and vocational training programs for incarcerated individuals. Studies have shown that individuals who receive GEDs, college degrees, or vocational certifications while in prison are significantly less likely to reoffend upon release.

The logic is simple: when offenders gain job skills and credentials, they have a higher chance of securing stable employment and achieving financial independence, reducing their motivation to engage in illegal activities. Programs that provide job readiness training, apprenticeships, and access to higher education courses inside prisons have yielded positive long-term results.

Employment is one of the strongest predictors of recidivism. Many former offenders struggle to find work due to **stigma, lack of experience, and legal restrictions on hiring individuals with criminal records**. Policies aimed at removing employment barriers—such as Ban the Box legislation, which prevents employers from asking about criminal history in initial job applications—have been shown to increase job opportunities for former offenders. Some states also offer tax incentives to businesses that hire formerly incarcerated individuals, encouraging companies to provide second-chance employment opportunities. Workforce reentry programs that provide career counseling, resume building, interview preparation, and job placement assistance further support individuals in their transition back into the workforce.

Stable housing is another crucial factor in preventing recidivism. Many formerly incarcerated individuals experience **homelessness, unstable living conditions, or difficulty securing rental agreements due to criminal records**. Without stable housing, individuals are at higher risk of reoffending because they lack a safe, structured environment that supports their reintegration. Policies that fund transitional housing programs, rental assistance, and reentry housing initiatives provide former offenders with temporary stability while they search for permanent housing and employment. Housing-first models, which prioritize placing individuals in stable housing before requiring them to meet other conditions such as employment or sobriety, have been particularly successful in reducing recidivism.

Mental health and substance abuse treatment are essential components of recidivism reduction strategies. Many incarcerated individuals suffer from **undiagnosed or untreated psychiatric disorders, trauma, and substance addiction**, which contribute to criminal behavior. Upon release, without proper mental health care or addiction treatment, individuals often relapse into old patterns. Expanding access to community-based mental health services, medication-assisted treatment for substance abuse, and therapy programs ensures that individuals receive the continued care they need. Drug courts, which divert nonviolent offenders into treatment programs instead of traditional sentencing, have been shown to reduce recidivism by addressing addiction as a public health issue rather than solely a criminal justice issue.

Community supervision policies, including **probation and parole reforms, also impact recidivism rates**. While parole and probation provide structured oversight for individuals transitioning out of incarceration, overly restrictive supervision conditions can set individuals up for failure.

In many cases, technical violations—such as missing a meeting, failing a drug test, or violating a curfew—result in reincarceration, even when no new crimes have been committed. Shifting from a punitive model to a rehabilitative approach in probation and parole—by focusing on support services rather than punishment—can significantly reduce reincarceration rates.

Restorative justice programs have gained momentum as an alternative to traditional punitive measures. These programs focus on **repairing harm, fostering accountability, and providing opportunities for reconciliation between offenders and victims**. Victim-offender mediation, community conferencing, and restorative justice circles provide spaces for dialogue, responsibility-taking, and restitution agreements. Studies have shown that offenders who participate in restorative justice programs are less likely to reoffend because they develop a greater understanding of the consequences of their actions and build stronger social ties to their communities.

Early intervention and youth diversion programs help prevent recidivism before it begins. Juvenile offenders who enter the criminal justice system at an early age are **far more likely to continue engaging in criminal behavior as adults**. Investing in community mentorship programs, school-based interventions, and alternative sentencing for young offenders helps redirect at-risk youth before they become entrenched in the criminal justice system. Programs that pair youth with positive role models, provide educational support, and offer recreational alternatives to crime are among the most effective at preventing long-term criminal behavior.

Cognitive-behavioral therapy (CBT) programs in correctional facilities have also been highly effective in reducing recidivism. Many offenders engage in criminal behavior due to impulsive thinking, poor emotional regulation, and cognitive distortions. CBT-based interventions focus on teaching offenders how to identify high-risk situations, recognize harmful thought patterns, and develop problem-solving skills. When paired with social skill development and emotional regulation training, these programs help individuals transition back into society with improved self-control and decision-making abilities.

Support networks and peer mentorship programs are important in reintegration. Many former offenders **lack strong social ties, family support, or community connections**, making reintegration difficult. Peer mentorship programs, where successful former offenders guide individuals through their reentry process, have been shown to reduce recidivism by reinforcing positive behavior and providing emotional support. Community organizations that offer reentry support, legal aid, financial planning assistance, and counseling services ensure that individuals have a structured system to help them navigate the challenges of reintegration.

Expanding eligibility for record expungement and sealing policies can help reduce recidivism by **removing barriers to employment, housing, and social mobility**. Many states allow individuals with nonviolent convictions to petition for record expungement after a certain period of demonstrated rehabilitation. Automatic expungement policies for low-level offenses, particularly for drug-related charges, further help individuals move past their criminal history and reintegrate more successfully.

Policy reforms aimed at **reducing incarceration rates for nonviolent offenses** have also contributed to lower recidivism. Many individuals serve prison time for drug possession, theft, or parole violations, offenses that could be better addressed through rehabilitation rather than incarceration.

Sentencing reform policies that divert low-risk offenders into treatment, community service, or probation rather than prison have proven to be more effective in reducing repeat offenses. Expanding alternative sentencing options, such as mental health courts and community service programs, helps prevent unnecessary incarceration while still ensuring accountability.

Investment in post-release monitoring and early reentry planning significantly impacts recidivism rates. Studies have shown that offenders who receive structured pre-release planning—such as employment placement, housing arrangements, and treatment referrals—are far more likely to reintegrate successfully.

Many community-based organizations provide "step-down" reentry models, where individuals transition from incarceration to supervised halfway housing before full reintegration. These transitional programs help individuals adjust to freedom gradually, minimizing the shock of release and reducing the likelihood of reoffending.

Reducing recidivism requires a multi-faceted approach that integrates education, employment, mental health care, substance abuse treatment, housing support, and strong community connections. Research consistently demonstrates that punitive approaches—such as longer sentences, harsh parole conditions, and strict supervision—are less effective in preventing reoffending compared to rehabilitative strategies. By investing in evidence-based policies that support reintegration, provide opportunities for personal growth, and remove structural barriers to success, societies can break the cycle of crime and build safer communities. The shift from a punishment-driven model to a restorative, rehabilitative, and reintegration-focused approach offers the best path forward in reducing repeat offenses and ensuring long-term public safety.

Chapter 11: Contemporary Challenges and Future Directions

Cyberpsychology and the Impact of Digital Crime

The rise of digital technology has fundamentally changed the way crime is committed, investigated, and understood. Cyberpsychology, the study of how human behavior is influenced by digital environments, is essential for understanding online criminal activity. Unlike traditional crimes, digital offenses do not always require physical presence, direct confrontation, or geographic limitations.

Cybercriminals exploit **anonymity, automation, and global connectivity** to engage in fraud, hacking, cyberstalking, identity theft, and even more complex crimes such as digital extortion and online radicalization. Understanding the psychology behind these offenses is critical for developing effective prevention and intervention strategies.

One of the defining features of digital crime is the psychological **detachment from real-world consequences**. In traditional crime, offenders face immediate risks—physical capture, social judgment, or direct retaliation. Online, the perceived distance from victims and authorities reduces empathy and fear of punishment.

A cybercriminal committing fraud or distributing malicious software may not experience the same moral conflict as someone robbing a person in the street. This detachment encourages individuals who might otherwise avoid criminal activity to engage in fraudulent schemes, cyber harassment, or online manipulation.

Cybercriminals take advantage of **cognitive biases and psychological vulnerabilities**. Many online scams rely on **social engineering**, a manipulation tactic that exploits human trust. Phishing attacks, where individuals are tricked into providing sensitive information, rely on authority bias (trusting official-looking emails), urgency bias (rushing decisions under pressure), and familiarity bias (responding to emails that seem recognizable). Hackers and scammers understand how to manipulate human behavior just as well as they understand software vulnerabilities.

Anonymity online encourages **disinhibition, aggression, and unethical behavior**. In face-to-face interactions, people regulate their behavior due to social norms and the potential for real-world consequences. The **online disinhibition effect** reduces these barriers, allowing individuals to engage in cyberbullying, doxxing, hate speech, and even online blackmail without the psychological burden of immediate confrontation. Some individuals use anonymity as a shield to experiment with sadistic or criminal impulses they would suppress in real life.

Radicalization and extremist recruitment have thrived in digital spaces due to **psychological manipulation, echo chambers, and targeted persuasion techniques**. Terrorist organizations, hate groups, and ideological extremists use online forums, encrypted chat platforms, and social media algorithms to recruit vulnerable individuals. Cognitive psychology explains how repeated exposure to extremist messaging, combined with isolation from counter-narratives, fosters ideological commitment. The internet enables groups to find and influence individuals predisposed to conspiracy thinking, resentment, or violent impulses, accelerating their transformation into offenders willing to act on digital or real-world violence.

Cyberstalking and online harassment exploit the **persistent and omnipresent nature of digital life**. Unlike physical stalking, where a victim may find refuge at home or change locations, digital harassment follows individuals wherever they go. Perpetrators use doxxing (publicly exposing private information), revenge porn, swatting (calling false emergency threats to someone's home), and deepfake technology to exert power over victims. The lack of physical presence often emboldens aggressors, allowing them to escalate their behavior without fear of immediate confrontation. Many online stalkers rationalize their behavior, convincing themselves that their actions are harmless or justified.

The gamification of cybercrime has further expanded the number of participants engaging in digital offenses. Some hacking communities **reward members with social status, reputation points, or monetary incentives** for successful cyberattacks.

Ransomware groups offer affiliate programs, where individuals with no technical expertise can deploy malware for a share of the profits. These incentives lower the psychological barriers to criminal participation, transforming hacking into an accessible, structured activity rather than an impulsive act of defiance.

Dark web markets create **a psychological separation between buyer and seller, reducing ethical concerns about criminal transactions**. Unlike traditional black markets, where participants may face violence or legal exposure, digital black markets provide encrypted anonymity, escrow services, and a review system that mimics legitimate commerce. This structure makes it easier for individuals to rationalize buying illegal drugs, weapons, stolen data, or counterfeit documents because the process feels transactional rather than overtly criminal.

The psychological impact of cybercrime extends to victims, who often experience **long-term emotional, financial, and reputational damage**. Unlike traditional theft, where stolen goods can be recovered, digital crimes often leave victims with **permanent consequences**—identity theft can take years to resolve, cyber harassment can destroy reputations, and financial fraud can leave individuals bankrupt. Victims frequently report **paranoia, depression, and trust issues**, as digital violations feel invasive and inescapable.

Law enforcement faces psychological challenges in cybercrime investigations. Digital crimes require a different mindset than traditional policing, as they demand technical expertise, deep psychological analysis, and an understanding of online subcultures. Many cybercriminals operate in tight-knit, anonymous communities that require infiltration tactics similar to organized crime investigations. Law enforcement officers must understand hacker psychology, behavioral patterns in cyber fraud, and the motivations behind online radicalization to anticipate and disrupt cybercriminal activities.

Prevention efforts in cybercrime rely on **psychological education, behavioral interventions, and technical safeguards**. Security awareness training helps individuals recognize **manipulative tactics used in phishing, scams, and fraud schemes**. Cognitive training in critical thinking and digital skepticism reduces susceptibility to social engineering attacks. Organizations use behavioral biometrics (monitoring typing speed, mouse movements, and login patterns) to detect suspicious activity before cybercrimes occur. These measures combine psychological understanding with technological solutions to create more resilient individuals and organizations.

Cybercriminal profiling uses **behavioral psychology, linguistic analysis, and digital forensics** to predict and identify offenders. Investigators analyze the language patterns in phishing emails, the choice of attack methods, and behavioral clues left behind in cyber intrusions to link crimes to specific perpetrators. Some cybercriminals display narcissistic traits, seeking attention for their exploits, while others operate with calculated detachment, motivated solely by financial or ideological goals. Understanding these motivations helps law enforcement anticipate attack patterns, infiltrate online criminal networks, and disrupt digital threats before they escalate.

Emerging technologies in cyberpsychology are expanding the way investigators approach digital crime. AI-driven sentiment analysis detects **potential threats in online forums, identifying individuals expressing violent intent**. Behavioral tracking algorithms monitor suspicious activity in financial transactions, predicting fraud attempts before they occur.

Neural networks analyze dark web traffic, identifying shifts in criminal behavior based on linguistic changes, transaction patterns, and user activity. These tools help bridge human psychology and machine learning, creating predictive models that assist in cybercrime prevention and investigation.

The future of cyberpsychology in criminal justice will require **a fusion of psychology, cybersecurity, law enforcement, and artificial intelligence**. As digital crime continues to evolve, so too must investigative strategies. Cybercriminals are constantly adapting their methods, using deepfake technology, AI-generated phishing attacks, and decentralized financial networks to evade detection. Law enforcement, psychologists, and researchers must remain ahead of these developments, refining digital investigative techniques and psychological analysis methods to combat online criminal behavior effectively.

Globalization's Effect on Crime Patterns and Offender Behavior

Globalization has fundamentally altered crime patterns, creating new opportunities for offenders while complicating law enforcement efforts. The increasing interconnectedness of economies, rapid technological advancements, and the ease of cross-border movement have expanded the scope of criminal activity. Crimes that were once localized now operate on an international scale, allowing offenders to exploit legal loopholes, evade capture, and conduct illicit operations across multiple jurisdictions. Understanding how globalization has shaped modern crime provides insight into offender behavior and the evolving challenges faced by criminal justice systems worldwide.

One of the most significant impacts of globalization on crime is the expansion of organized crime networks. Criminal organizations now operate beyond their home countries, forming transnational syndicates involved in drug trafficking, human smuggling, financial fraud, and cybercrime.

Traditional mafias and cartels have adapted to globalization by establishing connections with international counterparts, increasing their operational efficiency and access to global markets. This expansion has made it more difficult for law enforcement agencies to dismantle criminal enterprises, as leaders and key figures often reside in different countries than where their crimes are committed.

Human trafficking has surged as a result of globalization. With increased migration due to economic hardship, conflict, and instability, traffickers exploit vulnerable populations by offering false employment opportunities or using coercion. **Victims are often transported across multiple borders, making detection and intervention challenging**. Trafficking organizations use advanced technology, encrypted communication, and fraudulent documentation to evade authorities, making it necessary for international law enforcement agencies to collaborate closely to track and dismantle these operations.

Cybercrime has become one of the most pervasive consequences of globalization. The rise of digital technology has enabled offenders to conduct financial fraud, identity theft, hacking, and online scams from anywhere in the world.

Many cybercriminals operate from countries with weak legal frameworks for digital crime, making extradition and prosecution difficult. The anonymity provided by the internet further complicates efforts to trace perpetrators, as offenders use cryptocurrency, encrypted messaging platforms, and sophisticated malware to carry out their crimes undetected.

Financial crime has also evolved with globalization. Money laundering, tax evasion, and corporate fraud have become easier as financial transactions cross international borders. Criminals exploit offshore banking systems and shell companies to obscure the origins of illicit funds, making it difficult for authorities to track money flows. The rise of decentralized finance and cryptocurrency has further complicated financial investigations, allowing offenders to move money without relying on traditional banking systems.

Terrorism has been influenced by globalization, with extremist groups using online platforms to recruit, radicalize, and coordinate attacks across continents. The ability to share propaganda, communicate securely, and transfer funds internationally has allowed terrorist organizations to expand their reach without physical movement. Global travel and immigration patterns have also raised concerns about the movement of radicalized individuals between countries, leading to increased security measures and intelligence-sharing among nations.

The drug trade has adapted to globalization by developing more sophisticated distribution networks. Synthetic drug production has expanded, with chemicals sourced from different regions and assembled in decentralized locations to avoid detection. The use of encrypted marketplaces on the dark web has allowed drug traffickers to sell narcotics without direct contact with buyers, reducing the risk of law enforcement intervention. These changes have made it harder to track and disrupt global drug operations.

Cultural shifts caused by globalization have also affected crime rates. In some regions, exposure to global economic inequality has fueled criminal activity as individuals seek financial opportunities through illegal means. In others, the **erosion of traditional social structures has contributed to increases in violent crime**, as communities struggle to adapt to rapid societal changes. The spread of Western consumer culture has influenced organized theft and counterfeit goods markets, with criminals exploiting demand for luxury items by producing and distributing fake products on an international scale.

Law enforcement agencies have had to adapt to globalization by strengthening international cooperation. Interpol, Europol, and other global policing organizations facilitate information-sharing, coordinate joint investigations, and assist in extradition processes.

However, **differences in legal systems, bureaucratic inefficiencies, and political obstacles often hinder seamless collaboration**. Countries with weak governance or corruption further complicate efforts to combat transnational crime, as some governments may be unwilling or unable to crack down on criminal networks operating within their borders.

Border security has become a major focus in response to global crime trends. Smuggling of weapons, drugs, and contraband has increased with the ease of international travel and trade. Law enforcement agencies have turned to advanced technology, including biometric scanning, artificial intelligence, and predictive analytics, to monitor and prevent cross-border criminal activities. However, balancing security concerns with human rights issues remains a challenge, particularly in regions where strict immigration policies conflict with humanitarian obligations.

The legal and ethical challenges of globalization in criminal justice are significant. Many crimes now involve multiple jurisdictions, requiring coordinated legal responses that may conflict with national sovereignty. Extradition treaties, differences in sentencing laws, and varying definitions of criminal activity create obstacles in prosecuting offenders who operate across borders. The ethical implications of mass surveillance, data collection, and privacy laws also present concerns, as governments attempt to monitor potential threats without infringing on civil liberties.

The future of crime in a globalized world will likely involve continued adaptation by both offenders and law enforcement agencies. Criminal organizations will refine their methods, using artificial intelligence, blockchain technology, and increasingly sophisticated cyber tools to evade detection. Law enforcement, in turn, must invest in advanced forensic technologies, data analysis techniques, and cross-border intelligence-sharing to stay ahead of evolving threats. The challenge will be to balance security, privacy, and legal protections while addressing the complex realities of crime in an interconnected world.

The Integration of Artificial Intelligence in Criminal Profiling

The use of artificial intelligence in criminal profiling has introduced new possibilities for identifying offenders, predicting criminal behavior, and streamlining investigative processes. AI has transformed law enforcement by automating data analysis, recognizing patterns in criminal activity, and assisting in decision-making. While traditional profiling relies on psychological theories and behavioral science, AI enhances these methods by processing vast amounts of data that human investigators would struggle to analyze efficiently. The integration of AI in criminal profiling has the potential to improve accuracy, speed up investigations, and reduce human bias, though ethical and legal concerns remain.

One of the most significant applications of AI in profiling is **predictive policing**, which uses machine learning algorithms to analyze crime patterns and forecast where crimes are likely to occur. By processing historical crime data, AI systems identify **hotspots for criminal activity, helping law enforcement allocate resources more effectively**. Predictive models consider factors such as **time of day, location, and past incidents** to determine where offenses are most likely to happen. While this method has proven useful in reducing crime rates in certain areas, it has also raised concerns about **racial profiling and the reinforcement of systemic biases in policing**. If the data fed into AI systems reflects biased policing practices, the algorithms may disproportionately target certain communities.

Facial recognition technology has become an integral part of AI-driven criminal profiling. Advanced image-processing algorithms scan faces captured in security footage and compare them against **national or global databases of known offenders**. Law enforcement agencies use these systems to identify suspects, locate fugitives, and verify identities in real time. However, facial recognition is not foolproof—studies have shown that these systems can be less accurate for certain demographic groups, leading to misidentifications and wrongful arrests. Privacy concerns also arise, as widespread surveillance could lead to mass tracking of individuals without their consent.

AI-driven **behavioral analysis** enhances traditional criminal profiling by identifying **subtle patterns in speech, writing, and movement** that may indicate deception or criminal intent. Natural language processing (NLP) tools analyze online communications, social media posts, and recorded interrogations to detect potential threats. Some systems are designed to identify patterns of aggression, coercion, or radicalization in digital communications, alerting investigators to potential criminal activity. However, the challenge lies in distinguishing genuine threats from false positives, as AI models cannot fully interpret human intention.

Text analysis tools are widely used to assess threatening messages, ransom notes, and online extremism. AI compares linguistic styles, word choices, and sentence structures to known offenders, helping law enforcement determine whether multiple crimes were committed by the same person. Forensic linguistics powered by AI has been applied in cases involving cyberstalking, anonymous threats, and extremist propaganda, allowing authorities to profile unknown individuals based on their writing patterns.

AI is also transforming forensic psychology by analyzing **nonverbal cues and physiological signals** to assess deception. Some AI systems monitor **microexpressions, voice stress levels, and pupil dilation** to detect signs of lying or psychological distress. These tools are used in interrogations and security screenings, assisting investigators in assessing whether a suspect is providing truthful statements. However, human emotions are complex, and no AI system has yet achieved 100% accuracy in detecting deception.

Another emerging application is AI-driven risk assessment for offender profiling. Machine learning models analyze criminal history, psychological evaluations, and behavioral reports to determine an individual's likelihood of reoffending.

Some jurisdictions use AI-based tools to assist with parole decisions, bail recommendations, and sentencing guidelines, aiming to reduce recidivism rates. However, reliance on AI in legal decisions has sparked controversy, as algorithms may perpetuate existing biases in sentencing disparities. Transparency in AI decision-making remains a major challenge.

Cybercriminal profiling has benefited significantly from AI integration. Cybercrime investigators use AI-driven tools to track hacking patterns, analyze malware behavior, and identify anonymous offenders operating in the digital world. Algorithms analyze the coding styles of different hacking groups, pinpoint their geographical locations, and predict their next moves. AI-powered cybersecurity systems detect and respond to cyber threats faster than human analysts, helping prevent financial fraud, ransomware attacks, and identity theft before they escalate.

Social network analysis is another powerful AI tool used in criminal investigations. AI scans online relationships, interactions, and behavioral patterns to map out criminal networks, terrorist organizations, and human trafficking rings. By identifying key figures and their connections, law enforcement can disrupt organized crime operations more effectively. These techniques have been instrumental in counterterrorism efforts, drug cartel investigations, and child exploitation cases.

AI also enhances **geospatial crime analysis**, allowing law enforcement to **predict movement patterns of serial offenders** and identify potential crime locations. Geographic profiling, traditionally done manually, is now supplemented by machine learning models that recognize spatial behavior patterns. These tools help investigators narrow down suspect lists, anticipate future crime sites, and track fugitive movements across regions.

The use of AI in criminal profiling also extends to **financial crimes and fraud detection**. Banks, credit agencies, and law enforcement agencies use machine learning algorithms to detect unusual transaction patterns, identifying potential money laundering schemes, tax evasion, and financial fraud. AI-powered fraud detection systems **flag suspicious activities in real time**, reducing response time and preventing large-scale financial losses.

Despite its advantages, AI-driven criminal profiling presents serious ethical and legal concerns. One of the biggest challenges is bias in AI algorithms. If the data used to train AI models reflects historical biases in policing, sentencing, or socioeconomic disparities, the system may produce discriminatory outcomes.

Ensuring fairness and transparency in AI decision-making is critical to preventing wrongful arrests and racial profiling.

Another concern is **privacy violations and mass surveillance**. AI-driven profiling often involves collecting and analyzing **massive amounts of personal data, including social media activity, biometric information, and digital footprints**. Critics argue that widespread surveillance could lead to civil liberties violations, unlawful monitoring, and government overreach. Striking a balance between security and personal privacy remains a key challenge in implementing AI-driven criminal profiling.

Legal frameworks governing AI in law enforcement remain underdeveloped. Many countries lack clear regulations on the ethical use of AI in criminal profiling, data collection, and surveillance. Courts must determine how AI-generated evidence should be weighed in legal proceedings and whether AI-based risk assessments should influence sentencing decisions. Without standardized guidelines, there is a risk of misuse, over-reliance on AI outputs, and wrongful convictions.

The future of AI in criminal profiling will likely involve more sophisticated algorithms, greater transparency, and improved accuracy. Ongoing research aims to reduce bias, improve interpretability, and enhance the reliability of AI-driven insights. As technology evolves, law enforcement agencies will need to develop robust oversight mechanisms, ethical guidelines, and public accountability measures to ensure that AI enhances justice rather than undermines it.

While AI has the potential to **revolutionize criminal profiling**, it should not replace human judgment, critical thinking, or ethical considerations. Instead, it should be used as a tool to support investigators, analyze complex data, and improve decision-making processes. The integration of AI in criminal profiling must be approached with caution, fairness, and a commitment to upholding human rights and due process.

Innovations in Forensic Research and Methodologies

Forensic science has undergone significant advancements over the past few decades, with innovations in technology, data analysis, and investigative techniques reshaping how crimes are solved. The increasing precision of forensic methodologies has improved the accuracy of criminal investigations, helping law enforcement identify offenders, exonerate the innocent, and reconstruct crime scenes with greater detail. New forensic research methods have allowed for deeper insights into criminal behavior, the preservation of evidence, and more reliable forensic profiling. These innovations have not only enhanced traditional forensic disciplines, such as DNA analysis and fingerprint identification, but also introduced new fields like forensic genomics, digital forensics, and artificial intelligence-driven forensic analysis.

DNA analysis remains one of the most revolutionary forensic breakthroughs. Initially, forensic DNA testing relied on relatively large samples and lengthy processing times. However, new methodologies such as **Rapid DNA testing and**

Next-Generation Sequencing (NGS) allow for **faster and more accurate analysis** of even degraded or minimal DNA samples. Rapid DNA devices can produce results in under two hours, significantly reducing delays in criminal investigations. NGS, meanwhile, enhances forensic profiling by analyzing non-coding regions of DNA, which can provide details about an individual's biogeographical ancestry, physical traits, and even age estimation. These techniques have been instrumental in solving cold cases, identifying unknown remains, and verifying suspect identities with greater certainty.

Forensic genomics has expanded the scope of DNA analysis beyond simple matching. By leveraging gene sequencing and familial DNA searching, forensic scientists can now identify potential suspects through distant relatives.

This approach was famously used in the Golden State Killer case, where investigators utilized a public genealogy database to trace familial connections and identify the perpetrator decades after the crimes were committed. Although this method has proven highly effective, it's also raised privacy concerns regarding the use of genetic information in criminal investigations.

Digital forensics has become an essential field as crimes increasingly involve electronic evidence. Cybercriminals leave **digital footprints in emails, social media accounts, encrypted communications, and financial transactions**, making forensic analysis of digital devices critical for investigations. Advanced forensic tools can now recover deleted data, analyze metadata, and detect file manipulation with greater accuracy. Cloud computing forensics has also emerged as a growing field, focusing on retrieving evidence from remote servers rather than local devices. Law enforcement agencies now employ AI-driven algorithms to sort, categorize, and analyze massive amounts of digital evidence, reducing human workload and improving investigative efficiency.

Artificial intelligence is transforming forensic analysis by enhancing pattern recognition, crime scene reconstruction, and forensic psychology assessments. AI-powered software can analyze **millions of forensic records, identify trends in criminal behavior, and compare new evidence to vast forensic databases**. Machine learning algorithms assist in latent fingerprint analysis, firearm ballistics identification, and handwriting recognition, increasing the accuracy of forensic conclusions. AI-driven forensic psychology tools help assess suspect behavior, detect deception in interviews, and analyze linguistic patterns in threats or confessions.

Crime scene reconstruction has benefited from 3D scanning technology and virtual reality modeling. Traditionally, forensic investigators relied on photographs, sketches, and physical measurements to document crime scenes. Now, high-resolution 3D scanners capture every detail of a scene in minutes, creating interactive digital reconstructions that can be revisited and analyzed at any time.

Virtual reality technology allows forensic experts, law enforcement, and even juries to experience the crime scene in an immersive environment, improving spatial understanding and case presentations in court. These advancements enhance accuracy in forensic analysis, reduce the risk of evidence contamination, and preserve crime scenes indefinitely for future examination.

Chemical forensics has made strides in **trace evidence analysis, toxicology, and explosive residue detection**. Miniaturized mass spectrometry devices enable field investigators to detect drugs, gunshot residue, or chemical traces at crime scenes in real time. Advanced chromatography techniques allow forensic toxicologists to identify toxins, poisons, and drug metabolites in biological samples with unprecedented precision. These advancements have improved the ability to determine cause of death, drug intoxication levels, and exposure to hazardous substances in forensic cases.

Forensic entomology, the study of insect activity on decomposing bodies, has become more precise with the integration of genetic barcoding and environmental analysis tools. By examining insect species, growth stages, and DNA markers, forensic entomologists can estimate time of death more accurately and even determine whether a body has been moved post-mortem. Recent studies have also explored how climate change impacts insect behavior, leading to updated forensic timelines based on environmental conditions.

Voice forensics has advanced with **deep learning algorithms and acoustic analysis techniques**. Investigators can now analyze **voice recordings to determine speaker identity, emotional state, and deception cues**. AI-powered forensic voice analysis is being used in extortion cases, ransom calls, and intelligence-gathering operations. However, the rise of deepfake audio technology has created new challenges, as criminals can now manipulate voice recordings to impersonate individuals or fabricate evidence.

Forensic anthropology has improved with **high-resolution skeletal analysis and facial reconstruction technology**. CT scanning and 3D modeling now allow forensic anthropologists to digitally reconstruct skeletal remains with greater accuracy, helping identify unknown victims and determine cause of death. Advances in isotope analysis have provided insights into where individuals lived, what they ate, and potential migration patterns, aiding in missing persons cases and historical forensic investigations.

Gunshot wound analysis has evolved with high-speed imaging, wound ballistics research, and forensic acoustics. Forensic experts can now simulate bullet trajectories with 3D modeling, assess gunshot residue with nano-level precision, and analyze sound wave patterns to determine firearm discharge locations. These tools have been instrumental in shooting reconstructions, officer-involved investigations, and terrorism-related forensic cases.

Forensic psychology has embraced biometric analysis, eye-tracking technology, and cognitive neuroscience to assess suspect behavior, deception, and psychological profiling. Eye-tracking studies have revealed how individuals process crime scene photos, mugshots, and interrogation questions, providing insights into memory recall, stress responses, and emotional recognition. Neuroimaging studies have explored **brain activity patterns in psychopaths, violent offenders, and individuals with impulse control disorders**, offering potential insights into criminal motivation. However, ethical concerns remain regarding the use of neurobiological markers in criminal profiling and legal decision-making.

Cold case investigations have benefited from forensic advancements, as old evidence can now be reanalyzed with **more sensitive DNA techniques,**

enhanced fingerprint processing, and digital record cross-referencing. Genetic genealogy and forensic phenotyping have helped law enforcement solve decades-old cases by identifying suspects through family DNA matches and generating facial composites from DNA markers. These breakthroughs have helped bring justice to victims' families and provided answers in unsolved homicide cases.

Forensic science will continue to evolve, with innovations in **nanotechnology, quantum computing, and artificial intelligence** expected to further refine forensic methodologies.

Researchers are exploring molecular forensic techniques to analyze genetic material at an even smaller scale, as well as automated forensic laboratories capable of processing evidence with minimal human intervention. As forensic technology advances, legal and ethical considerations will remain at the forefront to ensure that forensic science remains a tool for truth, rather than a means of wrongful conviction or privacy invasion.

The ongoing integration of cutting-edge forensic research, AI-driven analytics, and interdisciplinary collaboration will shape the future of forensic investigations. As forensic methodologies become more precise, reliable, and efficient, law enforcement agencies will be better equipped to solve crimes faster, prevent wrongful convictions, and uphold the principles of justice with scientific accuracy. However, with every advancement, forensic scientists and policymakers must carefully navigate ethical challenges, data security concerns, and the potential for forensic misinterpretation to maintain public trust in the field of criminal investigations.

Navigating Ethical Dilemmas and Shaping Policy for Tomorrow

The integration of forensic science, artificial intelligence, and behavioral analysis into criminal investigations has brought undeniable benefits, but it has also introduced complex ethical dilemmas. Law enforcement agencies, policymakers, and forensic researchers must navigate the **fine balance between technological advancement and the protection of civil liberties**. Ethical concerns surrounding privacy, bias, accountability, and the potential misuse of forensic tools raise fundamental questions about the role of technology in justice. As forensic and investigative methodologies become more sophisticated, the need for clear ethical guidelines and sound policies becomes even more pressing.

One of the most significant ethical concerns in forensic science is **the risk of wrongful convictions due to faulty forensic methods, misinterpretation of evidence, or biased expert testimony**. While DNA analysis has exonerated many innocent individuals, other forensic disciplines—such as bite mark analysis, microscopic hair comparisons, and even some aspects of fingerprint identification —have been criticized for lacking sufficient scientific validity. Errors in forensic interpretation can result in misidentifications, unjust incarcerations, and a loss of public trust in the criminal justice system. The challenge for policymakers is determining which forensic methods meet rigorous scientific standards and should be admissible in court.

Artificial intelligence in forensic investigations presents another ethical dilemma. AI-driven tools are increasingly used for criminal profiling, predictive policing, and digital forensics, but these systems rely on historical crime data that may reflect biases in past law enforcement practices. If AI models are trained on data that overrepresents certain racial or socioeconomic groups as offenders, the algorithm may reinforce discriminatory policing practices. Ensuring transparency in AI decision-making, regular audits of forensic AI tools, and accountability in algorithm design is critical for preventing automated biases from influencing arrests, sentencing, and investigative focus.

Privacy concerns have intensified as forensic science becomes more reliant on **biometric data, genetic profiling, and mass surveillance technologies**. The **widespread collection of DNA, facial recognition data, and digital footprints** raises the question of how much personal information law enforcement should have access to without individual consent. In many jurisdictions, law enforcement agencies can obtain DNA samples from commercial genealogy databases to identify criminal suspects through familial matching, a method that has solved major cold cases but also raised concerns about genetic privacy and the ethical implications of using private DNA data for criminal investigations. Striking a balance between solving crimes and protecting individual rights remains an ongoing challenge for policymakers.

Another major ethical debate centers on **predictive policing**—the use of AI algorithms to anticipate criminal activity based on past crime patterns. While predictive policing has been praised for improving **law enforcement resource allocation**, it has also been criticized for **leading to over-policing of specific communities and reinforcing systemic biases**. If certain neighborhoods are historically over-policed, crime reports from these areas may be disproportionately high, causing AI models to direct even more law enforcement presence to these locations. This can create a self-reinforcing cycle where certain populations are over-scrutinized, while others receive little attention regardless of their crime rates. The future of predictive policing will depend on whether it can be implemented in a way that is fair, unbiased, and effective without violating civil liberties.

The ethical challenges of forensic science extend to **interrogation techniques and suspect treatment**. Some forensic tools, such as **polygraphs and voice stress analysis**, have been widely used in criminal investigations despite limited scientific support for their reliability.

While these methods can sometimes help identify inconsistencies in a suspect's statements, they can also produce false positives, misinterpret anxiety as deception, and pressure innocent individuals into making false confessions. Courts and law enforcement agencies must set clear policies on the admissibility of forensic tools in interrogations to prevent wrongful convictions based on flawed deception detection methods.

Cyber forensic investigations also raise new ethical concerns. Law enforcement agencies regularly access encrypted communications, track online activity, and analyze social media behavior to detect criminal intent. However, this level of digital surveillance can conflict with constitutional rights to privacy and free speech. Some governments have passed laws requiring tech companies to provide law enforcement with backdoor access to encrypted communications, arguing that such measures are necessary for national security. Critics warn that such laws weaken encryption standards, endanger data security, and allow for potential government overreach. Policymakers must determine how much access law enforcement should have to private digital communications without compromising the rights of innocent individuals.

The use of **facial recognition technology in forensic investigations** has sparked debates about **accuracy, racial bias, and the ethics of mass surveillance**. Studies have shown that some facial recognition systems have higher error rates when analyzing faces of people of color, increasing the risk of misidentifications and wrongful arrests. Additionally, the expansion of facial recognition databases raises concerns about how this data is stored, who has access to it, and how it can be used beyond criminal investigations. While facial recognition has been valuable in tracking fugitives and identifying victims, unchecked use could lead to pervasive government surveillance and civil rights violations.

Gene editing and forensic biotechnology present emerging ethical questions for the future. Scientists are researching **how genetic markers influence criminal behavior**, with some studies suggesting that **certain genetic traits may be linked to aggression or impulsivity**.

However, the idea of using genetics to predict criminal behavior is ethically controversial, as it raises concerns about biological determinism, discrimination, and the potential misuse of genetic data in legal proceedings. Future policies will need to ensure that genetic research in forensic science is not used to justify biased legal practices or unethical preemptive policing strategies.

Another pressing issue is **the commercialization of forensic science**. Many forensic technologies are developed by private companies that sell software, DNA testing kits, and digital forensic tools to law enforcement agencies. The lack of transparency in proprietary forensic algorithms raises concerns about how these tools make decisions and whether they are scientifically valid. Courts are increasingly scrutinizing forensic evidence presented by private vendors, questioning whether defendants have the right to challenge the algorithms used in their cases. Policymakers must establish clear regulations to ensure forensic technologies are subject to independent validation and judicial oversight.

The future of forensic science will also involve the ethical implications of **autonomous surveillance systems**. AI-driven drones, automated license plate readers, and predictive behavioral monitoring systems are being tested in criminal investigations. These systems have the potential to increase surveillance efficiency and detect crimes in real-time, but they also raise concerns about constant monitoring, lack of human oversight, and potential errors in identifying suspects. If AI surveillance is not properly regulated, it could lead to mass data collection on innocent individuals, undermining civil liberties.

To address these ethical challenges, policymakers must **develop comprehensive legal frameworks that balance technological advancements with the protection of human rights**. Regulations should require independent forensic oversight, strict data protection laws, and public transparency in the use of AI-driven investigative tools. Courts must ensure that forensic evidence presented in trials is scientifically validated, free from bias, and subject to rigorous cross-examination. Law enforcement agencies should implement bias mitigation strategies, ethical AI training, and privacy safeguards to prevent forensic technology from being misused.

The evolving landscape of forensic science presents both opportunities and ethical dilemmas. If managed responsibly, forensic innovations can enhance criminal investigations, improve accuracy, and reduce wrongful convictions. However, without proper oversight, these advancements could erode civil liberties, reinforce systemic biases, and compromise the integrity of the justice system. The challenge moving forward is ensuring that forensic science serves the pursuit of justice while upholding the fundamental rights of all individuals.

Chapter 12: The Future, Historical Timeline, and Terminology in Criminal Psychology

Emerging Areas of Inquiry

Criminal psychology is evolving rapidly as technological advancements, neuroscience, and social changes reshape how criminal behavior is studied, predicted, and managed. Traditional profiling and behavioral analysis are expanding to include artificial intelligence, neuroimaging, and genetic research. Investigators are exploring new ways to detect deception, assess criminal risk, and prevent violent behavior before it occurs. The intersection of psychology, law enforcement, and technology is leading to **more sophisticated methods of crime prevention, intervention, and rehabilitation**.

One of the most significant areas of development is the **use of artificial intelligence in behavioral analysis and risk assessment**. Machine learning algorithms process massive datasets to identify patterns in criminal behavior, psychological traits of offenders, and factors contributing to recidivism.

AI-driven risk assessment models analyze prior offenses, social environment, employment history, and psychological evaluations to predict the likelihood of reoffending. Courts in some jurisdictions have begun incorporating AI-driven sentencing recommendations, though concerns remain about bias, transparency, and due process. AI is also being used in forensic linguistics, analyzing verbal cues, writing patterns, and speech irregularities to detect deception, intent, or criminal planning in suspect communications.

Neuroscience is pushing the boundaries of **how criminal psychology understands aggression, impulsivity, and moral reasoning**. Functional MRI (fMRI) studies show that certain brain structures, particularly the prefrontal cortex and amygdala, are linked to violent behavior and emotional regulation. Researchers are investigating whether brain abnormalities, trauma, or neurochemical imbalances contribute to antisocial behavior. Advances in brain stimulation techniques, neurofeedback, and psychopharmacology may lead to targeted treatments for impulse control disorders and aggressive tendencies. However, ethical concerns regarding neuro-interventions in criminal justice, the potential for coercive treatment, and questions about free will remain unresolved.

Genetic research in criminal psychology is becoming **increasingly controversial**. Studies suggest that **certain genetic markers may influence aggression, risk-taking behavior, and antisocial tendencies**. Some researchers argue that a combination of genetics and environment determines criminal behavior, rather than genetics alone. The study of epigenetics—how environmental factors affect gene expression—has led to new theories on how trauma, abuse, and early-life stress influence brain development and criminal tendencies. However, concerns about genetic determinism, discrimination, and ethical use of genetic information in criminal profiling have made this a contentious area of research.

Cyberpsychology is emerging as **a critical subfield of criminal psychology**, focusing on **how digital environments influence criminal behavior**. Cyberstalking, online radicalization, internet fraud, and digital deception are fundamentally different from traditional crimes due to anonymity, global reach, and the ability to manipulate digital identities. Researchers are analyzing the psychological profiles of cybercriminals, the cognitive processes behind online deception, and the factors that drive individuals toward cybercrime. Law enforcement agencies are also investing in AI-powered behavioral analysis to detect radicalization, predatory behavior, and cyberthreats in real time.

Virtual reality and simulation-based training are revolutionizing how criminal psychologists assess and rehabilitate offenders. VR therapy is being used for trauma rehabilitation, empathy training, and exposure therapy for violent offenders. In some correctional programs, offenders participate in VR-based conflict resolution exercises, allowing them to experience scenarios from a victim's perspective. Psychologists are also testing VR as a tool to assess behavioral responses in controlled environments, giving insights into impulse control, decision-making, and aggression triggers.

The study of **psychopathology and criminal behavior is shifting toward early intervention**. Traditionally, criminal psychology has focused on analyzing individuals **after they commit crimes**.

Now, researchers are working on identifying early warning signs in childhood and adolescence that may predict violent tendencies, antisocial behavior, or psychopathic traits. Psychological assessments in schools, juvenile detention centers, and mental health clinics are being refined to detect at-risk youth before they engage in serious criminal behavior. Some governments are exploring policies that provide early mental health support, educational interventions, and mentorship programs to divert at-risk individuals from the criminal justice system.

The growing recognition of **trauma's impact on criminal behavior** is influencing legal defenses, sentencing guidelines, and rehabilitation programs. Trauma-informed care is being integrated into correctional facilities, recognizing that many offenders have histories of physical abuse, neglect, or PTSD. Courts in some jurisdictions are considering neurological and psychological evidence of trauma when determining sentencing and parole decisions. The long-term goal is to shift criminal justice from purely punitive measures toward rehabilitative models that acknowledge the psychological damage underlying many criminal behaviors.

Behavioral profiling is being **refined with advancements in big data analytics and cross-jurisdictional intelligence sharing**. Law enforcement agencies worldwide are collaborating on psychological databases of offenders, using predictive modeling to anticipate crime patterns based on behavioral markers. New methods for identifying serial offenders, analyzing crime scene behaviors, and linking unsolved cases based on psychological signatures are making investigations more data-driven and precise. However, the reliance on predictive analytics in policing raises ethical concerns about privacy, bias in data selection, and the risk of wrongful suspicion.

The role of **social and cultural psychology in crime prevention** is gaining more attention. Crime is not just an individual phenomenon—it is influenced by social structures, cultural norms, and economic conditions. Researchers are examining how societal attitudes toward aggression, authority, and punishment shape criminal behavior. Studies on the psychology of mass movements, groupthink in violent mobs, and the spread of extremist ideologies are providing new insights into collective criminal behavior. Understanding **how social environments create conditions for crime** is helping policymakers develop interventions that target root causes rather than just individual offenders.

Forensic psychology is expanding its scope beyond criminal profiling and courtroom testimony. Psychologists are now being called upon to assess competency to stand trial, witness credibility, and post-traumatic stress in victims and first responders. The role of forensic psychologists in jury selection, expert testimony, and rehabilitation planning is growing as legal systems recognize the need for psychological expertise in shaping fair trials and humane sentencing.

The future of criminal psychology also involves the ethical regulation of emerging forensic technologies. As AI, neuroimaging, and genetic research become more common in criminal investigations, legal frameworks must ensure these tools are used responsibly, without infringing on civil liberties. Psychological assessments will need to adapt to incorporate technological advancements while maintaining ethical integrity and scientific rigor.

As criminal psychology continues to evolve, its **interdisciplinary nature will become even more pronounced**. The future will require collaboration between psychologists, neuroscientists, AI researchers, forensic experts, and policymakers. The challenge will be ensuring that new advancements enhance justice rather than create new ethical dilemmas. Criminal psychology's ability to adapt to emerging technologies, integrate new research, and apply scientific knowledge to crime prevention will shape the next generation of criminal investigations and forensic psychology practices.

Historical Timeline: Key Milestones and Influential Figures

The study of criminal psychology has evolved over centuries, shaped by shifting social attitudes, legal frameworks, and scientific advancements. While early theories often relied on superstition and moral reasoning, the field gradually incorporated empirical research, psychological assessment, and neuroscience. The timeline below traces key developments and influential figures who contributed to our modern understanding of criminal behavior.

Ancient and Pre-Scientific Views on Crime and Criminal Behavior

Before the scientific study of psychology, crime was often explained through **superstition, religion, and moral reasoning**. Early societies attributed criminal acts to **demonic possession, sin, or divine punishment** rather than individual psychology.

- **Ancient Babylon (circa 1750 BCE)** – The Code of Hammurabi, one of the earliest legal codes, outlined a system of strict punishments based on the principle of lex talionis ("an eye for an eye"). It reflected a retributive approach to justice, where crime was punished in proportion to its severity.

- **Ancient Greece (5th–4th Century BCE)** – Philosophers like **Plato and Aristotle** debated the nature of human behavior, morality, and justice. Plato suggested that criminal behavior stemmed from ignorance and a lack of reason, while Aristotle emphasized habit and character formation in moral development.
- **Ancient Rome (1st Century BCE – 5th Century CE)** – Roman legal scholars introduced the idea of mens rea ("guilty mind"), recognizing that intent had a role in determining guilt and punishment. This concept remains fundamental in modern criminal law.

The Middle Ages and Early Theories of Crime (5th–17th Century)

During the medieval period, crime was still largely seen as **a sin against divine law**. However, legal and philosophical shifts began laying the groundwork for more secular understandings of criminal behavior.

- **1486 – Publication of *Malleus Maleficarum*** – This infamous text on witchcraft fueled moral panic and persecution of accused criminals, particularly women, reflecting how crime was still viewed through religious and supernatural lenses.
- **17th Century – Thomas Hobbes and Social Contract Theory** – Hobbes argued that humans were naturally selfish and prone to disorder, but a strong government could curb criminal tendencies through strict laws. His ideas influenced later theories of deterrence and punishment in criminal psychology.

The Enlightenment and the Birth of Criminology (18th Century)

The Enlightenment introduced **rationalist perspectives on crime**, challenging superstition and emphasizing **individual reasoning, free will, and social contracts**. This period marked the beginnings of modern criminology and legal reforms.

- **1764 – Cesare Beccaria Publishes *On Crimes and Punishments*** – Beccaria, an Italian philosopher, rejected torture and capital punishment, arguing that crime was a rational choice influenced by potential consequences. He advocated for proportional punishments and crime prevention, ideas that influenced modern deterrence theory.
- **1792 – Jeremy Bentham and Utilitarianism** – Bentham introduced the idea of "the greatest good for the greatest number", suggesting that punishment should be designed to prevent future crimes rather than exact revenge. His work influenced rehabilitative approaches to criminal behavior.

The 19th Century: The Rise of Scientific Criminology

With the rise of **biology, psychiatry, and psychology**, the study of criminal behavior shifted toward **scientific explanations and empirical research**.

- **1876 – Cesare Lombroso and the "Born Criminal" Theory –** Lombroso, an Italian physician, argued that criminals were biologically predisposed to crime and could be identified by physical features such as skull shape and facial asymmetry. While his theory was later debunked, it pioneered the use of empirical observation in criminology.
- **1895 – Havelock Ellis and Psychological Factors in Crime –** Ellis explored sexuality, mental disorders, and deviant behavior, moving beyond purely biological explanations of crime.
- **1899 – Establishment of the First Juvenile Court in the U.S. –** Recognizing that children were psychologically different from adults, reformers pushed for a separate legal system focused on rehabilitation rather than punishment.

Early 20th Century: Psychoanalysis and Behavioral Theories

The early 20th century saw the emergence of psychological theories of crime, shifting focus from biological determinism to personality, environment, and learning.

- **1909 – Sigmund Freud and Psychoanalysis –** Freud's theories suggested that unresolved childhood conflicts, unconscious desires, and personality imbalances could contribute to criminal behavior. While not a criminologist, his ideas influenced early forensic psychology and criminal profiling.
- **1920s – Behavioral Psychology and Learning Theories –** Psychologists like John Watson and B.F. Skinner argued that criminal behavior is learned through conditioning and reinforcement. Skinner's work in operant conditioning influenced behavior modification programs in criminal rehabilitation.
- **1939 – Edwin Sutherland and Differential Association Theory –** Sutherland proposed that crime is learned through social interactions, meaning that individuals become criminals if they are exposed to more pro-criminal attitudes than anti-criminal ones.

Mid-20th Century: Advances in Criminal Profiling and Forensic Psychology

As forensic psychology developed, criminal behavior became viewed through the lens of **mental health, cognitive processes, and personality disorders**.

- **1950s – Hans Eysenck and Personality Theories of Crime –** Eysenck studied links between personality traits and criminality, arguing that impulsivity, low anxiety, and risk-seeking behavior were associated with crime.
- **1964 – Development of Criminal Profiling –** The FBI began developing offender profiling techniques to identify patterns in criminal behavior, particularly for serial offenders.
- **1970s – The Study of Psychopathy and Antisocial Behavior –** Psychologists like Robert Hare studied psychopathy, sociopathy, and the role of lack of empathy in criminal behavior, leading to the development of the Psychopathy Checklist (PCL-R).

Late 20th Century: The Expansion of Criminal Psychology as a Discipline

By the late 20th century, criminal psychology was widely recognized as a legitimate field, with research focusing on mental disorders, criminal motivations, and cognitive processes.

- **1984 – FBI's Behavioral Science Unit Expands** – The development of criminal profiling, crime scene analysis, and investigative psychology became central to modern law enforcement.
- **1990s – The Rise of Neuroscience in Criminal Behavior** – Brain imaging studies showed differences in brain structure and function between violent offenders and non-offenders, advancing neurocriminology as a subfield.

21st Century: Integrating Neuroscience, AI, and Cyberpsychology

Modern criminal psychology now integrates **technology, big data, artificial intelligence, and neurobiological research** to predict and prevent crime.

- **2002 – First Use of fMRI in Criminal Psychology** – Functional MRI studies revealed brain activity linked to deception, impulse control, and aggression, leading to discussions about its use in lie detection and risk assessment.
- **2010s – Growth of Cybercriminal Psychology** – Researchers study online deception, cyberbullying, digital radicalization, and the psychology of hacking as internet-based crimes become more prevalent.
- **2020s – AI and Predictive Crime Analysis** – Machine learning models are now used to analyze criminal behavior, predict reoffending risk, and assist in forensic investigations. However, concerns about bias, ethics, and privacy in AI-driven policing remain unresolved.

The field of criminal psychology continues to evolve as new technologies, psychological theories, and legal policies shape our understanding of criminal behavior. Future research will likely focus on **the intersection of genetics, neuroscience, digital behavior, and artificial intelligence in crime prevention and rehabilitation**.

Terms and Definitions: An Essential Lexicon for Practitioners

- **Actus Reus** – The physical act of committing a crime, as opposed to the mental intent.
- **Mens Rea** – The mental intent or knowledge of wrongdoing in a crime.
- **Antisocial Personality Disorder (ASPD)** – A mental health condition characterized by disregard for others, impulsivity, and chronic rule-breaking.
- **Behavioral Profiling** – The analysis of behavioral patterns to predict or identify criminal actions.
- **Biopsychosocial Model** – A framework that considers biological, psychological, and social factors in criminal behavior.
- **Classical Conditioning** – A learning process where a neutral stimulus becomes associated with a reflexive response (e.g., Pavlov's dogs).

- **Cognitive Dissonance** – Psychological discomfort caused by conflicting beliefs or behaviors, sometimes leading to rationalization of criminal acts.
- **Cognitive-Behavioral Therapy (CBT)** – A treatment method focused on altering negative thought patterns and behaviors.
- **Criminal Profiling** – The process of constructing a behavioral and psychological sketch of an offender based on crime scene evidence.
- **Crime Scene Analysis** – The examination of physical evidence at a crime scene to reconstruct criminal events.
- **Criminal Intent** – The purposeful or knowing state of mind that leads to criminal actions.
- **Cybercrime** – Criminal activities conducted via digital platforms, including hacking, fraud, and cyberstalking.
- **Deindividuation** – Loss of self-awareness in group settings, leading to behavior that might not occur in isolation.
- **Deterrence Theory** – The idea that punishment prevents future crimes by discouraging criminal behavior.
- **Diagnostic and Statistical Manual of Mental Disorders (DSM-5)** – A classification system for mental disorders, including those linked to criminality.
- **Disinhibition Hypothesis** – The theory that reduced self-control, often due to substance use, increases impulsive and criminal behaviors.
- **Dark Triad** – A psychological framework consisting of narcissism, Machiavellianism, and psychopathy, often linked to criminal behavior.
- **Domestic Violence** – Physical, emotional, or psychological abuse occurring within intimate relationships or family units.
- **Forensic Psychology** – The application of psychological principles to legal and criminal justice settings.
- **Forensic Psychiatry** – The branch of psychiatry that evaluates and treats individuals within the criminal justice system.
- **Frustration-Aggression Hypothesis** – The idea that blocked goals lead to frustration, increasing the likelihood of aggressive or criminal acts.
- **General Strain Theory (GST)** – The theory that stressors, such as financial hardship, increase the risk of criminal behavior.
- **Geographic Profiling** – The analysis of crime locations to determine an offender's likely home base.
- **Habitual Offender** – An individual who repeatedly engages in criminal activity despite legal consequences.
- **Hedonistic Calculus** – A principle in criminology suggesting that individuals weigh the pleasure and pain of actions before committing crimes.
- **Hostile Attribution Bias** – The tendency to perceive ambiguous interactions as threatening, increasing aggressive responses.
- **Impulse Control Disorder** – A condition where individuals struggle to resist urges that may be harmful to themselves or others.
- **Insanity Defense** – A legal argument stating that a defendant was unable to understand the criminality of their actions due to mental illness.
- **Juvenile Delinquency** – Criminal behavior committed by individuals under the legal adult age.
- **Labeling Theory** – The idea that individuals become criminal when society labels them as such, reinforcing deviant behavior.
- **Latent Trait Theories** – Theories that suggest criminal tendencies are influenced by stable, underlying personal traits.
- **Locus of Control** – The extent to which individuals believe they control their own actions versus external influences shaping behavior.

- **Low Arousal Theory** – The hypothesis that low physiological arousal levels contribute to risk-taking and criminal behavior.
- **Machiavellianism** – A personality trait involving manipulation, deceit, and exploitation for personal gain.
- **Malingering** – The act of faking psychological or physical symptoms to avoid legal consequences.
- **Mass Murder** – The killing of multiple people in a single event, often in one location.
- **Modus Operandi (MO)** – The characteristic method or pattern a criminal follows when committing offenses.
- **Moral Disengagement** – A cognitive process where individuals justify unethical behavior to avoid guilt.
- **Motive vs. Intent** – **Motive** refers to the reason behind a crime, while **intent** refers to the conscious decision to commit the act.
- **Neurocriminology** – The study of how brain structure and function influence criminal behavior.
- **Operant Conditioning** – A learning process where behavior is reinforced through rewards or punishments.
- **Organized vs. Disorganized Offenders** – A classification system distinguishing criminals based on planning, crime scene behavior, and psychological traits.
- **Paraphilia** – A pattern of abnormal sexual desires that may lead to criminal behavior.
- **Parole vs. Probation** – **Parole** is conditional release from prison, while **probation** is a court-ordered alternative to incarceration.
- **Pathological Lying** – Chronic, compulsive dishonesty often seen in individuals with psychopathy.
- **Pattern Theory of Crime** – The theory that crimes follow identifiable behavioral and environmental patterns.
- **Pedophilia** – A psychiatric disorder involving sexual attraction to prepubescent children.
- **Personality Disorder** – A mental health condition marked by rigid, maladaptive patterns of thinking and behavior.
- **Phrenology** – A discredited theory that suggested skull shape and bumps could determine personality traits, including criminality.
- **Post-Traumatic Stress Disorder (PTSD)** – A condition often found in both victims and perpetrators of crime, affecting emotional regulation.
- **Prefrontal Cortex Dysfunction** – Impairments in the prefrontal cortex, linked to impulsivity and lack of inhibition in criminals.
- **Primary vs. Secondary Psychopathy** – **Primary psychopathy** refers to innate emotional deficits, while **secondary psychopathy** arises from environmental factors.
- **Profiling vs. Stereotyping** – **Profiling** is an investigative technique based on behavioral analysis, whereas **stereotyping** relies on biased generalizations.
- **Psychopathy Checklist-Revised (PCL-R)** – A diagnostic tool for assessing psychopathic traits in individuals.
- **Psychotic vs. Neurotic Disorders** – **Psychotic disorders** involve delusions and hallucinations, while **neurotic disorders** involve anxiety and distress.
- **Rational Choice Theory** – The belief that individuals commit crimes after weighing the risks and benefits.
- **Recidivism** – The likelihood of a previously convicted individual reoffending after release.

- **Rehabilitation vs. Punishment** – **Rehabilitation** focuses on reforming criminals, while **punishment** seeks retribution or deterrence.
- **Reinforcement Theory** – The idea that behavior is shaped by rewards and punishments over time.
- **Restraint Theory** – The idea that crime occurs when social and personal restraints (such as morality or law) are weak.
- **Risk-Need-Responsivity (RNR) Model** – A framework for designing offender rehabilitation programs based on risk assessment.
- **Routine Activity Theory** – The theory that crime occurs when a motivated offender, a suitable target, and lack of guardianship converge.
- **Serial Killer vs. Spree Killer** – **Serial killers** commit multiple murders over time, while **spree killers** commit multiple murders in a short period without a cooling-off phase.
- **Situational Crime Prevention** – Strategies aimed at reducing crime opportunities rather than changing offenders' behaviors.
- **Social Learning Theory** – The belief that individuals learn criminal behavior through observing others.
- **Strain Theory** – The idea that social pressure and lack of opportunity contribute to criminal behavior.
- **Victimology** – The study of victims, their relationships with offenders, and the psychological effects of crime.
- **White-Collar Crime** – Non-violent crimes committed in business or professional settings, such as fraud or embezzlement.
- **Zone of Transition** – Areas in cities with high crime rates due to economic instability and social disorganization.

Afterword

As we come to the end of *Criminal Psychology Step by Step*, I hope this book has given you a deeper understanding of the psychological forces that drive criminal behavior. Crime isn't a simple matter of good versus evil—behind every act, there are layers of motivation, emotion, and circumstance that shape a person's choices. By exploring the biological, social, and psychological factors behind crime, we begin to see the bigger picture of why people offend, how they are investigated, and what can be done to rehabilitate them.

Criminal psychology is a constantly evolving field. Every year, new research expands our understanding of criminal minds, and technological advancements like artificial intelligence and neuroimaging are revolutionizing the way we study and analyze behavior. What we know today may be refined or even challenged by the discoveries of tomorrow. This is what makes the study of criminal psychology so fascinating—it's a field that never stands still.

One of the key takeaways from this book is that crime is rarely caused by just one factor. A violent offender may have both a biological predisposition to aggression and a history of childhood trauma. A fraudster may be motivated by both greed and social pressure. A teenager who falls into gang activity may be influenced by both peer pressure and economic hardship. Understanding crime requires looking at all of these influences together.

It's also important to remember that while criminal psychology focuses on offenders, victims are just as much a part of the story. Studying criminal behavior is about learning how to better prevent it, supporting those who have been harmed, and improving the way justice is served. The more we understand about why people commit crimes, the better we can create solutions—whether through better law enforcement strategies, rehabilitation programs, or policies that address the root causes of crime.

If this book has sparked your interest, I encourage you to keep learning. Criminal psychology is a vast field with many branches, from forensic psychology to criminology to victimology. Whether you pursue further reading, take courses, or even consider a career in this field, there is always more to discover.

Thank you for taking this journey step by step with me. I hope this book has given you not only knowledge but also a new perspective on crime and human behavior. seeking to understand, we take the first step toward making a difference.

Made in United States
North Haven, CT
05 July 2025

70391927R00095